In the Footsteps of the
RUSSIAN
SNOWMAN
Dmitri Bayanov

Typeset by Jonathan Downes, Cover art by Gareth Shaw
Cover and Layout by SpiderKaT for CFZ Communications
Using Microsoft Word 2000, Microsoft Publisher 2000, Adobe Photoshop CS.

This revised edition published in Great Britain by CFZ Press

CFZ Press
Myrtle Cottage
Woolsery
Bideford
North Devon
EX39 5QR

Text and images © Dmitri Bayanov
Latout and cover © CFZ MMXV

ISBN: 978-1-909488-30-4

CONTENTS

PREFACE

- EASTERN KAZAKHSTAN AND KIRGHIZIA
- A FIELD INVESTIGATION INTO THE RELIC HOMINOID SITUATION IN TAJIKISTAN

Part III . SIBERIA

- DOES SIBERIA HAVE ITS OWN SASQUATCHSKI?
- THE TRAIL BLAZED BY VLADIMIR PUSHKAREV
- NEW TESTIMONY, By Vladimir Pushkarev
- REPORT BY MAYA BYKOVA, April 1988
- REPORT BY DMITRI BAYANOV, June 1988
- THE SECOND ENCOUNTER WITH MECHENY, By Maya Bykova
- FOLLOW-UP

Part IV. EUROPEAN RUSSIA

- VOICES AND PICTURES FROM THE PAST
- FROM THE STORY *FEAR* BY GUY DEMAUPASSANT
- COMMENT ON TURGENEV'S TESTIMONY
- LETTER FROM Moscow, August 1991
- THE URALS
- REPORT BY NIKOLAI AVDEYEV, May 1987
- REPORT BY LEONID YERSHOV, August 1989
- COMMENT BY DMITRI BAYANOV
- INCREDIBLE CASE IN SARATOV REGION
- REPORT FROM Moscow, February 1993

Part V. THE RUSSIAN FAR EAST

- REUTER REPORT, August 16, 1990
- REPORT BY DMITRI BAYANOV, February 1991
- BIGFOOT PLAYING WITH FIRE
- MORE INFORMATION ON SNOWMEN
- IN THE FAR EAST AND BEYOND

PREFACE

ussia was described by British Statesman Sir Winston Churchill as "a riddle wrapped in a mystery inside an enigma." Could, then, anything be *more* mysterious than the Russian snowman? Not anymore, for here is the world's first English-language book on the subject, written by Russian snowman researchers. In fact, there are a dozen books by foreign authors dealing, in part, with snowmen in Russia - but that, of course, is quite different.

The lateness of this book needs some explanation. Russia - or to be exact, the Soviet Union - was the first country to probe the snowman riddle on a scientific basis. In 1958, in the post-Stalinist political thaw, the Soviet Academy of Sciences diverted itself for a time with the exotic and sensational subject of the Himalayan yeti. As the Academy had received reports of similar creatures in the mountains of Soviet Central Asia, it set up a special commission to collect evidence on the subject and launched a major expedition to the Pamirs to establish the existence of snowmen there. The expedition was a failure (this book explains why), and this put an end to official interest in the matter. Snowman studies (or 'hominology,' to give its modern term) was declared by the academic establishment to be a pseudo-science, along with astrology and parapsychology.

As the State had the monopoly in both science and book publishing, it followed that no book on the snowman, except ones that were derogatory, in accordance with the official point of view, could be published in Russia. Professor Boris Porshnev's scientific monograph, *The Present State of the Question of Relic Hominoids,* was allowed to be printed in a limited circulation of only 180 copies. It contained a wealth of information on relic hominoids (i.e., snowmen) in the USSR, obtained by the Snowman Commission, but that information remained largely unavailable and unknown not only to the world public, but even to the scientific community in Russia.

When the commission ceased to exist, Boris Porshnev and some of his colleagues, convinced of the reality of snowmen and their great importance to science, continued their studies unofficially within the framework of the Relic Hominoid Research Seminar organized at the Darwin Museum in Moscow, by museum curator Pyotr Smolin. I joined the seminar in 1964 and, since 1975, after Smolin's passing, have been its chairman.

Our group had no access to book publishing or scientific journals in the USSR, but the pages of some newspapers and popular-science magazines were open to us from time to time (depending on the daring of the particular editor). Another outlet into print was provided by our contacts with colleagues abroad; thus over the last three decades our materials have appeared in English, mainly in U.S. scholarly and popular-science publications; and, in the last decade, on a regular basis, the *Bigfoot Co-op* newsletter, edited and printed by anthropologist Constance Cameron of California State University.

As these materials provide a coherent picture of our research from the beginning up to the present time, I decided to combine them into a single volume, add some commentary, and offer the whole to the reader. The contents are arranged geographically, in keeping with areas of fieldwork, and from each area, testimonies, reports and articles are presented, more or less chronologically, from the past to the present. I have selected materials that seemed to me to be of sufficient interest for the public at large. The bibliography suggests further reading materials for those seeking a deeper understanding of the scientific aspect of the matter.

Part I

THE CAUCASUS

A hirsute couple in the Kelermes mirror of gold and silver
dug up from a Scythian tomb (VII-V centuries B.C.), near the
village of Kelermes in the North Caucasus. The presence of a
female hominoid is significant. Devoid of clothes, both male
and female sport a protective coat of hair, just like the other
wild animals of the Caucasian fauna depicted by the artist in
the treasure piece.

VOICES FROM THE PAST

I n the 10th century A.D., the Caucasus was visited by Abul Hassan Ali Masudi, an Arab traveller and historian known as "the Herodotus of the Arabs." In his historical narrative *Meadows of Gold and Mines of Gems*, he wrote:

> Behind these four mountains on the sea coast is another ring near the precipice: in it are forests and jungles, which are inhabited by a sort of monkey having an erect stature and round face; they are exceedingly like men, but they are all covered with hair. Sometimes it happens that they are caught. They show very great intelligence and docility: but they are deprived of speech by which they could express themselves, although they understand what is spoken. (One copy reads that they do not understand what is spoken. - *D.B.*) But they express themselves by signs. Sometimes they are brought to the kings of those nations, and they are taught to stand by them and to taste what is on the table; for the monkeys have the peculiar quality of knowing if poison is present in food or drink. Some part of the food is given to the monkey, who smells it, and, if he eats it, the king eats; but if not, he knows that it contains poison. The same is the practice of most Chinese and Hindu sovereigns. We have given in this book an account of the Chinese missions which came to el-Mahdi, and we related what they said of the use which their kings make of monkeys for testing their food[1].

This gem of information makes it perfectly clear that long before modern scientists, journalists and cartoonists took a theoretical interest in bipedal "monkeys" which "are exceedingly like men," sovereigns of many nations, without much ado, put these "monkeys" to a practical use concerning the matter of life and death.

Douglas William Freshfield, an outstanding English explorer and mountaineer, and president of the Alpine Club, who travelled in the Caucasus in 1888 and climbed some of its highest peaks, has this to say in his book, *The Exploration of the Caucasus*:

1. Ali Masudi's Historical Encyclopaedia, entitled *Meadows of Gold and Mines of Gems*, translated from Arabic by Aloys Sprenger. London, 1841, V.I, p.440.

I had for years been possessed by a strong desire to penetrate the "No Man's Land" west of Svanetia and between the rivers Ingur and Kodor. Mr. Grove, in 1875, had quoted the tales told by the Urusbieh hunters of their great hunting-ground. He had written on his last page of a great tract of magnificent country, scored by deep valleys, watered by powerful streams, and covered by a mighty forest. It has no in habitants whatever, so far as we could learn, and the solitude of the entire district is disturbed only when a few hunters from the north venture into it after the game, in which it is said to abound...

Such a description was in itself well calculated to stir curiosity. And all we had heard in our travels had added to the mystery of the Great Forest. *Russian officials gravely repeated strange tales of a race of wild men, who had no villages or language, but appeared naked and gibbering in the depths of the woods, who lived on berries and were without fire-arms.* (italics added. - D.B.).

Fifty years ago an Englishman, a Mr. Spencer, one of those who instigated the Circassians in their struggle with Russia by holding out expectations which they had no power to fulfill, wrote a distressingly-vague account of his passage through this region, where he described the chamois as looking down on the traveller from every crag, as squirrels might from English trees.

An object long in my mind had been attained. The mystery of the great forest, which Grove, Moore and I had so often discussed, was at last solved. I had learned what truth underlay the strange tales current in the Caucasus. We had not met with the wild men of the woods, living apart, without villages, clothes, or fire-arms, clad in skins and feeding on berries, concerning whom Mr. Jukoff (one of the Russian officials. - *D.B.*) had repeated the legends, but we had visited the secret lodges of the wilderness and their denizens. We had not been as fortunate as Mr. Spencer, who saw chamois looking down on him from every crag, as numerous as the squirrels in an English park; but we had had frequent proofs of the proximity of bears. We had ascertained that the forest paths were not impassable when found; but we had discovered the difficulty of finding them. [2.]

By way of comment, I must remark that "strange tales" gravely repeated by Russian officials during the last century aptly describe some of the wildman's main characteristics. Whatever the nature of the truth learned by Freshfield concerning these tales, his failure to meet with "the wild men of the woods" comes as no surprise to those who have studied the subject more closely.

In 1976, my son and I backpacked through "the Great Forest" of Svanetia, mentioned by Freshfield, and found the scenery just as magnificent as described by the English travellers. We met no Russian officials there, but the Svans (local inhabitants) we interviewed told us about recent sightings of dav (local variation of *dev* or *div*), the wild man of the Caucasus. The eyewitness accounts were factual and down-to-earth, with no fairy-tale or legendary embellishments whatsoever. I believe Freshfield was rash to write off those "strange tales" as mere legends.

2. Douglas W. Freshfield. *The Exploration of the Caucasus.* London and New York, 1896, Vol.2, pp.191,210.

The book's compiler at the Klukhor pass on the way to Svanetia, August 1976. *Photo by Ivan Bayanov.*

• TESTIMONY BY LIEUTENANT-COLONEL VAZGHEN KARAPETIAN

In 1966, a Soviet popular-science magazine, *Tekhnika Molodyozhi* (Technology for Young People), No. 8, carried the following article:

In December 1941, Vazghen Sergeyevich Karapetian, a Lt. Col. in the Army Medical Corps, happened to observe a strange hairy man in the Caucasus. Our correspondent asked Karapetian to tell our readers about that incident and his attitude to it, 25 years on.

"The man I saw," said the army doctor, "is quite clear in my memory, as if standing in front of me now. I was inspecting him at the request of the local authorities. It was necessary to establish whether the strange man was an enemy saboteur in disguise. But it was a totally wild creature, almost fully covered with dark brown hair resembling a bear's fur, without a moustache or beard, with just slight hairiness on the face. The man was standing very upright, his arms hanging down. He was taller than average, about 180 centimetres. He was standing like an athlete, his powerful chest put forward. His eyes had an empty, purely animal expression. He did not accept any food or drink. He said nothing and made only inarticulate sounds. I extended my hand to him and even said 'Hello.' But he did not respond. After this inspection I returned to my unit and never received any further information about the fate of the strange creature."

I heard Karapetian's story many times, as told by him at our seminar and to other audiences that invited him. Here's what should be added in summation - Karapetian stressed the fact that the whole thing happened during the war with Germany, in fact at a critical moment of it, which explains, firstly, why the authorities (a group of local home guards) became interested in the creature, captured and investigated it (suspicious of an enemy ploy), and secondly, why there was no follow-up, the records of the incident having been lost or concealed. Nobody at

A monthly session of the Relic Hominoid Research Seminar at the Darwin Museum in Moscow. The seminar was formed in 1960 and headed by Museum chief curator Pyotr Smolin until his passing. Today it is called the Smolin Seminar.

the time gave a thought to the potential scientific value of such freaks of nature.

Looking back, Karapetian mused that, besides its beastlike hairiness, the captured subject differed from humans in three respects.

- Firstly, he was resistant to the cold; in fact, he preferred cold to the warmth of normal room temperature. The creature was shown to Karapetian in a cold shed, and when he asked why it was kept in such cold conditions the answer was 'because he sweats very much in the room.'
- Secondly, the subject's eyes and face held a very non-human, animal-like expression.
- Thirdly, the army doctor noticed that the creature had lice of a much bigger size and of a different kind than found on humans. As a result of the medical check-up, Karapetian gave the home guards his conclusion to the effect that it was not a man in disguise, but a really "very, very wild" subject and "all that hair is his own."

He asked the guards what they were going to do with the captive, and they answered: "We shall report your conclusion to our superiors and, depending on their order, shall either dispatch him or set him free."

Subsequently, proceeding from the possibility that the hairy man was shot by a firing squad, my colleagues addressed the Minister of the Interior of Daghestan, where the incident took place, with the request to provide information on the case. The Minister's reply was to the effect that after so many years of Soviet power in Daghestan, the entire population had become fully civilized, and it was pointless to search for any wild men. The captive was, according to the Minister, just a saboteur, to which the law of war-time had been applied (i.e., he was executed). No details were supplied.

In 1958, when the USSR Academy of Sciences set up a commission to investigate the problem of the snowman, Karapetian was one of the first to supply information, which took the commission by surprise since nobody at that time could accept the possibility of such creatures in the Caucasus (the idea was considered just as absurd as snowmen in California).

Following Karapetian's report and some others, as well as initial trips to investigate the situation on the spot made by Marie-Jeanne Koffmann and zoologist Dr. Alexander Mashkovtsev, the Caucasus, of all places, became for many years the main site of our fieldwork.

The book's compiler with the founders of the
hominoid research in Russia. From left to
right: Boris Porshnev, Alexander Mashkovtsev,
Pyotr Smolin, Dmitri Bayanov and Marie-
Jeanne Koffmann. January 1968.

REFLECTIONS ON THE POSSIBLE SURVIVAL OF A POPULATION OF RELIC HOMINOIDS IN THE CAUCASUS[3]

By Dr. Marie-Jeanne Koffmann

Translated from the French by E. B. Winn

An investigation, carried out over many years among various peoples of the Caucasus, has made possible the compilation of a file containing more than 500 statements by witnesses, who claim to have observed hominoid creatures personally, sometimes for lengthy periods of time. These hominoids are described as bipedal, covered with hair, and having no language. They are described in the local languages as '*men of the woods*' or '*wildmen.*'

An analysis of the descriptions of the wildmen discloses very precise anatomical, ecological and ethological criteria. This evidence, as well as certain observations collected in the field, indicate that these reported observations are real and are well-founded in fact.

Reports in the Soviet press in 1956 of Anglo-American expeditions searching in the Himalayas for bipedal, hairy creatures, termed '*yetis*,' unexpectedly gave rise to a multitude of letters from the mountainous provinces of the USSR addressed to scientific authorities and to editors of major publications. School teachers, physicians, shepherds, and military personnel, among others, all were astonished at the interest being shown in the foreign-led expeditions, whereas in the USSR itself, similar anthropomorphic creatures, well-known to the writers of the letters, apparently evoked no interest on the part of Soviet science.

Such reports and correspondence, of course, are not usually in the slightest degree capable of arousing most scientists. However, on this occasion, chance decreed that Professor B. Porshnev would take a look into the matter. Historian, philosopher and esteemed humanist of world renown (Doctor *honoris causa*, among others, from the University of

---

3 A complete text of this material in French is carried by *Archeologia*, Juin 1991.

15

Montpellier), Porshnev was struck by the simplicity of the reports and by the realism of the descriptions, all of which tallied despite the diversity of their origins.

The energy and authority of Professor Porshnev were sufficient to overcome the resistance, and even the indignation, of the academic community.

Brought to the notice of the Presidium of the Academy of Sciences of the USSR, the ensuing debate led to the creation in 1958, under the auspices of the Presidium, of a Commission to study the question of the snowman, and to the organization of a research expedition to the Pamirs. Responsibility for this expedition was assigned to the Botanical Institute of the Academy, which had its own scientific base in that region, and the personnel, some of whom claimed to be informed about the existence of strange anthropomorphs. The USSR was thus the only country to attempt a serious investigation of this unusual problem.

The Commission mounted a series of intensive activities: bibliographical research, which was to turn up numerous descriptions of these creatures by naturalists and explorers, from numerous places and points in time; the alerting of the Chinese authorities, to whom were sent a number of reports concerning their Western territories, and who reacted favourably to such an extent that a joint Sino-Soviet expedition was projected for 1959; cooperation with the Academy of Sciences of Mongolia, of which two leading members had been studying the problem since the 1920s, as well as with Western zoologists who had reported the existence of yetis or who had led Himalayan expeditions (Drs. B. Heuvelmans and G. Russell based in France, and I. Sanderson in the USA); and annual publication of monographs in which were presented, without modification and without commentary, reports, as they had arrived from different parts of the world and over a wide span in time.

The expedition to the Pamirs, dominated as it was by the interest of its leaders in plant life and, above all, having only a very vague idea of the target of its research, returned empty-handed. Conceived too hastily in the first flush of enthusiasm, the 1958 expedition of the Academy of Sciences, of which I was the physician, was premature.

The expedition's failure was vigorously exploited by its powerful "opponents." Thus shaken, the Commission, among whose members were numerous prominent people who were indifferent to the problem, broke up slowly of its own accord, and expired definitively in 1960.

Thereafter, research was in the hands of several individuals who were totally deprived of all material, technical and financial resources, a situation which was singularly difficult in the USSR, where all activity was structured by the State.

Nonetheless, in 1963, the Academy of Sciences agreed to publish under its seal a total of 180 copies of the voluminous monograph *The Present State of the Question of Relic Hominoids,* in which Porshnev set forth the analysis and the synthesis of the exceptional documentation, collected up to that time, on these man-like bipeds distributed over several regions of the globe, and in which he advanced the hypothesis of their paleoanthropic nature.

It was at this point that the matter of the Caucasus arose. In November 1958, the Presidium of the Academy received an official visit from a physician with the rank of Lieutenant-Colonel.

This person, Dr. Vazghen Karapetian, considered it his duty to report an anomalous sighting which he had made personally, and for which the recent publications finally had supplied an interpretation. In the winter of 1941, in Daghestan, he had been called to examine a creature of human appearance, male, covered with thick fur, and described as having a brutish expression.

Shortly afterwards, a similar report was submitted by the Chief Game Warden of the Republic of Daghestan, V. K. Leontiev. In August 1958, in the high mountains, he had sighted very briefly an identical creature. He described in great detail its footprints, which had been left in a snowfield.

Almost simultaneously, we discovered an analogous report. Dated 1899, it came from an eminent zoologist, Professor Satunin, whose works on the fauna of the Caucasus are considered to be the most exhaustive to this day. In the course of an expedition to the Eastern Caucasus, he reported having observed briefly a "wild woman, covered with hair."

It is to be noted that all three of these persons who recorded their observations are:

> a) non-native; i.e., foreign to the Caucasus; and
> b) especially well-qualified to judge zoological phenomena.

Nonetheless, these first Caucasian communications gave rise to profound contention and divergences of view. The very idea of the survival into the twentieth century, in areas regularly visited by human beings, of an unknown hominoid population, appeared absurd and totally unacceptable; the search for the snowman thus took on an aspect of the ridiculous.

As an alpinist and veteran of the Battle of the Caucasus in 1942, I felt especially concerned by this disastrous turn of events.

In August 1959, I left for the southern slopes of the Great Caucasus, on the border of Daghestan, with the intention of explaining and putting these disputes to rest.

When I returned to Moscow a month later, I had collected the verbal reports of 40 witnesses who had personally observed the 'men of the woods.'

Results of the Investigation Carried out among the Caucasian Peoples

At present I have available the verbal statements taken from more than 500 witnesses, who stated that they had observed these creatures personally.

My paper deals with the Caucasus, and this should be specially stressed. The particularities of the Caucasus habitat have produced a unique situation for the hominoids, and have deeply affected the ecology and ethology of their local population. In the Caucasus, a theatre of the earliest civilization, the hominoid population, pressed by *Homo sapiens* to the lifeless uplands of rocky ranges, turned out to be surrounded and imprisoned by humans, as it were. The hominoid's resemblance to man aroused in the latter both fear of, and pity for, the creature. Not feeling particularly menaced by them, though fearful of their great physical strength - and above all of their strange nature

Marie-Jeanne Koffmann with Caucasian herdsmen,
her major source of information on almasty.

(neither man nor beast) - people preferred to maintain peaceful relations with the hominoids. The creatures even used to be offered food and old clothes by humans. Special sympathy used to be extended to their "women" with babies. The hominoids have had enough presence of mind to profit fully from the proximity of man. The kind of relationship that exists between man and hominoid in the Caucasus is not equalled, as far as I know, anywhere else in the world at present.

Despite the wide variety of ethnic groups, tongues, religions and cultures, the people of the Caucasus as a whole are characterized by the deeply-antiquated nature of their customs and traditions. For thousands of years their livelihood has depended on the breeding of sheep, and even today they retain the traits of ancient pastoral peoples, such as spiritual rectitude and simplicity, great hospitality, and keenness of observation.

Covering a wide range of nationalities, ages, educational abilities and social standing, my informants are, for the most part simple people - shepherds, farmers, and hunters. Their knowledge of nature and their faculties of observation are beyond reproach.

Reports obtained second-hand were innumerable, but are not included in this list.

It should go without saying that the name given to the creatures described varied according to the language of the area; however, it is always to be translated as 'man of the woods' (*meshe-adam* in Azerbaijani, *tskhiss katsi* in Georgian, *agatch-kishi* in Karachai, etc.), 'wildman,' or 'hairy man.'

I use here the Kabardian *almasty*, which is familiar to me since it was Kabardino-Balkaria especially, at the foot of Mt. Elbrus, which served as the base for our research.

The reports obtained vary in both extent and value, depending upon the circumstances of the sighting, its duration, the subject's distance away, the ambient light, the interest shown by the observer, his state of fear or curiosity, and the posture and behavior of the almasty. One witness would be struck by a secondary detail and would come back to it persistently, while dismissing other essential points. The next stressed a completely different aspect, and a third was able to examine these creatures at leisure and, repeatedly, to approach them and to give them food.

The following are some examples of the type of verbatim report which I have available. Their selection from among hundreds was not an easy matter.

Administrative map of Caucasus in USSR, 1952-1991

S.S.R.	Soviet Socialist Republic
A.S.S.R.	Autonomous Soviet Socialist Republic
A.O.	Autonomous Oblast (province)
-----	Boundaries of Soviet Republics

STAVROPOL KRAI

KARACHAY-CHERKESSIA

Baksan

Prokhladnyy

Dugulubgey

Mayskly

Chegem

Nartkala

KABARDINO-BALKARIA

Terek

Nalchik

Tyrnyauz

NORTH OSSETIA ALANIA

GEORGIA

Kabardino-Balkar Republic

Eyewitness Reports
Republic of Kabardino- Balkaria

- **Communication by Talib Kumyshev, 67;** *Kabardian, a highly respected elderly man of the village of Kamennomost:*

…It was probably in 1930, or 1931, or 1932, in June or at the end of May, when our cattle left for the alpine pastures of Elbrus. I was chief of the group. We had left to inspect the herds with the veterinarian.

Well, rain had surprised one of my shepherds, Shaghir Zagureyev, very high up on the slopes, and he had gone to take refuge under a rocky overhang. As he approached it, he saw there were three almastys sitting under it. Shaghir was a little frightened, but as the rain was by then falling much harder, he decided to stay there anyway, though at a distance from them. They looked at one another. Then, the rain stopped and Shaghir came down to the farm. He

An artist's impression of almasty based on eyewitness accounts collected by M. J. Koffmann

did not say anything to anyone.

Very early in the morning, I was awakened by cries, a tremendous noise, and I saw that the shepherds were running to assemble their herds and were taking the cattle down the valley. "Why are they leaving?" I asked. "There are almastys under the rock, up there." At that moment Shaghir declared, "It's true, there are three almastys sitting up there, I saw them yesterday evening." I was then really angry. I said to Shaghir, "You're an idiot. You were frightened by a bush." "No," said Shaghir, "I saw them." "Well, why didn't you tell anyone?" "Because the old people have warned that, when you see an almasty for the first time, if you tell anyone about it you'll get a bad headache. Well, for me, it was the first time that I have seen one."

I continued not to believe all this. They said to me, "OK, go ahead, go see for yourself."

We were about 10 to 15 people making a half-circle around that rock. We stayed there until dinnertime. Some went away, and others came up. Three almastys were seated under the overhang, two of medium size, and the other bigger. The one which was the biggest was in the middle. They were sitting on rocks, facing us, hunched over, with their heads down. From time to time they raised their heads slightly, and looked at us from under their brows.

Their heads were very ugly, not nice at all. Their faces resembled human faces, but the nose is shorter and flattened. The eyes are slanted and reddish. The cheeks are very prominent, like those of a Mongol or a Korean, but more so. The lips are thin. The lower jaw is receding, as though cut on a bias.

The hair is long, like that of a woman, and tangled. The entire body is covered with shaggy hair, resembling that of the buffalo. In some places this is long (torso, chest) and in other places it is shorter (arms, legs).

The big one had the chest of a man. The others had the breasts of a woman, but extremely long and covered with hair. The hair was very dirty. The stink was so strong that we could not stand it. The odour was like that of wild flax, when it grows thickly.

Once, the one seated on the right mumbled something.

I did not see their hands clearly, as they were held between their legs. The legs are rather short and bowed. The foot is like that of a man, but more spread out. All were wearing, wrapped around their waists, an old piece of a shepherd's cape.

A young shepherd proposed to throw a lasso around one of them and bring it into the village. But all the others cried out that it is forbidden, that they must not be harmed, and that they must not be disturbed.

I watched them from a distance of three or four metres, and I even approached to within about one metre. Did I touch them? I should say not! If you touch them, as Allah is my witness, you could no longer eat with your hands afterward, they are so dirty, stinking and repulsive. I remained 1.5-2 hours. When I left, other shepherds were arriving.

I have heard my father recount that they suckle on cows.

- **Communication by Erjib Koshokoyev, *70, Kabardian, inhabitant of Stary Sherek:***

Before the war, there were many almastys around our area. Today, evidently, very few are encountered. I am somewhat informed about almastys, because I have heard a great deal spoken about them. I have personally seen them three times.

The first time was in October 1944. Our detachment [of police] was on horseback, crossing a field of hemp on the steppe. Suddenly, the horse of the first man stopped so abruptly that I almost ran into it. I was riding second in line. He said to me, "Look! An almasty!" Just in front of us, a few metres away, an almasty was stuffing into its mouth the ends of stalks of hemp, with the grains on them. Behind us, the detachment was gathering around and making some noise. It saw us and ran away very rapidly - it ran extraordinarily fast - towards a shepherd's cabin which was not far away. While it was running, several men of our detachment took their rifles from their shoulders and prepared to fire, but our chief, a Russian officer from Nalchik, cried out, "Don't shoot, don't shoot! Let's capture it alive and take it to Nalchik."

We dismounted and surrounded the shepherd's cabin. We were quite numerous, and were able to form a solid circle around the cabin. I was just opposite the door, and saw everything very well. When we approached, the almasty came out of the cabin two or three times, in one bound. It appeared very agitated; it came out, moved around, jumped to one side, but then saw the men. It went back in one jump, immediately leaping out again, jumped to another side, but there also it saw the men. In doing this, it grimaced, with its lips moving very, very fast, and it mumbled something.

Meanwhile, our cordon was approaching. We had closed ranks and were advancing elbow-to-elbow. At this moment the almasty appeared again, jumped in all directions and, suddenly, gave a terrible cry and ran straight at the men. It ran faster than a horse. To tell the truth, the men were taken by surprise. It easily broke through our cordon, jumped into the ravine and disappeared in the brush surrounding the river.

It was about 1.80 metres in height, and very robust. One could not see its face well because of the hair. Its breasts hung down to its middle. It was covered with long shaggy red hair, like that of the buffalo. The hair could be seen clearly through the pieces of the old handmade Kabardian caftan which it was wearing, and which was completely in tatters.

One must look for almastys at night, near fields of hemp, when it is ripe. They love hemp. They eat a great deal of it, walking around in the fields and stuffing themselves with clusters of the grain. While doing this, they mumble all the time, "Boom, boom, boom!" They chew noisily, they blow from their noses, and they rustle the stalks. When an almasty is eating hemp at night, it can be heard at a great distance. How many times in the past have I heard them mumbling this way? In recent years I have not heard them at all.

Almastys also like watermelons. In the past they came into the plantations and did a great deal of damage. I had a friend, an old man; he was guardian of a melon field on the kolkhoz (collective farm), and lived in a hut there. It was before the war. One day, I went to see him and I noticed that many of the melons had been damaged; they had been chewed on in a strange way, and were eaten in the middle. I picked up a melon and saw the marks of very large teeth. I then understood that it was an almasty which had done this.

I arrived at my friend's, I laughed and I said, "You're a fine guardian! Look at your plantation, look what has happened to it!" He answered me, "Be quiet! This almasty takes all my strength. Every night it comes and eats the watermelons. I go out to meet it with my stick, but I don't dare come too close. I shout at it, "Aren't you ashamed! Go away!" It says to me, "Boom, boom, boom." I shout again, "You have no conscience! Me, I'm the guardian here. I'm responsible for the watermelons." It answers me, "Boom, boom, boom." And there you are - we chat like that all night.

Q. Do you know of any cases where an almasty has been killed, or a carcass has been found?

A. Thirty or forty years ago, two shepherds came and told how they had found in the forest the carcass of an almasty which must have died a short time before and was half devoured by wolves or dogs. In. fact, there was not even a carcass anymore, as only the head remained. The shepherds were very upset. They kept repeating, "That will bring a lot of trouble! That will bring a lot of trouble!"

Q. Why do certain almastys wear human clothing?

A. First of all, our people take pity on almastys. Earlier, it was often the case that almastys came into the houses, for us to give them something to eat. At the same time they would be given some clothing so that they would not be cold.

Secondly, the almastys take things themselves. That happened very often in former times. Let's say someone goes into the forest or into the fields to collect wood or to cut hay. He hangs his food and some of his clothing on a branch or somewhere, in order not to be too warm. He comes back a few hours later: his food has been eaten and his clothing has disappeared. The almastys have stolen everything.

The almastys watch humans very closely. For example, a man is walking in the forest. It's hot. He sees a river. He undresses, puts his things on the bank and goes for a swim. Then, he comes out, dresses, and goes on his way. Immediately, as soon as he has left, at the very same moment, out of the forest comes an almasty; that is, of course, if there was one watching nearby. Usually, it will come to the place where the clothing was put down. It will feel around the ground, and will sniff at it. The almasty is very curious.

Communication by Khuzer Bekanluk Akhaminov, *55; Kabardian, farmer, village of Planovskoye:*

A month ago, on the 10th of August (1964), about three kilometres from the village, I was scything in a field of sunflowers where there remained some open places where seeds had not been sown. Suddenly I heard a strong noise, as if someone were snorting noisily, like a dog when a fly gets into its nose. When the sound occurred a third time, I put down my scythe and went to look. Suddenly, two arms, like human ones, but long, black and hairy, extended out of the foliage in my direction. I ran immediately to my cart, which was about 10 metres away, and climbed up onto it. Standing on the cart, I saw a silhouette; it resembled a human one and was bending over pushing into the sunflowers. I only saw the back clearly; it was covered with long reddish fur, like that of the buffalo, and the long hair of the head. I did not see its face. When the almasty had left (I recognized it at once, because before this I had seen others), I got down from my cart and returned to my scythe.

At that moment I heard a squealing coming from the same place. I advanced carefully, and pushed the stalks apart.

On the packed-down grass, as if in a nest, were lying two newborns. It was clear that she had just given birth. They were exactly like human babies, except that they were smaller. They must have weighed around two kilos, no more. Apart from that, you would not have been able to distinguish them from our little ones. They had rosy skin, like human infants, exactly the same head, the same arms and legs. They were not hairy. No, I stress this - they were not hairy. They looked like newborn humans or newborn rats: bare, and with rosy skin. They were waving their little arms and legs, just like our newborns, and squealing.

I got away from there in a hurry. I quickly hitched up my donkey and returned to the village. Two or three days later I came back, but there was no one around.

Q. Why did you not tell anyone about this?

A. What do you mean - not tell anyone? I told my wife and my neighbours about it.

Q. I mean, why did you not report it?

A. But, report it to who? For what reason?

Q. To the authorities, to the police, to the village Soviet! (The idea of reporting such foolishness to the authorities - an almasty giving birth! - aroused great hilarity among the small group present.)

Q. But, didn't you know that this was of interest, that scientists were studying the almasty?

A: Who knew that it was important? Never in my life have I heard it said that such a thing could be of interest to anyone.

Administrative map of Caucasus in USSR, 1952-1991

Republic of Azerbaijan

- **Communication by Khadji Murat, 23;** *Azerbaijanian, driver from Belokany:*

In the autumn of 1950, I was walking at night along the edge of the Belokan-Chay River. I was carrying a sack of rice which I had "pinched" down there at the old mill. It weighed some twenty kilos. Plainly, I didn't want to meet anyone. As if intentionally, the moon was shining as brightly as possible. Also, I had not taken the main street, but rather the back alleys of the village, along the river. Suddenly, I heard a noisy splashing. I thought at first that the wind was carrying the sound of the rapids, but there was no wind and, also, the rapids were quite small. The splashing was repeated regularly, as if someone were emptying a bucket at one go. I said to myself, "That must be the neighbour across the way, who is taking a bath; the devil take him. What am I going to do to get by?" I came up to the riverbank carefully, and looked around from behind a rock. In the moonlight, I saw a person, very tall, standing in the water. He was standing upright and throwing enormous handfuls of water over himself. That's curious, I thought, the neighbour isn't that big. At that moment I saw the long hair on the head. Bah, that's better, I said to myself, it's not the neighbour, it's his wife! Well, I said to myself, I'm going to watch her take a bath. I was a young fellow and still a bachelor, so in any case it was interesting to see a good-looking woman!

I put down my sack and crept up carefully. I arrived at the water's edge, but just at that point there were bushes which got in the way so that one could only see very poorly. I had to retreat. She was just behind a rocky outcropping.

I went down on my chest, crawled toward the rock, and raised my head slowly, exactly at the level of the water, right beside her. I almost gave up the ghost right there. In the water was standing a dreadful-looking woman, abominable. It wasn't a face that she had, but a frightful muzzle. And enormous hands - long ones. She was filling them with water and throwing it on her shoulders. On my word of honour, it was a half-bucketful that she scooped up each time. Then, she took her breasts and began to throw them on the water. Her breasts were enormous, very long, and made a loud slapping sound on the water.

Then, she started to throw water over herself again.

My hair was standing up on my head. I crawled slowly backward, then I jumped to my feet and ran across the road to get the neighbour, the one I thought was - himself or his wife - bathing. I knocked at his door for quite a long time. Finally, he came out. I said to him: "Get your rifle and come quickly, there's a kaptar[4] taking a bath, come and see." At first, he hesitated, and then we left. When we arrived, there was no one in sight.

The neighbour helped me to carry the rice, which I had to share with him after all.

4. *Kaptar* - a popular name for hominoid in Azerbaijan and Daghestan.

Republic of Daghestan

- **Communication by Ramazan Omarov,** *37; Lakh, director of the veterinarian station of the district of Tlyarata:*

On August 20, 1959, I was coming back across the mountain to Antzug. It was about six o'clock in the evening. The visibility was very good. I was coming down a small valley where the trees were quite sparse.

When I reached the big white rock, I noticed an animal that was moving at the base of it. I thought it was a bear, and so I hid behind a bush. I had no firearm of any sort on me. I had only my bridle and the bag in which I carry the supplies needed for vaccinations.

While hiding behind the bush, I began to observe. The animal, which as far as I could see had been seated, got up suddenly and started in my direction on its two legs. It was a creature which resembled both a man and a monkey at the same time. Since my childhood I had heard stories of kaptars, but I did not believe in them. Well, this was a kaptar that I was seeing with my own eyes.

Its fur was long and black, like that of a goat. The neck was virtually non-existent, the head resting directly on the shoulders. Long hair hung down from it.

The kaptar was approaching, not directly toward me, but somewhat to one side. It was a male. The head was long and tapering to a point toward the top; in other words, it was conical or ovoid in shape. Its long arms hung almost to the knees. It swung them while walking, and they jerked, as though they were articulated on bolts. They gave the impression of having been assembled in joints, like a child's plaything.

At about 200 metres from where I was, this strange creature crossed the path and sat down again. It remained seated two or three minutes, with its hands touching the ground. It reminded me of an athlete doing warming-up exercises. Then, it got up again and went toward a bush on the other side of the crest and disappeared. I did not see it again. I abandoned my bush and came calmly back to the house. What struck me the most? It went up the slope very quickly, taking steps of a metre and even more. A man would not be able to go up such a steep slope with such great strides.

Administrative map of Caucasus in USSR, 1952-1991

I thought of the chimpanzee which I had seen in the zoo at Tbilisi. The fur of the chimpanzee is shorter, and its head more round. Its arms and legs are also shorter. It must be said, it is true, that its size is much smaller. The kaptar did not measure less than 1.80 metres, and it resembled more a man than a monkey. It walked erect, with just the head inclined a little forward from the shoulders. There was no tail. Another typical thing - with wolves and bears, one always sees the ears, even if they have short ones, whereas here the hair covered the ears, and they were not visible.

Clearly, I was afraid, but my curiosity was even stronger than my fear. I have lived 37 years, and I had always thought that the kaptar was the invention of superstitious people. Now, I know that to be false; I saw it myself.

--0--

Having presented more sighting reports and thoroughly analyzed them from a morphological point of view, Koffmann comes to the following conclusions:

> Extrapolated from hundreds of eyewitness reports, classified and subjected to statistical analysis and to anatomical dissection, the data and information concerning the morphology of the almasty - the only body of information considered here, that relating to the ecology and to the ethology[5] not being presented - constitute authentic and precise reference points, the convergence of which produces the appearance of an anatomically concrete, well-defined, balanced and visible personage, devoid of any element of fantasy.

> The morphological realism, the biological verity, the anthropological authenticity conceivable concerning this personage are indisputable. This is a fact.

> Now, this personage is out of the ordinary. The criteria which characterize it belong to a very specialized domain of science: human paleontology.

> Moreover, this personage cannot be the expression of scientific knowledge by our informants; it goes without saying that the old Caucasian shepherds, for the most part illiterate, do not have this knowledge.

> This personage cannot be the fruit of imagination or of fraud; we would be obliged to accept the postulate that a lie repeated many times engenders authenticity. A third hypothesis remains: if there can be

5. Ethology - study of animal behaviour

neither lie nor exceptional knowledge on the part of our informants, there remains the supposition that their descriptions of the man of the woods correspond to a reality.

What reality? Great anthropoid for some, or backward Neanderthal for Professor Porshnev, the almasty certainly presents many more *hominian*[6] traits than *simian*[7]. However, in the present state of the research, it seems to me more in line with wisdom and scientific rigour to abstain from even a preliminary diagnosis.

Nevertheless, it would seem that the species supposed to exist in the Caucasus belongs to the human phylum, or to a parallel and neighbouring line. Need one dwell upon the repercussions in the human sciences which its confirmed discovery would have?

DR. KOFFMANN REPLIES
TO PROFESSOR AVDEYEV

Literaturnaya Gazeta (Literary Gazette), October 1, 1964, published a letter from Professor Valeri Avdeyev under the heading *Almastys - Where Are the Traces of Them?* He wrote:

In popular-science literature, from time to time the question is raised of the existence of hitherto unknown wild men. An article signed by four correspondents of the TASS news agency and Nedelya weekly has been published in Nedelya under the heading of *Do Almastys Exist?*.

They maintain that official science is wrong in rejecting the possibility of the existence of a wild man-like creature, unknown to science, that is hiding in places difficult of access, because more and more testimony is being gathered to the effect that natives of the Caucasus have long known about him and some have seen him in our own times. Since the wild man, according to the article, is "nothing extraordinary" to the inhabitants of the Caucasus, the various nationalities there have different names for him. A list of these names is given in the article, and all of them mean *man of the woods or wild man...*

It is perfectly clear that it will be possible to talk seriously of the existence of the almasty only after unquestionable material traces of their presence have been found.

6. Hominian - manlike
7. Simian - apelike

After my personal talks with her, I sincerely wished - and continue to wish - Jeanne Koffmann and her assistants the best of luck in their fascinating search. In the meantime, however, like many others, I do not believe in the existence of the almasty.

M.-J. Koffmann's *Reply to Prof. Avdeyev* was published in the April 1965 *Nauka i Religia (Science and Religion)* magazine:

> Esteemed Professor, I would like to comment on your views on the so-called snowman, which are shared by many others.
>
> It is true that we do not yet possess serious material proofs that man-like creatures live in the Caucasus. The stories of eyewitnesses are as yet almost the only material we go by.
>
> This means that our claims are built entirely on their accounts. Do we have any reason to question them?
> You, and those who think like you, solve that problem very simply. All reports concerning wild men, whether they originate from Tibet, the Pamirs, North America or the Caucasus, are dismissed as false. Discussion is thus closed.
>
> But there is no unanimity among you, even in arriving at such an unsophisticated conclusion. Some of you think hundreds of eyewitnesses lie just like that, from a depravity inherent in human nature. Others see our informants as practical jokers, glad of a chance to put one over the scientists. Still others consider that all our witnesses are cowards who simply see things out of fright. Kinder critics are disposed to regard them as suffering from hallucinations. Finally, there are those who consider them to be backward ignoramuses, given to superstitious fears.
>
> Two years ago, a well-known Moscow scientist, asked to at least look at my record of evidence, flatly refused to examine "old wives' tales gathered in the marketplace." Yet the file contained:
>
> 1)   the record of a two- hour talk in one of the largest party district committees of Azerbaijan, signed by the second secretary of the committee, Dr. Kuliyeva, and a livestock specialist Akhadov;
> 2)   the report of milita captain Belalov;
> 3)   an affidavit by Tairov, a research worker of the Academy of Sciences of Azerbaijan;
> 4)   the testimony of Dyakov, an officer (Georgia);
> 5)   the testimony of Shtymov, a Kabardian, dean of the faculty

of pedagogics and psychology of the Pedagogical Institute in Kustanai;

6)   the statement of Lt. Col. Karapetian of the Medical Corps, to the Academy of Sciences of the USSR; and

7)   the testimony of Kardanov, a Kabardian, a deputy to the Supreme Soviet of the USSR, etc.

The idea that the wild man is just a figure of folklore is ruled out by the testimony of witnesses not belonging to the local population. The view about ill-intentioned deception is incompatible with the testimony of persons who were unaware of the scientific controversy, and who enjoy considerable authority among the local inhabitants. The suggestion that it is a question of hallucination is refuted by the very nature of these hallucinations - the same in the case of hundreds of people at various times and in different localities.

I agree with you that if one wishes, one can collect any number of rumours about anything. However, people not only hear, but they have the ability to evaluate what they hear. There is a method of ascertaining scientific truth by holding polls. A strictly worked-out system of compilation, analysis, comparative evaluations, verification and summarising of information guarantees a definite trustworthiness of the data received.

When I left for the Caucasus some years ago to verify the first reports that had reached us, I considered the possibility of wild men living there to be ridiculous, just as you and thousands of others do. It took a long time and hundreds of conversations before I reached the conclusion, and later the conviction, that I was dealing with realities.

You underline that you don't believe in the devil. I don't want to yield to you on this point, so I hasten to announce that I also don't believe in the devil. What is more, I don't believe in the almasty. I possess sufficient data to simply say that he *exists!*

REPORT BY DMITRI, BAYANOV

Bigfoot Co-op, April 1981

Marie-Jeanne Koffmann's achievement in 1978, in fact her major achievement over the years, was the finding of a set of good tracks which she photographed and made casts of. The footprints, by our best judgement, were truly left by an almasty. Regrettably, Koffmann has not published her photographs or any description of them yet, and this prevents others from doing anything about her findings.

**An expedition member trying to keep in step with almasty tracks.
Dolina Narzanov, March 1978.**

Expedition head M. J. Koffmann carefully extracting from the ground an intact almasty track hardened with glue. It was one of a set found in March 1978 in the Dolina Narzanov valley in the North Caucasus.

Fortunately, a young hominologist, Andrey Kozlov, a physician by profession, who lives in the Urals, is doing some research in this respect, i.e., studying the creature's anatomy as revealed by their tracks.

Another recent development there is that an instructor in mountain climbing from Leningrad named Leonid Zamyatnin became interested in our subject and started to collect reports of hominoid sightings from his friends and acquaintances among the local mountaineers (sort of Caucasian "Sherpas"), including Joseph Kakhiani, a hero of Soviet mountain climbing, who, it turns out, is a hominoid eyewitness himself, as are his relatives and friends. Considering Kakhiani's high reputation and disinterestedness, this is a trump for us in our never-ending bickering with unbelievers. Zamyatnin has access to local editors and may have his findings published in a local magazine. According to one bizarre tale from his collection, a local mountaineer on horseback was once accosted by an amorous hirsute female of appropriate size and strength. She grabbed his hand and started to pull him to herself. He managed to hold his ground for some time because his other hand was held fast in the loop of the rein. He may have been torn apart by horse and hominoid, but luckily a truck came round a bend on the mountain road where they were struggling and the man was saved.

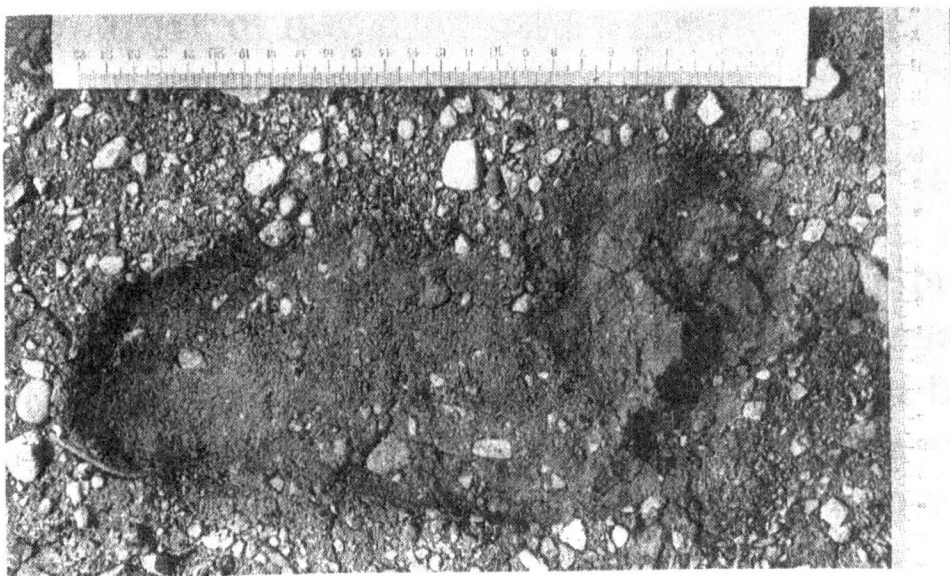

One of the footprints (the same place).

Koffmann's search goes on in the foothills of the North Caucasus, and hominoids there, judging by the sighting reports and footprints, are of human sizes. From time to time, though, we hear of giant creatures living high in the mountains. A presumed description of their bones is contained in the book *Home, and Home Again* by George and Helen Papashvily. Recently we've obtained two separate, unambiguous and weighty reports from two ethnic Russians (not the locals with their suspected folklore proclivity) who were in the Caucasus on a short visit, who had never heard of the matter, who saw the giants at close range in daylight and nearly died of fear. One encounter happened in August 1967, the other in September 1979. The creatures were about three metres (10') tall! These sightings do not abound in details of anatomy, but, all things considered, I find them credible and very important for the clear indication of the creatures' gigantic size. Both encounters took place high in the mountains, one even on eternal snow where the giant left his footprints. These sightings are pretty dramatic in human terms, but they add nothing of value to our knowledge of hominoid anatomy and behaviour.

The latest sighting report, collected by Alexandra Bourtseva, in the area of Koffmann's search, tells of two local teenagers mowing grass in July 1980 in an open space some 500 yards from the Nalchik - Pyatigorsk Highway. There is an open water duct raised above the ground and running across the field in which the boys took dips from time to time. At one moment they looked in the direction of the duct and saw a hairy creature, not much taller than themselves, standing on the edge of the duct looking at them. The boys stood, motionless and surprised, while the creature entertained them with all sorts of jolly antics: running with great speed to and fro on the edge of the duct, jumping from it, somersaulting, etc. The boys received the impression that the creature was inviting them to take part in the merriment, but it was too much for the humans, and after awhile a disappointed hominoid took leave and disappeared into a nearby hemp field. The boys went home and told their mothers what they had seen. "It was a young almasty," said the mothers. It happened at noon and in full view from the Nalchik-Pyatigorsk Highway, often travelled by tourists from all over Europe and sometimes from America. So keep your eyes open next time you come to the Caucasus.

WHERE ARE THEIR BONES?

The following is an extract from an autobiographical book, *Home and Home Again*[8]. The late George Papashvily, a sculptor, who migrated to the US, tells of his life as a boy in a Georgian village in pre-revolutionary Russia. The village boys, including the author, went on a hike to the mountains and found their way into a secluded cave with an underwater entrance wherein they discovered the following (italics added. -*D.B.*):

From cracks in the ceiling ghostly vines trailed, and a pale green light filled the room. The floor was covered with bones, bleached white - huge bones, ribs that would have made a cage for a hen and all her chicks, hips wider than an ox yoke, skulls like wine jugs with eye sockets our fists could go in, bulging foreheads, huge jaws.

I pointed at the teeth. "As big as a horse's."

"But these aren't horses," Teddua said, "or cows."

Not water buffalo and not stag," Bootla said.

"I know that. Bones from those animals we saw dozens of times. These are men, I think. *Some kind of men.*"

"Men like us", Bootla said. "Look. They had long arms with five- fingered hands and feet with toes, not paws."

"And not hoofs." Teddua picked up a leg bone. It was half as tall as he. Carefully, he laid it back. "These men could take apples from the top of the highest tree. Without stretching."

"And cover six feet in a single step," Bootla said.

---

8 George and Helen Papashvily. *Home, and Home Again.* New York, 1973, pp.128-131.

George Papashvily with his American wife, Helen. As a boy he learned first-hand where snowmen go to die.

The light from the roof was fading. "I think we'd better go," Teddua said. We took a last quick look around. The eyes in the skulls watched us as we went through the passage and swam to the shore. Walking home, we could talk of nothing else, of course, but the men in the cave. Who were they? Where did they come from? Why were they buried there? How long ago? We had no answer.

"We will have to ask the old men," Teddua said. "If anybody knows, surely it must be one of them…"

When we came home, my father was there, and we told our story to him and to the parents of Teddua and Bootla. They, as puzzled as we, agreed that we certainly must talk to the old men.

So we told our story again while the old men listened carefully. When we were through, they asked us questions.

"Were their swords and daggers beside them?"

"Any bowls or tools in the cave?"

"Pieces of jewelry or scraps of cloth near the bones?"

"No," we said.

"And the upper leg bone was how long?"

Teddua marked two feet on the floor.

"And the lower one?"

He added another two.

"I think," Miriani said, *"you found the place where the Giants came home to die."*

"Were they men?"

"Yes," Miriani said, different from us, but men. *Long ago they lived on earth."*

"Some call them Narts," Vachtang said. "Some say *they were the first men. We came afterward."*

"What happened to them?" Bootla said.

"Slowly, one by one, they disappeared. Nobody knows where or how, for *they left no graves, no bones."*

*"*But now I think you found their resting place," Miriani said. "Perhaps *as some animals do, the Giants knew when their time had come, and when they grew old or sick they went to their cave to die."*

"Did you ever see one of the Giants?" Teddua asked.

"No, but my great-great-grandfather did. At least, he saw a Giant's footprint in the snow up above Mleti."

"Are all the Giants dead?" Bootla said.

Otar shrugged. "So they say, but who knows?"

"I have heard a few, *a very few still live* at the top of Mount Kazbeck," Vachtang said. "But unfortunately I never had the pleaure to meet one. At least so far."

Igor Bourtsev 'goes underground' in
search of Zana's bones in Abkhazia.

A SKELETON STILL BURIED AND A SKULL UNEARTHED:
THE STORY OF ZANA

By Igor Bourtsev

I n Abkhazia, Western Caucasus - relic hominoids are called abnauayu. While collecting reports in 1962, a colleague of Boris Porshnev, zoologist Prof. Alexander Mashkovtsev, heard and studied the story of Zana. Subsequently, Porshnev took over where his late companion left off. The following information is borrowed from Porshnev's work *The Struggle for Troglodytes*[9].

Zana was a female abnauayu who had been caught and tamed and who lived and died within the memory of a number of people still alive at the time of the research. She was buried near the village of Tkhina in the Ochamchiri District of Abkhazia in the 1880's or 1890's.

The manner of her capture is vague. Some said it was not a chance catch. Hunters familiar with an age-old technique tied her up, and, when she furiously fought back, hit her with cudgels, gagged her mouth with felt, and shackled her legs to a log. Probably she had already changed hands by sale when she became the property of the ruling prince D. M. Achba who was the titular head of the Zaadan region. She passed into the possession of one of his vassals, named Chelokua and still later she was presented to a nobleman, Edgi Genaba, who visited the region. He took her away, still shackled and chained, to his estate in the village of Tkhina on the Mokva River, 78 kilometres from Sukhumi.

At first Genaba lodged her in a very strong enclosure and nobody ventured in to give her food, for she acted like a wild beast. It was thrown to her. She dug herself a hole in the ground and slept in it, and for the first three years she lived in this wild state, gradually becoming tamer. After three years she was moved to a wattle-fence enclosure under an awning near the house, tethered at first, but later she was let loose to wander about.; however she never went far from

---

9. Boris Porshnev *The Struggle for Troglodytes*. In the *Prostor* magazine, July 1968 pp.113-116 (in Russian).

---

the place where she received her food. She could not endure warm rooms and the year round, in any weather, slept outdoors in a hole that she made herself under the awning.

Villagers teased her with sticks thrust through the wattle-fence, and she would snatch them with fury, bare her teeth and howl.

Her skin was black, or dark grey, and her whole body covered with reddish-black hair. The hair on her head was tousled and thick, hanging mane-like down her back.

She could not speak, over decades that she lived with people, Zana did not learn a single Abkhaz word; she only made inarticulate sounds and mutterings, and cries when irritated, but she reacted to her name, carried out commands given by her master and was scared when he shouted at her - and this despite the fact that she was very tall, massive and broad, with huge breasts and buttocks, muscular arms and legs, and fingers that were longer and thicker than human fingers. She could splay her toes widely and move apart the big toe.

From remembered descriptions given to Mashkovtsev and Porshnev, her face was terrifying; broad, with high cheekbones, flat nose, turned out nostrils, muzzle-like jaws, wide mouth with large teeth, low forehead, and eyes of a reddish tinge - but the most frightening feature was her expression which was purely animal, not human. Sometimes, she would give a spontaneous laugh, baring those big white teeth of hers. The latter were so strong that she easily cracked the hardest walnuts.

She lived for many years without showing any change: no grey hair, no falling teeth, keeping strong and fit as ever. Her athletic power was enormous. She would outrun a horse, and swim across the wild Mokva River even when it rose in violent high tide. Seemingly without effort, she lifted with one hand an eighty-kilo sack of flour and carried it uphill from the watermill to the village. She climbed trees to get fruit, and to gorge herself with grapes she would pull down a whole vine growing around the tree. She ate whatever was offered to her, including hominy and meat, with bare

The exhumed skull of Zana's son, Khwit, exhibits a combination of modern and ancient features which aroused great interest amongst anthropologists.

hands and enormous gluttony. She loved wine, and was allowed her fill, after which she would sleep for hours in a swoon-like state.

She liked to lie in a cool pool side by side with buffalos. At night she used to roam the surrounding hills. She wielded big sticks against dogs and on other perilous occasions. She had a curious obsession for playing with stones, knocking one against another and splitting them.

She took swims the year round, and preferred to walk naked even in winter, tearing dresses that she was given into shreds. However, she showed more tolerance toward a loincloth. Sometimes she went into the house, but the women were afraid of her and came near only when she was in a gentle mood; when angry she presented a scary sight and could even bite. But she obeyed her master, Edgi Genaba, and he knew how to bring her to heel. Adults used her as a bogy figure with children, although Zana never actually attacked children.

She was trained to perform simple domestic tasks, such as grinding grain for flour, bringing home firewood and water, or sacks to and from the watermill, or pull her master's high boots off.

But she became the mother of human children, and this is the wonderous side of her life story, very important for the science of genetics. Zana was pregnant several times by various men, and, giving birth without assistance, she always washed the newborn child in the cold water-spring. The half-breed infants, unable to survive these ablutions, died.

So, when subsequently Zana gave birth, the villagers began taking the newborn babies away from her in good time, and reared them themselves. Four times this happened, and the children, two sons and two daughters, grew up as humans, fully-fledged and normal men and women who could talk and possessed reason. It is true that they had some strange physical and mental features, but nonetheless they were fully capable of engaging in work and social life.

The eldest son's name was Dzhanda, and the eldest daughter was Kodzhanar. The second daughter was named Gamasa, and the younger son Khwit, who died in 1954. All had descendants of their own, scattered across Abkhazia.

There were rumours that the father of Gamasa and Khwit was in fact Edgi Genaba himself, but in the census they were put down under a different surname, and their family name became Sabekia. It is significant that Zana was buried in the family cemetery of the Genabas, and that the two youngest children of Zana were brought up by Genaba's wife.

Gamasa and Khwit were both powerfully built, had dark skins, but they inherited scarcely anything from Zana's facial appearance. The complex of human features, inherited from their father, was dominant in them, and overruled the mother's line of descent. Khwit, who died at the age of 65 or 70, was described by his fellow-villagers as little different from the human norm, except for certain small divergences. He was extremely strong, difficult to deal with and quick to pick a fight. In fact, he lost his right hand after one of the many fights he had with his fellow villagers, but his left hand sufficed him to mow and do other work on a collective farm, and even climb trees. When old, he moved to the town of Tkvarcheli, where he eventually died, but he was taken back for burial at Tkhina.

The next stage of the Zana case was taken up by attempts to find her grave and skeleton. Here is what Boris Porshnev says about his first effort in that direction:

> In September 1964, the archaeologist V. S. Orelkin and I made our first attempt to find Zana's grave. The cemetery was wildly overgrown and only the ten-year-old mound over Khwit's grave could be picked out among the bracken covering the hillside. Nobody else had been buried since then. Zana must be somewhere near. We asked the old residents and the last scion of the Genaba clan, seventy-nine-year-old Kenton. He was clear that we should dig under a pomegranate tree. What was found there turned out to be the remains of one of Zana's grandchildren who had died early, for the profile that we established from the skull was extraordinarily like the profiles of Zana's two living grandchildren, whom I myself had met.

> After two more expeditions the search party had still not found Zana's bones, though in a third attempt in October 1965, they found what are probably the bones of Gamasa, as they present slight, but definite, paleoanthropic features.[10.]

> After the passing of Porshnev, it fell to my lot to continue the search. I headed three expeditions to Abkhazia in search of Zana's skeleton, in 1971, 1975 and 1978, which merits a separate story. Our difficulty was that by that time the last scion of the Genaba clan had passed away and nobody knew exactly where Zana's grave was. We put in a tremendous amount of spadework on that hillside, digging sticky clayey earth under almost daily downpours. During the second expedition I was taken seriously ill with an illness which doctors failed to identify. We never found a skeleton that would fit Zana's features as described by witnesses.

> It was then decided to exhume the skull of Khwit, Zana's younger son, whose grave was still well-indicated. Professor N. Bourchak-Abramovich assisted me in that digging. I brought the skull to Moscow, where it was studied by two physical anthropologists, M. A. Kolodieva and M. M. Gerasimova. The results of the study were reported by me at the Relic Hominoid Research Seminar and the

10 Archaeologist Yury Voronov, who later became Vice Premier of Abkhazia and was killed in September 1995, participated in the search at the time. *(IB)*

Igor Bourtsev examines the skull of Zana's son, Khwit.

Moscow Naturalists' Society and published in 1987.[11.]

Anthropologist M. A. Kolodieva compared the skull of Khwit with the male skulls from Abkhazia in the collection of the Moscow State University Institute of Anthropology, and found that Khwit's skull was significantly different. Indicating it as the Tkhina skull, she writes:

> The Tkhina skull exhibits an original combination of modern and ancient features. The facial section of the skull is significantly larger in comparison with the mean Abkhaz type. All the measurements and indices of the superciliary cranial contour are greater not only than those of the mean Abkhaz series, but also than those of the maximum size of some fossil skulls studied (or rather were comparable with the latter). The Tkhina skull approaches closest the Neolithic Vovnigi II skulls of the fossil series.

On her part, anthropologist M. M. Gerasimova came to the following conclusions:

> The skull discloses a great deal of peculiarity, a certain disharmony, disequilibrium in its features, very large dimensions of the facial skeleton, increased development of the contour of the skull, the specificity of the non-metric features (the two *foramina mentale* in the lower jaw, the intrusive bones in the sagittal suture, and the Inca bone). The skull merits further extended study.

So the bottom line of the Zana case today is this: we have nothing but the words of witnesses to describe Zana's peculiar nature, but the hard and specific evidence of her son's skull goes a long way in making the testimony of witnesses more solid and trustworthy.

---

11 I. D. Bourtsev, M. A. Kolodieva. *Results of a Preliminary Investigation of a Skull from the villlage of Tkhina, Abkhaz, ASSR.* In: *Papers of the Moscow Naturalists Society.* Moscow, 1987 (in Russian).

REPORT BY DMITRI BAYANOV

Bigfoot Co-op, February 1992

In the August 1991 issue I informed Co-op readers of Marie-Jeanne Koffmann's publication on the almasty (wildman) of the Caucasus in the French science journal *Archeologia*, June 1991. Koffmann tells me her next publication is due in the February 1992 issue. She has been staying in Paris for several months while preparing these materials. She was born in France and has relatives there. Let me remind you that Koffmann is chairperson of the Russian Society of Cryptozoologists[12] (RSC), as our organization is newly named, and the main authority on the wildman of the Caucasus.

Last summer, with Koffmann in France, fieldwork in Kabarda (Northern Caucasus) was headed by her close colleague and RSC Board member Gregory Panchenko, a very able young biology researcher, residing in Kharkov, Ukraine. On August 26, Panchenko had a close encounter with an almasty, which he reported in detail at the September session of our seminar in Moscow. The incident is connected with the wildman/horse relationship, and so I intend to dwell on this matter first.

In his fundamental monograph *The Present State of the Question of Relic Hominoids*, in the section "Biology," Prof. Porshnev discusses ecological and ethological connections of relic hominoids with different wild and domestic animals, including horses. Here's a relevant passage in my translation:

> Of much interest are the observations of the relic hominoid approaching horses, so that in the dark he is sometimes mistaken for a horse-stealer. Horses are afraid of the relic hominoid, but there is no information that he does them harm, except the popular belief spread in diverse geographic regions that he can get onto a horse's back and ride the animal to exhaustion. What biological stimulus could, in the hominoid's evolution, have formed his interest in horses - in the first instance, obviously, wild horses of one or another species, and later, in domestic horses? There are stories claiming that he can suck the milk of mares and just for this purpose approaches herds of

12. Cryptozoologists are engaged in collecting evidence for the existence of animals whose presence in general or in a particular time or place is not recognized by zoology.

ABOVE AND OPPOSITE: Photographs taken by Igor Bourtsev whilst trying to solve the riddle of plaits in horses' manes during his expeditions to the Talysh Mountains in Azerbaijan in the early 1970's.

horses. Here is, for example, a testimony by A. M. Markova, researcher at the Horse-Breeding Department of the Timiryazev Agricultural Academy, regarding stories she heard from Kazakhstan herders. In the southern steppes of Kazakhstan, herders complain that the man-like bipedal creature sucks the mare's milk at night. It is alleged that the creature plaits the mane, using hair loops as stirrups, and, lying on the stomach on the horse's back, facing backward, and holding with one hand to the base of the tail, hangs down under the horse's belly, sucking the udder on the move. Despite the fairy-tale flavor of the story, researchers of the said department pointed out that only such a trick of "fancy riding" could have provided access to a mare's udder for an alien creature. It is too early to judge whether such stories contain factual biological substance. It may be simply that the hominoid used to make long journeys following herds of wild horses, having developed them, and retained ever since the habit of tackling horses with an ape-like or even more-than ape-like nimbleness. In any case, the biological links of relic hominoids with horses deserve serious study.

In a footnote, Porshnev writes that the above information was received and passed on to him by Koffmann in December 1959, and I know from Koffmann that she consulted horse specialists after hearing similar stories in the Caucasus.

The next relevant quotation, showing the ubiquity of the theme, is from the article *Unknown Hominids and New World Legends* by Bacil F. Kirtley, published in *Western Folklore* (April 1964).

In 1925 Aime F. Tschiffely, an intrepid English school-teacher, journeyed, using two Argentine Creole horses, from Buenos Aires up the length of South America, Central America, and into the United States as far as Washington, D.C. He narrates the following experience, which occurred in the Colombian Andes. Victor, mentioned in the account, was an illiterate Ecuadorian peasant, and was Tschiffely's *mazo*.[13]

> One morning when I brought the horses from pasture, I noticed that one had his mane plaited. I tried to undo it, but found it tightly knotted. I asked a boy, Victor, if he knew anything about this or if he had done it, and he immediately told me El Duende had been with the horses during the night. I had never heard this name and asked for an explanation. In the meantime a half-caste Indian with whom I had spent the night had come up and assured me that the boy was right.
>
> It appears that El Duende, according to these people, is a dwarf who lives in deep canyons and desolate valleys, where he can often be heard crying like a baby or, when he is in a boisterous mood, making noises rivaling thunder. Natives firmly believe that he is very fond of horseback riding, but, being so small, is unable to sit on the horse's back, so he sits on the animal's neck, making stirrups by plaiting the mane in such a way as to be able to put his feet in it.

Tschiffely concludes the episode with the following words, which are not cited by Kirtley:

The only explanation I can give for this extraordinary plaiting is the dampness in the air, which may twist the hair in such a way as to form these knots; or perhaps the horse does it by rubbing against a tree. [14]

Worth mentioning is also the following information supplied by Kirtley:

> *"... that very Mab That plaits the manes of horses in the night..."*
> (William Shakespeare, *Romeo and Juliet*, I, iii, 88-89.)

For our part, we were rather intrigued by the riddle of braids in horses' manes, and paid much attention to it in the 60's and early 70's. We learned that manes may get plaited under conditions whereby the presence of wildmen is definitely excluded. A noted zoologist suggested that may be caused by weasels that come to stables for mice and, running all over the place, climb onto horses

---

13 *Mazo* (Spanish) – servant.
14 Aime F. Tschiffely. *Tschiffely's Ride*, New York, 1933, p.182.

Biologist Gregory Panchenko, who spent a night in a barn in the company of a young almasty and an old mare.

and entangle their manes.

Igor Bourtsev devoted much effort to the problem of watching horses on pastures at night through a night-vision device during his expeditions in the Talysh Mountains, and seemed to have solved the riddle. In an article in the July 1975 *Znanye - Sila (Knowledge is Power)* magazine, he argued, with the help of photographs and a drawing, that manes get plaited "on their own" due to the horses' habit of incessantly shaking the head and the neck. Why, then, aren't manes always plaited?

Because one more condition is needed to get the process of "self- plaiting" under way: a piece of mud, a burdock seed, anything that ties together the ends of strands in the mane, so that the knot gets through the loops from time to time as the horse shakes the neck. Bourtsev's explanation was so convincing that I congratulated him on the solution of at least one of our numerous problems, and the matter was put to rest... until last August.

On August 25, 1991, Gregory Panchenko, having collected yet another portion of sighting evidence from the locals encountering almasty in Kabarda, was all set to go home when someone told him that an almasty had been plaiting a horse's mane over the past weeks in a place called 'the ravine of Kuruko.' Being young and not as convinced as Bourtsev and I of the process of "self-plaiting," Panchenko decided to put off his departure, shouldered his pack and hastily hiked the several miles across the hills to Kuruko.

Having arrived at the place, he found a mare with a plaited mane and talked to the man in charge. This man, Ali Mukov, aged 60, guards the grain and machinery of a collective farm which are kept in a barn there, as well as the crop fields nearby. Panchenko had met with Mukov some days before, but the guard never mentioned the "braiding" business. Now, pressed by Panchenko, he admitted the matter and related that he had two horses, a gelding which he rode, and the mare with a plaited mane and a sore hind leg, for which reason she was not then being used for riding. Over the previous two weeks, braids had appeared in the mare's mane time and again - but not every night. At first, Mukov tried to unplait them in the morning, but then gave up. To his surprise, Panchenko discovered a braid in the gelding's short mane as well. That evening, Mukov rode off on the gelding to spend the night in the village, leaving the key to the barn with Panchenko. Above the door of the barn, more than 3 metres off the ground, there was a paneless window, used, according to Mukov, as an entry to the barn by whoever plaited the mare's mane.

Getting ready for his vigil in the barn, Panchenko prepared his observation post under a couch standing by the wall opposite a manger to which the mare was tied. Hidden from view by a blanket hanging down from the couch, he could see both the mare and the opening above the door. He left food gifts in the barn: bread, dried meat, sour milk. (Incidentally, the mare had no lactation.) He had no time to prepare a control spot for footprints, and, besides, was not sure it would not deter a visitor.

As for photography, the situation was hopeless. He had a camera with a flash, but no batteries: they are not available under the current crisis conditions here. What's more, would it be wise to use a flash being locked up in a barn with a strong creature that may be provoked by such a trick? Says Panchenko: "Unfortunately, starting the vigil I was pretty tired after my hasty march through the hills with a heavy pack. As a result, I fell asleep and nearly missed the whole visit." (Let me remark in brackets that recalling my own vigils in Kabarda, including that very ravine of Kuruko, I only wish my nerves were as strong as Panchenko's.)

He was awakened by the snorting of the horse. Looking in that direction, Panchenko discerned an upright figure standing by the horse. The visitor seemed to be plaiting the mane. Quote: "I was surprised by the sounds he made. Instead of the often-described mumbling sounds, I heard a kind of high-pitched and excited twittering, almost a bird-like chirping. From time to time, it was interrupted by a smacking of the lips and sounds produced by a swallowing of saliva." (The only other mention of twittering sounds made by relic hominoids known to me is from as remote a place as Indochina.)

The horse strained the tether but did not offer any resistance. Despite a close range (about six metres), visibility was very poor. Panchenko neither had a night-vision device, nor dared to shine a flashlight. Fortunately, there was a full moon, and some light coming through the window made the outlines of objects in the barn visible. So the only thing Panchenko could definitely see was the size and upright stance of the visitor. He was 170-175 centimetres tall, the head sunk in the shoulders, which were wider than the hips, and the arms seemed longer than in humans.

Some minutes later, the creature left the horse and disappeared from Panchenko's line of sight. A little later he reappeared, silhouetted against a light-coloured part of the wall, but visible only from the shoulders to the middle of the thighs because the rest of the body was projected against dark parts of the wall. At that moment the visitor stood at a distance of four metres from Panchenko. Unfortunately, the most informative part of the figure - the head and face - were not visible. After some seconds in that position, the visitor made a step toward the locked door and again disappeared from view. Then Panchenko heard the sound of a double leap and saw the creature in the window opening. Panchenko surmised that the creature first leaped onto a ledge of the wall, and from there to the window. In that position his outline was well visible, but again, as the body was in a crouching stance, few details could be seen. Somehow Panchenko got the impression that the visitor's figure resembled that of a youngster. With some difficulty, he thrust himself through the opening and jumped to the ground outside. Panchenko heard the sound of the landing and retreating steps. To my mind, the creature beat a hasty retreat, having somehow felt the presence of a peeping human in the barn.

(Top) The barn in the ravine of Kuruko, the scene of Panchenko's sighting; (Lower) his sketches illustrating what he saw in the barn.

For about half an hour after that, Panchenko continued to lie still under the couch, hoping that the guest might return; then he shined a flashlight on his watch to see the time. The visitor left the barn about 3 a.m.; how long he was there is not known. Panchenko thinks he woke up 7-8 minutes before the creature's retreat and the total time of observation (near the horse, against the wall, and in the window opening) lasted 5 minutes.

No tracks were found in the morning; the ground was hard, and there was no manure in places where the creature stood and stepped in the barn. No hairs were found in the window opening. Of the food gifts, only the bread was missing, apparently consumed on the spot. The state of the mare's mane differed from what Panchenko observed the evening before: there appeared new and very clumsily-plaited braids. Panchenko's theory is that the better braids were plaited by an adult almasty, perhaps the mother of the youngster he observed (there is some indirect evidence to that effect), and she plaited them when the horse spent nights in the open; but, when the mare was locked up in the barn, it was only the youngster who could get inside through the relatively narrow opening. Panchenko spent some more nights in the barn, but the visitor did not return. Although he did not see any features that would allow to definitely draw a line between the almasty and a human, Panchenko is convinced that it was not a practical joke by some local inhabitant. Firstly, that would be utterly out of character for the local population. Secondly, the nocturnal visitor made such peculiar sounds and showed such an "ape-like nimbleness" by leaping to the window that they sufficiently betray his non-human nature.

The lessons of this event are momentous and have to be thoroughly learned. The Occam's razor rule, much revered in science, proved wrong in the explanation of plaited manes. Both ways of plaiting, natural (explained by Bourtsev) and artificial (explained by folklore), must be real, and we should learn to identify them by the look of the plaits (Bourtsev and Panchenko already claim to be able to do so). Gregory Panchenko is the second of my colleagues, after Maya Bykova, to have had a close and, what's more, premeditated encounter with a hominoid; that is something really new in our research. Two factors made this possible: 1) the researchers' courage and energy, and 2) good contacts with local inhabitants.

Ever since Rene Dahinden paid us a visit in 1971, I've been advocating the method of "an animal farm" as the most promising way in hominology. Panchenko's experience gives more weight to this idea. Wildmen are fascinated by horses and other hoofed animals, so it is pure logic to make full use of this in a bid to befriend a wildman. Panchenko dispatched his report, illustrated with photographs and a drawing, to Koffmann to be published in France, in *Archeologia*. Koffmann's own article has already brought her offers of Western technical aid in the search for almasty in the Caucasus. If the social situation in the region does not get worse, we can expect a well-equipped expedition in Kabarda this year; but I never tire in stressing that the solution of the hominoid problem lies, first and foremost, in biology, and only in the second place, in technology.

CRIMEA PENINSULA
THE BLACK SEA

Bigfoot Co-op, December 1985

We received this surprising account this year (1985), surprising because the Crimea, although next to the Caucasus, and with a good archaeological record of Neanderthal finds, with woods, grottos and caves in the mountains, is believed to have been a civilized and populated area for a long time. When our opponents dismiss the Caucasus as a hominoid habitat, they often say, "Ha! Next you will be seeing them in the Crimea!" It now appears that we have.

One day in September 1974 or 1975, our female witness was in the mountains west of Feodosia (a coastal city in eastern Crimea), gathering wild-growing Cornelian cherries in a deep ravine. Suddenly she heard the sound of breaking branches and a kind of mumbling sound in the brush. Looking in that direction, she saw an unusual creature walking towards her. It was over two metres tall, covered all over with short black hair, had no neck, had very

wide shoulders, long arms and long fingers. It walked in big strides, lifting its feet "unnaturally" high, so that she glimpsed its enormous hairless soles, and bringing the feet down with force. It also waved its arms "unnaturally," slapping the head, the body, and one arm against the other. The creature was looking down and sideways and making mumbling sounds in a low male voice, interrupted two or three times by louder utterances which sounded phonetically like OO-RUK (first long OO like in CHOOSE, U as in BOOK). The witness gained the impression that the creature was irritated and did not notice her. Having watched for a few seconds, the woman took fright and ran away leaving her bag of cherries. Later she returned with three men, and found her bag intact, but no trace of the wildman.

Sculptured portrayal of silenus found in excavations of Nymphaion, an ancient Greek colony town in the Crimea. The term "silenus" in ancient Greece meant "old satyr." The portrayal is remarkable, for it combines certain features (low cranium, bulging brow ridges, prominent cheekbones, deeply-sunken nose bridge) typical both of fossil man and relic hominoids, as described by witnesses.

Part II **THE PAMIRS AND TIEN SHAN**

VOICES FROM THE PAST

The following are extracts from two books by oriental authors of the 12th century A.D. The first is an Arab traveller, the second a Persian scholar.

A kind of nasnas ("faun") is found in the region of Bamir (Pamir) which is a desert stretching between Kashmir, Tibet, Vakhan and China. The nasnas are covered with fur except on their faces, and leap like gazelles; the people of Vakhan hunt them and eat them.

(From the book *Sharaf al-Zaman Tahir Marvazi on China, the Turks and India*.) ^

The highest animal is the Nasnas, a creature inhabiting the plains of Turkestan, of erect carriage and vertical stature, with wide, flat nails. It is very curious about man. Wherever it sees people it comes their way and watches them. And if it sees a lonely man it abducts him and is said to be able to conceive by him. This, after mankind, is the highest of animals, in as much as in several respects it resembles man: first in its erect stature, secondly in the breadth of its nails, and thirdly in the hair on its head.

(From the book *Chahar maqala* by Nizami al-Arudi.) **

In modern scientific literature, "nasnas" is treated as a "faun," i.e., a figment of the imagination, and this despite the clear anatomical characteristics to the contrary supplied by medieval authors. Genetic affinity between nasnas and man, hinted at by Nizami, is of the greatest importance, giving, incidentally, more weight to the Zana story. In a way, Nizami al-Arudi is a precursor of Linnaeus and Darwin, for he used the nasnas to fill in the gap between mankind and the animal kingdom.

---

* Sharaf al-Zaman Tahir Marvazi Sharaf (056/57–1124/25) was a physician and author of Nature of Animals. Al-Marwazi served as physician at the courts of the Seljuk Sultan Malik-Shah I and his successors. As a physician, he recorded observations of parasitic worms.

** Ahmad ibn Umar ibn Alī, known as Nizamī-i Arūzī-i Samarqandī and also Arudi ("The Prosodist"), was a Persian poet and prose writer who flourished between 1110 and 1161 AD. He is particularly famous for his Chahar Maghaleh ("Four Discourses"), his only work to fully survive.

ДИВЪ «АКВАНЪ» (въ Шахъ-нани)

A LESSON FROM ART

There are two kinds of portrayal of hominoids in art: realistic and "ritualistic," i.e., symbolic. The first is true to life and helps the hominologist to study the creatures' appearance and anatomy. The second may be a virtual caricature, which shows not so much the hominoid as the artist's attitude to the subject. When an obnoxious tyrant is pictured with horns, fangs and claws, nobody thinks the tyrant exists because such a monster is impossible. All understand it's grotesqueness, a caricature; yet portrayals of hominoids as grotesque monsters in ancient and medieval art have led scientists and art specialists into believing that these monsters are pure figments of the imagination and that nothing real stands behind them. Hominology puts an end to this self-deception.

Two drawings presented here illustrate this lesson. The first (opposite left) is borrowed from *The Anatomical Dictionary*, a textbook of natural history applied in Buddhist medicine, which was discovered in Mongolia and described in 1959 by the Russian zoologist G. Dementiev and the Czech anthropologist E. Vlcek. The accompanying text in Tibetan says that it is the wild man that lives in the mountains; his body resembles that of man and he has enormous strength. His meat may be eaten to treat mental diseases and his gall cures jaundice. E. Vlcek points out that the authenticity of this drawing of the wild man is supported by the fact that among tens of illustrations of animals in *The Anatomical Dictionary* - showing reptiles, amphibians, birds, and mammals - there is not a single instance of a fantastic or mythological animal; thus, this is a fairly realistic picture of our hero. Note his powerful breast muscles, bent knees, and absence of hair on the hands and feet. [15]

The second drawing is a traditional presentation of a *div* - in this case called 'Akwan,' an evil, devilish character in the Persian epic *Shah Namah by Firdausi*. Div (dev, dav) is a common name of the hominoid in Persia (modern Iran) and the adjacent countries.

---

15. Emanuel Vlcek, *Old Literary Evidence for the Existence of the 'Snow Man' in Tibet and Mongolia.* In: *Man*, August 1959.

Initially divs were worshipped like gods by heathen peoples, and this explains the fact that the words "Deus", "Divus" (meaning God in Latin), "Zeus" in Greek, and "divine" and "divinity" in English are etymologically related to the word "div." With the advent of the Zoroastrian religion, divs were relegated to the status of demons, when Persian rulers began a relentless struggle against divs which is vividly described by Firdausi in the epic *Shah Namah*.

In the picture of the div, such attributes as horns, claws, fangs and a tail, in addition to a real coat of hair, are designed to show him as an evil and terrifying character, a truly "bad guy" of beastly nature. Although hominoids are sometimes known to wear clothes (stolen or received from humans), the kilt sported by the div is certainly added for the sake of prudence. It remains to note that animalistic attributes of hominoids in art, such as horns, hooves and tails, were not always meant to be seen as reprehensible. In the heyday of the hominoid cult, these attributes were just symbols and identification marks in artistic presentations of these heathen deities.

TESTIMONY BY MAJOR GENERAL MIKHAIL TOPILSKY

In the autumn of 1925, together with a scouting party we were engaged in tracking down a gang of anti-Soviet guerrillas which was operating in the Western Pamirs. They were trying to shake us off by going to the Sinkiang via the Eastern Pamirs. On our way through the highland villages in the Vanch district, we had heard stories about hairy man-beasts, monstrous creatures (I don't remember the local name for them) that lived in the mountains. They were said to be hostile to humans; although they didn't usually attack first, they would kill a man or tear his head off if they came across one by accident on a mountain path. According to local belief, to meet the creature - to see it and hear its howling - was to bring misfortune and death. We didn't pay much attention to these stories.

Once, when we were following the gang's tracks along a mountain path and had already reached the permanent snow line, we saw some tracks running across the path. Our dog took up the scent but refused to follow the tracks. They were very clear and there could be no doubt they were the prints of bare human feet. They continued for some 150 metres and stopped at the foot of a sheer, barren cliff which a man could hardly have climbed. Our doctor studied the tracks thoroughly and decided that they were human footprints beyond all doubt. Additional evidence of this was found at a spot where the creature had defecated; the fecal matter was dry

Major-General Mikhail Topilsky inspected a slain snowman in the Pamirs in 1925. This photograph shows him speaking at a meeting with researchers in Moscow in February 1966

65

and consisted of the remains of dry berries.

Continuing our chase, we caught up with what was left of the exhausted gang, which had stopped for a rest at a place where the glacier was split apart by a stone cliff. The upper tongue of the glacier hung from the cliff, in which there was a crevice or cave. We surrounded the gang and took up a position above where they were resting. A machine gun was placed in position. When we threw the first grenade, a man (a Russian officer) ran out onto the glacier and started shouting that the shooting would make the ice cave in and that everyone would be buried. When we demanded that they surrender, he asked for time to talk it over with the other guerrillas, and went back into the cave. Soon after, we heard an ominous hissing as the ice began to move. At almost the same moment we heard shots, and, not knowing what they meant, decided that it was the beginning of an assault.

Pieces of ice and snow started falling down from the cliff, gradually burying the entrance to the cave. When it was almost buried, three men managed to escape, and the rest (we learned later that there were five) were buried under the debris. Our shots killed two of the guerrillas and seriously wounded the third. When we reached him, he showed us the spot where the body of the Russian officer was buried, and we dug it out. The wounded man turned out to be a Uzbek teahouse owner from Samarkand. We questioned him and he gave us the following information: while they were discussing our order to surrender, some hairy, man-like creatures, howling inarticulately, appeared in the cave through a crevice (which possibly led upwards from the cave). There were several of them, and they had staves in their hands. The men tried to shoot their way through. One of the guerrillas was clubbed to death by the creatures. Our narrator received a blow from a staff on his left shoulder as he rushed to the cave entrance with one of the monsters hard on his heels. It ran out of the cave after him, but was shot and buried under a snowslide.

To check up on this strange story, we made him show us the exact spot and cleared the snow away. We recovered the body all right. It had been shot three times. Not far off, we found a stick made of very hard wood, though it cannot be stated for certain that it belonged to the creature. At first glance I thought the body was that of an ape, as it was covered all over with hair - but I knew there were no apes in the Pamirs. Also, the body itself looked very much like that of a man. We tried pulling the hair, to see if it was just a hide used for disguise, but found that it was the creature's own natural hair. We turned the body over several times onto its back and its front, and measured it. Our doctor (who was killed later that year) made a long and thorough inspection of the body, and it was clear that it was not a human being.

The body belonged to a male creature 165-170 centimetres tall - elderly or even old, judging by the greyish colour of the hair in several places. The chest was covered with brownish hair, and the belly with greyish hair. The hair was longer but sparser on the chest and close-cropped and thick on the belly. In general, the hair was very thick, without any underfur. There was least hair on the buttocks, from which fact our doctor deduced that the creature sat like a human being. There was most hair on the hips. The knees were completely devoid of hair and had callous growths on them. The whole foot, including the sole, was quite hairless, and was covered by hard brown skin. The shoulders and arms were also covered with hair, which got thinner near the hands, and the palms had none at all, but only calloused skin.

The colour of the face was dark, and the creature had neither beard nor moustache. The back of the head was covered by thick, matted hair. The dead creature lay with its eyes open and its teeth bared. The eyes were dark, and the teeth were large and even, and shaped like human teeth. The forehead was slanting and the eyebrows were very powerful. The prominent cheekbones made the face resemble the Mongol type of face. The nose was flat, with a deeply-sunken bridge. The ears were hairless and looked a little more pointed than a human being's, with a longer lobe. The lower jaw was very massive. The creature had a very powerful, broad chest and well-developed muscles. We didn't find any important anatomical differences between it and man. The genitalia were like a man's. The arms were of normal length, the hands were slightly wider, and the feet much wider and shorter than a man's.

We did not know exactly where we were, because no accurate maps of the Pamirs were then in existence, but we must have been somewhere between the Yazgulem and the Rushan Ranges. As we had completed our task, we had to return. The last member of the gang died on the second day. The nature of the dead creature presented us with a problem, but it was impossible to take the body with us on the very difficult trek that lay ahead. Also, it could have caused complications with the local population; we could say, of course, that we were carrying the body of an animal, but the creature looked too much like a human being. We thought about skinning it, but it was too much like skinning a man. In the end, we decided to bury the creature where we had found it. We did not try to enter the cave because we were afraid of another cave-in. We went south, and at the first opportunity left the mountains and crossed a river (it might have been the Panj). The few inhabitants of the mountains there, the Baluchi, were amazed to see us, and asked us how we had come down from places which were supposed to be inhabited by man-like monsters. We heard a lot of new details from the Baluchi. They told us that the hairy man-like creatures had been observed not only singly, but also in twos and occasionally with a baby as well, but that they did not go around in large groups.

After presenting Topilsky's account in his monograph *The Present State of the Question of Relic Hominoids*, Porshnev describes the witness in these words: "The narrator impressed me as a well-educated person, fully conscious of his responsibility to science and in possession of a clear and accurate memory." This was my impression, and that of my colleagues, when, in February 1966, we met with General Mikhail Topilsky at a special conference in Moscow, attended both by researchers and eyewitnesses. Topilsky's testimony, like those of Karapetian and several others, is listed as a basic and "classical" one in our files, mainly on account of the abundant anatomical details supplied by the witness. As for its dramatic quality, the story really stands out and seems unrivalled. We should remember that the event took place during military action. We know of several cases when wildmen were captured or killed in wartime, but Topilsky's report is different in that it describes relic hominoids not only as suffering from warring humans, but also as offering - quite effectively - collective resistance. In modem times that is quite unusual; in fact, in almost all other cases known to us, the hominoid tries to retreat, usually with dignity, from its chance encounters with humans. John Green, an authority on the subject in North America, even titles one chapter of his book "Gentle Giants."

The picture is quite different when we look back into history. The epics of many peoples describe fierce battles waged by our ancestors against "man-like monsters." For example, the great Persian epic *Shah Namah* is almost entirely devoted to this theme. There must have been a time when humans were a minority and, gradually increasing in numbers, they pushed back their primate rivals and seized the earth for themselves, relegating the "monsters" to relics. Nowadays it is only in situations which resemble the erstwhile man-wildman feud that relic hominoids dare stand up and strike back. One such fight, across the ocean, is cited in John Green's book *Sasquatch: The Apes among Us.* The story broke in the Portland Oregonian, July 13, 1924, as follows:

FIGHT WITH BIG APES REPORTED BY MINERS; FABLED BEASTS ARE SAID TO HAVE BOMBARDED CABIN

Wash., July 12 (Special). The strangest story to come from the Cascade mountains was brought to Kelso today by Marion Smith, his son Roy Smith, Fred Beck, Gabe Lefever and John Peterson, who encountered the fabled "mountain devils" or mountain gorillas of Mount St. Helens this week, shooting one of them and being attacked throughout the night by rock bombardments of the beasts. The men had been prospecting a claim on the Muddy, a branch of the Lewis River about eight miles from Spirit Lake, 46 miles from Castle Rock. They declared that they saw four of the huge animals, which were about 400 pounds and walked erect. Smith and his companion declared that they had seen the tracks of the animals several times in the last six years and Indians have told of the "mountain devils" for 60 years. But none of the animals has ever been

OPPOSITE: A traditional Persian style illustration to the epic Iskander Namah by Nazami. The epic hero, Iskander, lassoes and captures a div whose image is far removed from biology into devilry.

Дивъ,

захваченный въ плънъ Искандеромъ.

seen before. Smith met with one of the animals and fired at it with a revolver, he said. Thursday, Fred Beck, it is said, shot one, the body falling over a precipice. That night the animals bombarded the men's cabin with showers of rocks, many of them large ones, knocking chunks out of the log cabin, according to the prospectors. Many of the rocks fell through a hole in the roof, and two of the rocks struck Beck, one of them rendering him unconscious for nearly two hours. The prospectors, having apparently violated the territory of the "mountain devils" (such terms as "bigfoot" or "snowman" were not yet in use), were the first to start hostilities and, as a result, encountered retaliation. In the case of Topilsky, the wildmen, whose territory was also violated, had no idea, of course, that on that occasion man was fighting man, and did not care in the least for his hairy cousins. The latter found themselves cornered in the cave and were forced to counter-attack. Separately each story is rather hard to swallow, but when studied in comparison they make sense. Incidentally, the place in the Cascades where the fight took place has since been known as Ape Canyon.

Fred Beck in 1967

TESTIMONY BY B. M. ZDORIK

B. M. Zdorik, a geologist and resident of Alma-Ata, Kazakhstan, worked in the Pamirs during 1926-1938. In a long account sent to Boris Porshnev in 1959 and published in *The Information Materials of the Snowman Commission*, he said, among other things, the following:

In the autumn of 1929, preparing for a hunt, I asked the locals about the fauna in the district. The chairman of the Tutkaul Soviet gave me the following list of local wild animals: wild boar, bear, red wolf, hyena, porcupine, jackal and dev. I was surprised to hear the last name as part of the animal kingdom, because, according to my previous information, "dev" or "div" was a character of Tajik fairytales - but here the headman of the locality told me that the dev resembled a thickset man, that it walked on two legs and was covered with brown or black hair. According to the headman, the dev was encountered very rarely in the Sanglakh Mountains, but did turn up now and again, either alone or in pairs, male and female. He had never seen young ones, but during the previous summer the Tajiks had caught a grown one alive at a mill on the eastern slopes of the mountain ridge, only a few kilometres from Tutkaul. They kept the dev chained up for two months, feeding it with raw meat and flatcakes of barley flour. Eventually the dev broke its chain and escaped. I did not believe the story, and the headman then showed me a villager, allegedly injured by a dev. The man had indeed a large scar on the head, but the encounter allegedly so much affected his mind that he was unable to tell me anything intelligible. I then decided that the injury could have been done by a wild boar.

Once, in 1934, I climbed with much difficulty one of the flat mountaintops in the upper reaches of the Dondushkan. My Tajik guide and I were making our way along a network of narrow paths made by a colony of marmots in the high alpine grass. Suddenly, a small area opened up in front of us on which the grass was completely flattened, and the ground dug up as if with a spade. On the path were drops of blood and scraps of what looked like marmot fur - and there, right at my very feet, on a heap of freshly-dug earth, an unknown creature lay asleep. It was lying fully stretched out on its stomach, about a metre and a half or so in length. I could not see the head and front limbs very well, as they were hidden by a bundle of withered grass. I did manage to see the legs and the bare black feet, which were too long and too well-shaped to be a bear's. And the back was too flat for a bear. The whole body of the animal was covered with shaggy fur. The hair colour was reddish-brown, redder than I have ever seen on a bear. The creature's flanks rose and fell rhythmically as it slept. I stood there, frozen with surprise, and at a loss as to what to do. I looked back at my Tajik guide, who was following close behind me. He was standing there stupified, his face as white as a sheet; then, with a gesture, he pulled me silently by the sleeve and indicated that we must run at once.

Never before had I seen such an expression of terror on a man's face. His fear communicated itself to me, and, beside ourselves, without glancing backwards at the creature, we both fled away down the path, enmeshing ourselves and stumbling about in the high grass....

It was only the following day that I learned from the Tajiks, who were rather alarmed by the event, that we had stumbled upon a sleeping dev. They also used some other name for the creature, but I don't remember it. According to the inhabitants of the Talbara and Saffedara valleys, there were several families of those devs - males, females, and young - living in the mountains. The creatures were considered to be of the animal kingdom, and not supernatural beings, but it was considered to be an evil omen to meet one.

Zdorik's testimony is remarkable in several respects; first, his discovery that certain legendary and fairytale names can indicate beings of flesh and blood (it is simply the failure of some orthodox scientists to make this discovery that prevents them from recognizing the reality of snowmen); second, the evidence given by the geologist that the "teenage" dev (judging by its size) had apparently been hunting and eating marmots (we have other cases testifying that marmots and other rodents form the staple of hominoids' protein food); and third, Zdorik's stumbling upon a sleeping hominoid is by no means a unique example. We know of similar cases in the Caucasus (I investigated one of them on the spot), and one famous historical case which will be cited later in this book. It should also be added that there are cases (some recorded in the literature) of other sleeping wild animals, some very cautious (wolves, wild boar, deer) that were stumbled upon by man.

TESTIMONY BY ALEXANDER PRONIN

On August 11th, 1959, when selecting a site for our camp on the edge of the Fedchenko Glacier, I sent my fellow workers with the horses to the settlement of Altyn-Mazar and remained alone. It was the peak time of the rainy season, and, as a hydrologist, I had more than enough work to keep me busy. On August 12th, at mid-day, I was following the course of the valley of the river Balyandkiik when I suddenly noticed a strange sight. On the southward slope of the valley, at a distance of approximately 500 metres, up on the permanent snow, a being of unusual aspect was moving, reminiscent of a man's figure. The figure was stooping while moving in wide strides, its arms being longer than in the ordinary man. Visibility was perfect, especially against a backdrop of snow; however, I was unable to make out the creature's hair. Five minutes elapsed. The figure then vanished, hidden behind a rock.

Three days later, just before sunset, returning from a reconnaissance, I again saw the figure in that same valley. This time the sighting was quite brief, as the figure vanished into a dark depression, possibly a cave. I think the animal noticed me.

A week later, my colleagues returned with all their equipment. The place began to be noisy. The work of the expedition went ahead. The strange encounter was forgotten, but, just before we left, our rubber boat suddenly disappeared from the riverbank, and all our attempts to find it were in vain. We just had to lump it. It was only when we were back in Leningrad, a month after leaving the research site, that we received word that our colleagues of the scientific post of the Uzbek SSR's Academy of Sciences, who were operating not far from us, had found the boat five kilometres upstream from where we had left it. It was fully intact. How could it have gotten up there? It would have been impossible to go in a boat up that boiling mountain torrent, abounding in rapids and shoals.

I must mention that I interrogated the local inhabitants - they were Kirghiz - and asked if they had seen a strange being, like a man, up on the rock faces. Some replied they had. They said that this being liked to be impudent. It happened that some of them had lost domestic utensils - troughs, basins, even clothing - and, later on, some of these things had been found a way up on the heights. Are these facts not linked with the loss of our boat? After publication of *Encounter with a Snowman,* many people have come to me with dubious questions, and that is only natural; for indeed, could I make out, from a distance of 500 metres, whether that was in fact a so-called snowman, or, as they call it, a 'gulbiyavan,' and not, say, perhaps some other living creature? Naturally not. I am far from making a categorical statement. I just told the facts as they were, that is all, and a few inaccuracies in the press item have given my words a different meaning.

People have said to me: "Why didn't you climb up there where the manlike creature was moving about and explore the depression where he seemed to take shelter?" Such a question can only be expressed by folk who don't know the Pamirs. The shape was at a great altitude and on an absolutely sheer cliff face. Even an experienced alpinist would have found it difficult to get up there.

Pronin's evidence came at a time when official interest in the snowman problem in this country was at its peak, and helped in the setting up of a Snowman Commission by the USSR Academy of Sciences and the mounting of its 1958 expedition to the Pamirs. The very choice of the Pamirs for a state-funded expedition in search of the snowman shows how little was known about the subject at the time. One of the main reasons for the choice was the geographical proximity of the area to Tibet and the Himalayas, which was where hot news of the yeti was emanating from during the 1950's, so the Pamirs was considered a possible habitat for the "Russian snowman," but other regions of the country were believed to be totally out of the question - today we know better. It should also be mentioned that, in response to newspaper articles telling of Pronin's sighting, he received several letters from retired frontier guards who once served at border posts in the Pamirs and witnessed similar sightings. Those letters were published in *The Information Materials,* and confirm our suspicion that the archives of the KGB (The State Security Committee), which was then responsible for the security of the USSR borders, may contain crucial information on our subject.

Incidentally, Boris Porshnev confided to us that the Pamirs expedition was under constant surveillance by a special detachment of border guards who used to amuse themselves by hunting mountain goats and other game, thus frightening off any possible snowmen.

The fate of the expedition is aptly described by M.-J. Koffmann, who took part in it as a physician (see Part I). When official Soviet science eventually lost interest in the matter, Professor Porshnev and his colleagues - in particular P. P. Smolin, A. A. Mashkovtsev and M.-J. Koffmann - set up a permanent Relic Hominoid Research Seminar under the auspices of the Darwin Museum in Moscow, which became and continues to be the venue of snowman research in Russia. Fieldwork was started in the Caucasus, and for many years was conducted under the guidance and leadership of M.-J.Koffmann. Almost all hominologists of the second generation, Bayanov and Bourtsev included, did their "apprenticeship" in Koffmann's self-funded expeditions. It was only at the end of the '70's that Soviet Central Asia, and Tajikistan in particular, made a comeback in our research, as is seen from the following.

Yeti sighting is reported by Soviets
Associated Press

Moscow. January 23, 1988. Researchers from the Ukrainian capital Kiev say they have come to within about 35 yards of a creature they believe to be an abominable snowman in the rugged Pamir Mountains.

The news agency TASS reported Wednesday that the group, led by Igor Tatsl, sighted the creature during a visit last year to the Hissar range in Soviet Central Asia near the Afghanistan border. "After watching the people for some time, it went back into the thickets," TASS said.

Tatsl and other group members noted several night visits to their camp by the creature, called a 'yeti,' during their last expedition. The group is preparing for another trip, TASS said.

Igor Tatsl, mountaineering instructor and leader of several
expeditions in search of the snowman.

BIGFOOT TRACKS FOUND IN TAJIKISTAN MOUNTAINS

By Igor Bourtsev

CANYON OF MYSTERY
Komsomolskaya Pravda, September 8, 1979.

Editor's Note: *An expedition from Kiev worked in the Hissar Range of the Pamir-Alai Mountains in Tajikistan during the latter part of this summer, continuing its search of many years for "snowmen" - representatives of a relic branch of man's ancestors that may still exist in hard-to-reach regions of the planet. Today we publish a report by our special correspondent, Candidate of History Igor Bourtsev, who took part in the expedition's work.*

The leader of our expedition, I. F. Tatsl, a worker at the Bolshevik Plarit in Kiev, spends his vacation every summer going to the Hissar Mountains with a group of people in search of 'relic hominoids,' the scientific name that has been adopted in our country for these mysterious bipeds. Tatsl chose a canyon in the upper reaches of the Varzob River for his search.

Unfortunately, no scientific institution will assume responsibility for this work. At the same time, the reports coming in from various places about encounters with mysterious two-legged beings not only arouse interest in the problem, but also spur enthusiasts to take up search. Thus, on August 4, the expedition pitched its base camp at the confluence of two mountain streams, and work began. At night we conducted observations with the aid of night-vision devices, and during the daytime inspected the slopes of nearby canyons in the hope of finding signs of the hominoids. Wherever possible, we scarified and smoothed the soil to make "track zones."

Shortly afterward, we noticed the first tracks, albeit very indistinct ones. Sometimes even identifying the size of the track was hard; in one place the heel would have left an imprint while the toe had touched rock, and in another place it would be the reverse. We soon noticed a pattern emerging - when we conducted vigilant observations at night, no tracks appeared; as soon as we slackened our attention and stopped standing watch all night, tracks appeared. We decided to remove our concealed nighttime observations and limit ourselves to observation from the tents, so as not to frighten any "visitors" away.

We had constant arguments about the tracks. Tatsl would claim that they had been left by hominoids, and I would say that maybe that wasn't the case. One time my obstinacy was shaken - on the morning of August 15, I clearly saw four tracks made by bare feet, two leading toward the camp and two away from it. The length of the stride was 120 centimetres, twice the average human stride. The tracks were 50 metres from the tents.

We had an interesting conversation with residents of the settlement of Khakimi, a seasonal settlement not far from Lake Temir-Kul. People live there only during the summer. Our guide, Kulbeddin Rajhabov, a forestry station employee, took us to the home of Gafar Jabirov, a huntsman who is about 60 years old. When we showed Gafar a picture of a hominoid in the magazine *Tekhnika molodyozhi*, he exclaimed, "I saw one like that myself, and even shot at him!" According to his story, one spring in the mid-1960s he went into a canyon six kilometres from Khakimi to mow reeds. When he had almost finished, he suddenly felt an uneasiness. Looking around, he saw some kind of wild, hairy man, almost black, sitting 15 metres away on a big rock and watching him. Frightened, Gafar grabbed his gun, closed his eyes and fired in the direction

Eyewitness Gafar Jabirov

of the creature. "It was five minutes later before I opened my eyes and saw that he was gone."

On August 21, after breakfast at the base camp, when most of the expedition members had gone off to inspect the surrounding area, I heard Eugenya Dobchinskaya shout. I rushed over. Eugenya was pointing to an enormous track, clearly visible in the loose black earth. It was an impressive sight! In the distance was another track, this one not so distinct. The other participants came running, and everyone looked, spellbound, at the track.

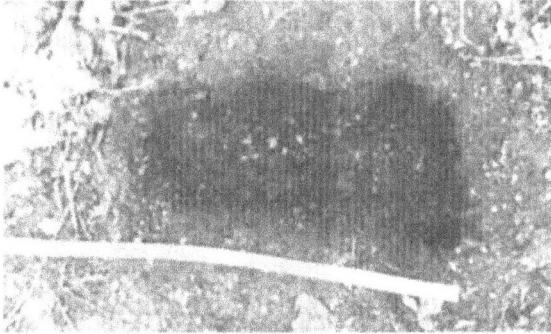

This was unquestionably the imprint of a bare foot, but it was inconceivable that a man had made it. The track was 35 centimetres long; for comparison, I wear a size 44 shoe, and my foot is 28 centimetres long and 16 centimetres wide at the toes. The toes were slightly spread, with the big toe considerably larger than the others, and the foot was flat.

We made a plaster-of-Paris cast of the track, first fixing the soil with lacquer. It most closely resembled the tracks of American hominoids, although there are some minor details that distinguish it from them. I should note that none of the members of this expedition except myself was familiar with the American materials. This cannot possibly be a forgery.

For the first time in our country, a rather decent cast of a large track, presumably left by a relic hominoid, has been obtained. Before, such casts had been obtained only in the US and Canada. It is necessary to continue the work of collecting information on hominoids. A broad range of volunteer helpers - tourists visiting the mountains, geologists, and field zoologists - can be of invaluable service to researchers. It is important that people keep an open mind about reports of wild creatures resembling human beings.

Igor Bourtsev demonstrating a cast of a hominoid footprint (shown above).

EXPEDITION "HISSAR-80"
Report by Igor Bourtsev
Bigfoot Co-op, June 1981

In 1979, Igor Tatsl led a dozen people to the mountains of the Hissar Range in Tajikistan to search for relic hominoids. They spent 20 days in the mountains and found a footprint 35 centimetres long and 16 centimetres wide. After publication of an article about the success of the search, many letters poured in, mostly offering to help with the next trip and requesting to be a part of it.

The 1980 search lasted two months, using three groups of volunteers, each group staying for twenty days in the mountains - a total of 120 people. To cope with logistics, preparations began in the fall with training, shopping, letter-writing and planning. The volunteers were students, workers, teachers, and engineers from Moscow, Leningrad, Petrozavodsk, Tashkent, Yaroslavl and many other towns, but the majority were from Kiev and other cities in Ukraine. The volunteers gave their money and their time; however, some were not familiar with hiking or the hominoid problem, and had to be trained. The group was equipped with phototraps, walkie-talkies and other gadgets, but firearms were not allowed. The ultimate aim of our search efforts was to give protection to and ensure the survival of these perhaps last "brothers" of *Homo sapiens*, whose study could help solve many problems of our own descent and potential.

Our goals in 1980 were:

- Number one: an intensive search in the area of last year's find of the footprint. The assignment was to try to contact the hominoid, whom Tatsl nicknamed "Gosha," who left his footprints last year. Here, observations were conducted from vantage points, track zones were prepared, and phototraps were put into place.
- Number two: observation in several gorges in different localities, where reports of sightings or prints have occurred. From three to six groups of searchers were engaged in this work. They also interviewed local herders and hunters.
- Number three: a search for new areas inhabited by hominoids. Tajikistan's Committee on Forestry, especially its department of hunting and natural reserves, helped with this, stimulated by a find of prints by the deputy chief hunting expert of the Committee, who had previously been a sceptic. Several new localities for hominoid searches were pinpointed, and the habitat area greatly enlarged.

On August 20, after hiking in the Karatag gorge, I went to the upper reaches of the Varzob gorge to see Igor Tatsl and other friends from whom I had parted two weeks before. I planned to fly to Moscow a few days later and, expecting no major developments before my departure, decided to unburden my rucksack for a two-hour hike along the mountain track, leaving my tape recorder in Dushanbe, though taking along my still and cinecamera.

When I reached Tatsl and his group, he told me they had no hot news, though Gosha had been

Igor Bourtsev interviewing a Tajik witness

visiting the campsite area, judging by indistinct tracks and certain other signs, which other members of the group did not find convincing. After supper we sat around a fire and I told them of the work of the other groups and about my search on the Surshku Ridge. The discussion we had was long; we brewed tea twice. At around 11 p.m., I asked, "Where is Zaichik (Bunny)?" It was the nickname of a cheerful and robust 18-year-old girl, Nina Grinyova, a library student in Voroshilovgrad (Lugansk) in Ukraine. Someone replied she had already turned in, and our talk continued. At about midnight, we began preparing to turn in. Suddenly, I heard sounds as if a cat was mewing; others said they heard a whistle. Svetlana Zaeka, a geologist from Kiev, who seemed to be agitated, whispered a few words to Tatsl, who called to Georgy Kirilyuk, and they dashed down the path to the river.

We shrugged our shoulders and went on preparing to go to bed, but, after some time had passed and our comrades had not returned, we began to worry. We then took flashlights and also made for the river. There we saw someone on the steep slope of the opposite bank leading another person by the arm. "That's Zaichik," someone exclaimed in surprise. Presently Georgy and Nina crossed the river, by the ropes especially hung there because it was deep and very rapid at that point.

When I took a close look at Nina I could hardly recognize her. There was no trace of her former cheerful self; she looked withdrawn and remote. She spoke with difficulty, and said, from time to time, "Why did he go away?". Though she was soaked in water to her waist and the night was very cold, she did not pay attention to that. She was made to change into dry clothes and then answer our questions. She found words only with difficulty.

I bitterly regretted that I had left my tape-recorder in Dushanbe, because Nina's first oral report was very impressive and its quality could not be reproduced later on. Here's what she said:

> At about 10 pm, Tatsl helped me to cross the river. Only he and I were in on our plan. When I was left alone on the other bank I was not afraid. At first the moon was shining. Through the trees I could see our campfire burning, then it went out. The sound of the river was coming up from beneath the slope. I sat singing songs,

and when I felt cold I danced. Then the moon went behind the cliff, but continued to illuminate the high rock wall above me, still giving me enough light to see around.

Soon after I heard a noise coming from the area of the bushes upstream, and began to look in that direction. Again there was a noise coming from the same area upstream, and I turned there. Then, as if urged to do so, I made a sudden turn in the direction of the stone-pounding sound I had heard earlier and saw him. It was Gosha. He was standing some 25 metres away, facing me and piercing my very soul with his gaze. It was not aggressive - rather well-wishing, but piercing. The eyes were big and glowing. They were not bright but did glow. In fact, all of his body was sort of glowing. He was dark and, at the same time, somewhat silvery. I could see his body was covered with hair, but it was not shaggy. Maybe it was wet; anyhow, the color had a silvery tinge. He was about two metres tall. (Nina said that Gosha was 10-15 cm taller than I. My height is 187 cm. -I.B.) His figure looked very hefty, square and straight from shoulder to hip, with a short neck, the head put forward; also, the arms were hanging down freely in a somewhat forward position.

When I saw him I was not scared, and began slowly to advance toward him. Having gone about five steps, I held out and pressed, two or three times, a rubber toy in the shape of a bird, which made a squeaking sound. It was given to me by Tatsl in order to attract Gosha's attention with its sound, but it was this that spoiled our contact. Gosha made a sharp turn and quickly slid down the slope to the river and disappeared beyond the steep bank. I noted the softness and grace of his walk, though he moved very fast. It was not a human walk, but as of an animal, as of a panther. Despite boulders and other obstacles, he moved quickly, softly and even gracefully. He must have a perfect sense of balance, because he negotiated the steep and uneven slope with no more difficulty than we would walk along a paved road.

I was greatly disappointed by his retreat, but nothing could be done. I turned around and started to walk in the opposite direction, towards the crossing. At that point my memory faded, and I don't remember what I did. No, I was not frightened; on the contrary, I regretted very much that he had gone. But I must have passed out. I don't know how I reached the water and what I did there. I came round only when Georgy was shaking me, then I showed Georgy where I had seen Gosha.

Judging by the fact that Nina was wet to her waist, she had walked into the river and been in mortal danger, but somehow she had escaped the worst. This is what Kirilyuk told us:

When we were preparing to turn in, Tatsl came up to me and said, "Take your

OPPOSITE: Nina Grinyova meeting a local eyewitness.

flashlight and come along!" I grabbed a miner's lamp and rushed after him to the crossing place. On the way I thought maybe a mountain climber had gotten into trouble or something. When I got to the other bank, I saw someone sitting there. Coming closer, I saw it was a girl, and she was sitting motionless. I shone the light into her face and realized it was Zaichik. She did not react to the light. I took her hand - her pulse was even but the hand was quite limp. I took her by the shoulders and began to shake her. She came to and her first words were, "Why did he go away?" I said, "How are you?", but instead of answering she said, "Do you want to see the place where I saw him?" I said, "If you're able to show me, go ahead." She got up and led me straight to the place, telling me what had happened. Then we returned to the crossing place and I helped her cross the river using the ropes.

Lastly, to dot the i's, here's what Igor Tatsl had to say:

The idea of a contact with Gosha was not a new one - that is the goal of our whole expedition. Taking into account his telepathic ability, I've always demanded that the expedition members "tune" themselves up accordingly. When we came to this place this summer, and it was my seventh visit here, we began, as usual, to make track zones in the vicinity of our camp and to install phototraps made by Igor Kolesnik. The track zones were also made on the other side of the river, which is practically inaccessible to humans. We loosened the soil as far as we could there and set up a pole with a red flag, hoping the bright colour might interest and attract any hominoids. Indeed, we noticed their footprints, but they were very indistinct - and no wonder, considering the hard soil in that place. It was then that Zaichik volunteered to "date" Gosha on the other side of the river. The two of us discussed the plan in detail, but, to avoid complications, did not tell anyone else. The experiment has proved that the hominoid can affect a human's mind and react to a human's thoughts or maybe feelings; otherwise, how can one explain the fact that, though Nina was not frightened by Gosha, she had experienced a blackout?

Tatsl also said that a fortnight earlier another member of the group spotted a silvery-grey creature during daytime, standing among bushes on a mountain slope, quite a distance from her in the vicinity of the camp. The sighting was short and perhaps questionable. She only told Tatsl, so Nina did not know of that sighting.

When I listened to Nina I asked myself, *Perhaps it had been a hallucination?* After all, she had been preparing herself for a rendezvous, and the tension and suspense of waiting in a lonely place at night may have played tricks with her senses - but the details she recalled and the circumstances of the encounter seemed to rule that out. When we inspected the place the next morning, we discovered indistinct hominoid tracks by the river, especially traces of heel marks where he had slid down the very steep slope of the bank, just where Nina had seen him do this, a place where no human would have risked going.

Just a few words regarding Gosha's "vibes" affecting Nina's mind. Besides Tatsl's belief in such a possibility, there are accounts of witnesses who claim to have experienced a certain sensation even before they actually saw a hominoid. There are also reports of people who have become sick after an encounter with a hominoid. (Another explanation could simply be their shock and fright. – D.B.) This raises the interesting question posed by Boris Porshnev in his monograph *On the Beginning of Human History*, published posthumously in 1974: "Has not the science of anthropogenesis overlooked the vast potential of man's highly-organized ancestors to affect the central nervous system of animals and their higher nervous activity? The speed and capacity of their [man's ancestors] nervous processes were greater than in other animals."

Thus, contact has been made. We must thoroughly ponder its significance and implications before proceeding with our search.

EXPEDITION "HISSAR-80"
Comment by Dmitri Bayanov
Bigfoot Co-op, August 1981

A clarification may be needed concerning one point in Bourtsev's report. He mentions a mewing (others said a whistling) sound which set Tatsl and Kirilyuk hurrying to help Nina. The origin of the sound remains unidentified. Svetlana Zaeka was the first to raise the alarm because she had noticed Nina's absence from camp and told Tatsl about it, but he had asked her to keep quiet about it. Still, she was very much on the alert.

As for Nina's presumed contact, we had two rather tense sessions of the seminar devoted to the event. At the September session, Bourtsev, Tatsl and Nina told a critical audience what had happened. The critical attitude was clear from the questions posed to the members of the expedition. The reports and questioning took a long time, and therefore discussion was transferred to the October session, at which Tatsl and Nina were absent because they live in Ukraine.

Summing up my impressions and voicing the opinions of many members of the seminar, I said in October that, if we can trust what we are told, and I am prepared to give it the benefit of the doubt, what happened in Tajikistan this summer is a real breakthrough. For the first time in the history of our expeditions, a planned and premeditated sighting of a hominoid has been made - but the way in which it was achieved by Tatsl and Nina was disapproved of by our seminar, and we object to its repetition in the future. Girl-bait may be a good subject on which humorists can exercise their wit (see Eric Nicol's piece in the Vancouver *Province,* cited by Green and Dahinden), but it's quite a different matter if practiced in reality. Nina's exploit could have ended in tragedy. We have lost Vladimir Pushkarev because he ignored all the rules of safety (he set out alone on a long hiking and boating journey through the Siberian taiga in 1978 and never returned). We cannot condone a repetition of playing, quite unnecessarily, with one's life. We believe that positive results can be achieved, with due provision being made for the safety of those who take part in the experiment, in making contact with a hominoid. If we take pains to ensure the hominoid's life, we must not fail to also ensure all human life as well. What was allowed of the Babylonian king Gilgamesh, who used girl-bait to lure half-man/half-beast Enkidu into captivity, cannot be allowed of the Kiev factory worker Tatsl, I said.

Putting aside the relic hominoid question, as pointed out by members of Tatsl's own group, he and Nina violated the basic rules of conduct of mountain climbers and hikers, in that she was left alone in a potentially very dangerous situation. As I have already mentioned, Tatsl and Nina were absent from our October session, which discussed the incident and Tatsl's methods, but there were present some other Kievites who later told Tatsl of our opinions. As a result, Nina paid a surprise visit to our session in November. As there were some new people in the audience who had not heard Nina's original report, she was asked to repeat her story, and was again asked many questions. (Interestingly, some members of our seminar disbelieved her report on account of her fearlessness; they said they could not imagine a girl being brave enough to be willing to face, alone, a "wild man" in the mountains at night.)

The thrust of Nina's message, and the purpose of her again coming to Moscow, was to protest at our labelling her "girl-bait." She said it was she who had suggested the experiment to Tatsl, and that she was never used by him as bait. She thinks her idea was correct, and she wants to try it again next year. (I must add that Tatsl and Bourtsev tried the "method" the night following the incident: they again left Nina alone on the other bank while keeping a constant watch on her from their side of the river, and nothing happened.) Asked if she was not afraid of suffering violence from Gosha, she said, "Don't judge him by your own standards. I believe he will never do me any harm if I wish him well." What can you do with that kind of idealism? So far, at least, and to believe Nina, it was the hominoid who had become frightened in a face-to-face confrontation with a girl and her squeaking toy. Also, note that our seminar has no influence, other than a moral one, over who conducts the hominoid research or how it is conducted.

One interesting detail that emerged from Nina's second visit to Moscow was that she said she and some others had heard striking-stone sounds from the base camp the night before her rendezvous, even during the day, but during the time preceding Gosha's appearance that night, the stone-pounding sounds were more frequent and insistent. Note that American researcher Archie Buckley also mentions a stone-pounding sound as a characteristic of the noises made by Bigfoot. As for the "vexing" question of the hominoid's presumed telepathic powers, this caused even more uproar and dissension at our seminar than the question of "girl-bait." Let me cite an appropriate extract from a paper by a Bigfoot investigator and Los Angeles area policeman, Ken Coon:

> I think we are all aware that as our fund of knowledge of the creatures continues to grow, we will all risk becoming self-appointed experts, and with that, suffer a loss of flexibility of our thinking. That would certainly be unfortunate, because it was our open-mindedness that got us into this fascinating study to begin with... I think if we will, each of us, retain an open mind and cooperate as fully as possible in exchanges of information, we may yet learn some things that will surprise us all. *(Sasquatch Footprint Variations, 1974)*

VOICES OF REPUTABLE SCIENTISTS

The weekly *Moscow News* No. 42, 1979, carried the following interview with Professor Nikolai Vereshchagin, D.Sc. (Biology):

Q. What is your view of the most recent expedition to Tajikistan and the discovery of what looks like a huge human footprint?

A. I can go only by a photograph, which was of a hazily-defined cast of a naked human foot. You can't say anything conclusive from looking at the cast. The cavity could have been formed absolutely naturally, since no consecutive footprints have been found.

Many of my colleagues believe, as I do, that anyone who talks about some kind of ape-man living in the snows is not thinking logically and has no idea whatsoever of how hard life is up there in the mountains, and no knowledge of how difficult it is to find food there, and the "abominable snowman", as reputed eyewitnesses say, has no traps or any other - even primitive -hunting implements.

Q. So what do you think feeds all the myths about the "abominable snowman"?

A. My opinion is that while legends about trolls, demons and witches have lost their credibility with modem Europeans, travellers and mountain climbers have probably fallen hook, line and sinker for similar legends and myths current among the peoples of the Himalayas and the Pamirs, giving enthusiasts the fuel they desire.

In April 1984, foreign news agencies carried the following item from Moscow:

Vadim Ranov, a leading Soviet explorer and expert on the Pamir Mountain Range, told TASS news agency that there was no evidence to back up stories of the existence of the Abominable Snowman. He said the theories put forth to justify the scientific expeditions hunting the

Snowman were nonsense. Alleged Yeti tracks are probably those of other animals distorted by the bright sun, and eyewitness accounts are all imagined.

EASTERN KAZAKHSTAN AND KIRGHIZIA
(Now Kyrgyzstan)
Report by Dmitri Bayanov

Bigfoot Co-op, June 1986

This is an age-old habitat of the hominoids, where zoologist Vitaly Khakhlov collected sighting reports back in 1914 and named the creature *Primihomo asiaticus*. As part of the feedback from the latest publications on the subject, we have received some fresh reports from that area.

Veteran zoologist and writer-naturalist Maxim Zverev, 84, residing in Alma-Ata, capital of Kazakhstan, was the first to respond. It turned out he was a friend and colleague of Khakhlov when the latter lived in Kazakhstan. Zverev published a piece on the subject in a local newspaper and forwarded to us fresh reports that he had received. Two activists of our seminar, Vadim Makarov and Mikhail Trachtenherz, with colleagues from other parts of the USSR, made trips to that area, interviewed witnesses, and found some tracks.

One of the more interesting reports of this series comes from a local teacher, Anatoly Pechersky, who was backpacking with two teenage pupils in July 1972 in the mountains of the Kirghiz Range and, according to him, for over a week they were followed, surreptitiously approached and had their food stolen by what appeared to be an old male hominoid who made sounds as if he was asthmatic. When the food was placed in the tent overnight, the creature

Zoology Professor Vitaly Khakhlov, who, as a college student, collected information on the wildman in Eastern Kazakhstan and Kirghizia, and who reported his findings in 1914 to the Russian Academy of Sciences.

tried to get it by thrusting his hairy arm through the tent flap. This was observed by Pechersky, who was awakened by the activity and who used a flashlight. Alas, Pechersky was too nervous and did not attempt to befriend the hominoid. When the creature became bold enough to step out of the night to their fire and stood facing them at a distance of four metres, Pechersky panicked, backed up to the tent, and got his gun; as a result, no more sightings - end of story.

Another teacher, Mstislav Kushnikov, who lives near Nor-Zaisan Lake in Eastern Kazakhstan, in his letter first gives praise to "that clever head that thought up of publishing your address in a newspaper" (in fact, the tightly-controlled official media hushed up our activities and our address). He has heard stories about the *ksy-gyik* (wild man) from the locals, and personally saw huge footprints at the place of one sighting. He opened a regional museum and, one of its paintings, done by a local artist, is an enlarged copy of a picture in a text-book of anthropology showing a Neanderthal in front of his cave.

Once a young tractor-driver from a nearby village, writes Kushnikov, scrutinized that painting for a long time and said, "I've seen a type of this kind, only female. She had dangling breasts and her skin was not as naked as in this one in the picture." The "prehistoric woman"

Drawing by Anatoly Pechersky, illustrating the sighting in the Tien Shan Mountains in July 1972.

Vadim Makarov, deputy chairman of the Russian Society of Cryptozoologists, Smolin seminar activist, and a keen field investigator specializing in hominoid footprint and hair identification.

encountered by the tractor-driver in 1977 at a mountain creek, where he went for a drink while working on the tractor, had her body covered with "long, shaggy, dark brown hair."

* * *

From August 17 to September 22, 1982, I made a fact-finding tour of some areas of Soviet Central Asia, namely one area of Eastern Kazakhstan along the Kurchum River, southeast of the city of Ust-Kamenogorsk, and three areas in Tajikistan which I shall name later. Except for one area in Tajikistan, I travelled in the company of Vadim Makarov, our seminar activist

A summer camp of Kazakh cattle-breeders we visited on our way. The hosts offered us a good meal but were reticent regarding the wildman subject.

The author and Kazakh guide Nurbopo Kopanov from the village of Kurchum, who had confidently led the way to the bone location

and an experienced field researcher. I had been to Central Asia previously, but not on a hominoid search. Historically, this part of our country was the first to attract the attention of what we call hominologists; thereafter, it has been on and off of our priority list, mainly because of its remoteness from Moscow. In the late 1970s, more fieldwork was carried out in Central Asia than in the Caucasus, so it was high time for me to go and take a look around there, remembering that it is better to see once than hear a hundred times.

Our trip to Eastern Kazakhstan was prompted by letters from two locals: one, a former teacher and now pensioner, Mstislav Kushnikov, 76, and the other, an anonymous woman teacher, reporting information of hominoid sightings made by the local people. One recent letter from Kushnikov mentioned a skeleton seen in a cave by a local man, which we wanted to check out. Besides, Eastern Kazakhstan is the area where our pioneer, Vitaly Khakhlov, then a young zoologist, collected data on the ksy-gyik (the Kazakh for "wildman") at the beginning of this century, and sent his report to the Russian Academy of Sciences in 1914. His search was interrupted by the First World War, and his report was "excavated" by Boris Porshnev half a century later from the file in the archives labelled "Papers of no scientific significance."

Alas, the area did not quite live up to our expectations during our six-day visit there. We reached the village of Kurchum, where Kushnikov lives, by plane on August 18th via Ust-Kamenogorsk, the region's main city. From there it took us two days by truck along a bumpy mountain dirt road to get to the upper reaches of the Kurchum River, where a local guide showed us the site of the aforementioned skeleton. The bones were there, but under stones beneath a rock shelf, not in a cave. The skull was missing, but even without it we immediately determined it to be a human skeleton and of ordinary proportions. We photographed the bones and took one for dating purposes, having put the rest under the stone slabs the way we found them. We had hoped that the bones would have clear signs that they were NOT those of Homo sapiens. As such signs were not visible that was disappointment number one.

Perched precariously on slanting rock, the author demonstrates weather-beaten bones that brought him and Vadim Makarov half way across the country to the Tien Shan Mountains. The find had been reported by a local hunter.

As for disappointment number two, we failed to find even a single eyewitness of the local "wildman." Kushnikov claims to have seen only tracks, and we met people who offered secondhand stories of sightings by their mostly-deceased relatives or acquaintances that did not happen to be around. In the first letter to us, Kushnikov wrote of a young tractor-driver who visited the local history museum organized by Kushnikov and, seeing a picture of a Neanderthal, said he had seen a similar being in the mountains, only more hairy. We also visited Kushnikov's museum, found it very interesting, and saw the Neanderthal in the picture, but there was no tractor driver to be found because Kushnikov did not write down his name; thus, we now have nothing but Kushnikov's word for that curious piece of information.

Disappointment number three was that the area we visited proved to be far less "wild" than I had expected from the letters of our informants. It does not mean there is no real wilderness down there, but we had neither the time nor the means to reach such places. When back in Moscow, I learned from the press that somewhat further east from where we had been, geological prospectors recently came across a family of hermits that had been out of contact with civilization for over forty years, and not a soul had suspected their existence.

On second thought, it was rash of us to expect quick results from such a short and cursory visit to the area. Re-reading Khakhlov's material, I noted with interest the following passage:

> "My father, who travelled much in Dzungaria at the beginning of the second half of the 19th century, and knew well the adjoining regions of China, had never heard of the "wildman." On my request, he questioned the old Kazakhs he knew, and none of them confirmed my information; yet, I kept up my interest in the subject, visited the adjoining regions of Dzungaria, and attentively listened to and recorded everything relating to the "wildman."

Visiting one area of Khakhlov's field work on our side of the border some seventy years later, I found old Kazakhs as reserved and reluctant to touch on the subject as they were in Khakhlov's day, whereas young people preferred to make jokes about it. On the positive side, I noted with satisfaction the richness of local plant and animal life, and an abundance of small and big game, the latter including deer, wild goats, sheep, pigs and bears; this was learned from the local hunters and a visit to the Regional Nature and History Museum in Ust-Kamenogorsk. On the whole, the scenery, terrain and flora of the area reminded me of the North Caucasus, the usual site of our previous (and current) fieldwork. We were also satisfied to have made acquaintance of two efficient and sober-minded outdoorsmen and nature lovers in Ust-Kamenogorsk, who have discovered interesting petroglyphs in the upper Kurchum district. We exchanged addresses and they promised to be on the lookout for our subject.

I found our main informant in the region, Mstislav Kushnikov, much

Ancient Chinese drawing showing a frolicsome wild-woman

too talkative for my taste. Other people we talked to described him as "prone to exaggeration." Still, I think he is capable of being to the point some of the time; after all, his information on the skeleton proved to be correct inasmuch as the skeleton really existed, and it was not really his fault that the bones were not the kind we dreamed of. With this reservation, I report two anecdotes from a stock delivered by Kushnikov, which sound more like folklore than real facts, but even so seem to be worthy of note as shedding light on man's attitude toward his hairy brothers and sisters. Here they are:

> In the village of Verkhnyaya Yelovka, on the edge of Lake Markakol, lived an old Russian man named Blokhin (he is now dead), who, for many years, used to go to the mountains every summer and live there with a ksy-gyik woman. When asked how he managed to befriend her, he answered, "Go alone to the mountains, strip naked, and wait quite some time - that way she'll come to you."

> One forester in the Kurchum district went hunting and waited in ambush on a game track. Suddenly he was almost bumped into by two male ksy-gyiks. Seeing a gun pointed at them, the wildmen trembled with fear, their "apparatuses" (Kushnikov's euphemism for male organs) shaking most conspicuously. Confronted by such a sight, the forester couldn't help laughing (whether it was a nervous or hearty laugh Kushnikov did not tell). Hearing the man laugh, the ksy-gyiks laughed even louder, then turned round and, still laughing, made off.

If only all encounters of hairy bipeds with armed bipeds could end in this laughable manner!

Here is one more tale from Eastern Kazakhstan, which plays interestingly on the difference of ethnic attitudes to our "wards" and their ambiguous status of "manimals," if I may borrow Jim McClarin's neologism. The story was told to us by the Kazakh editor of a local newspaper when we paid him a visit at his office; he said he'd heard it in his childhood.

> It happened in the old days, before the Revolution and Soviet power. One Kazakh, the proud owner of a hunting gun, went across the border to hunt in China. The Chinese had no guns, and asked him to lend them a hand in hunting. The Kazakh agreed and the party went to the mountains. The Kazakh stayed in ambush while the Chinese beaters chased the game towards him. Presently a wild woman holding a baby in her arms appeared in front of the ambush and stood in hesitation. The Kazakh waved her away, saying, "Hey, woman, get out of danger's way, quick!" The wild woman did not have to be asked twice, and as soon as she had disappeared into the undergrowth the Chinese arrived on the scene. "Why didn't you shoot the game?", they asked the Kazakh. "What game? I didn't see any game." "Why, it was right here. We saw it approach you." "That was a woman with a child. I don't shoot people," said the Kazakh. "No", said the Chinese, "that was game alright. Very tasty game. Yesterday you shared our meal. It was cooked with fat from the butt of such game."

Thus, we did not get any firsthand evidence of the hominoid's current presence in Eastern Kazakhstan, but our stay was too short for a totally negative conclusion. The area was valid as habitat in the past, and looks a possible habitat at present; hence, we must continue to watch the region and glean information from there. The mountainous country in Eastern Kazakhstan is the northernmost part of Soviet Central Asia that we investigate, while Tajikistan is its southernmost part. Tajikistan was next on our itinerary because I wanted to see for myself the sites of presumed hominoid encounters and finds of footprints claimed by our own people in recent years - but that will be the subject of my next report.

A FIELD INVESTIGATION INTO THE RELIC HOMINOID SITUATION IN TAJIKISTAN [16]
By Dmitri Bayanov

Introduction

From August 27 to September 22, 1982, the author visited three regions of Tajikistan [17] for the purpose of learning firsthand the hominological situation there. Tajikistan is about the size of Wisconsin or Nepal, and somewhat bigger than Greece. Ninety-three percent of the republic's area consists of high mountains, including the Pamirs.

The beginnings of hominoid research in Tajikistan is connected with the name of Professor Boris Porshev, who took part in a 1958 USSR Academy of Sciences "Snowman" expedition, and who later visited the area several times. The Scientific Commission to Study the Snowman Question that existed at the time received accounts from General M. S. Topilsky, who claimed to have examined a slain hairy wildman in Tajikistan in 1925; from prospector B. M. Zdorik, who claimed to have stumbled on a sleeping hairy "dev" in 1934; from hydrologist A. G. Pronin, claiming a hominoid sighting in 1957; and some others.

When the lack of physical evidence resulted in the evaporation of official interest in the problem, Tajikistan, being several thousand kilometres from Moscow, took second place after the Caucasus in our self-funded hominology research; but, in the late 1970's, Igor Tatsl, later supported by Igor Bourtsev, put much effort into bringing Tajikistan back to the forefront of hominological activity. In 1980, two hominoid sightings were claimed by Tatsl expedition members, the first ever reported by actual field searchers. These developments, given publicity in the USSR and abroad, met with enthusiastic acclaim from a segment of the public, and with silence or negative reaction from the scientific community. The Darwin Museum and newspaper editors received many pro and con letters from all over the USSR, including Tajikistan - hence my decision to undertake a fact-finding trip to the area in 1982.

16 *Cryptozoology*, Vol. 3, 1984.
17 Tajikistan is an ex-Soviet republic in Central Asia, lying at the latitudes of northern California. Today it is an independent state with an unstable political and economic situation.

Sampling the local wild fruits straight from the tree, which are plentiful in the mountains.

Narrative Description

Upon arriving in Dushanbe, capital of Tajikistan, my colleague Vadim Makarov and I consulted local hominoid researchers, including geophysicist Karl Yefremov, who advised us to visit the region of Sary-Khosor, some 100 kilometres southeast of Dushanbe, where he heard sighting accounts from the local population.

In the company of four associates from Dushanbe, Makarov and I trekked through the mountains for a week in the region of Sary-Khosor. Travelling along creek beds and hardly-discernible or very precipitous paths for several days, we encountered no human habitation. The fauna was most conspicuous by numerous and ever-present bear tracks of different sizes, left mainly in creek beds; I found this encouraging, as the bear and the supposed hominoid are about equal in weight and diet. The bear faeces we found were full of stones from wild plums *(Prunus divaricata)* and undigested plums. Occasionally we came across plum trees with branches broken and bent down, and a lot of fruit strewn on the ground - leftovers of bear feasts. Bears *(Urus arctos isabellinus)* are abundant in Tajikistan for two reasons - food is plentiful, and the Tajiks, being Muslims, do not eat bear meat. They trap bears only rarely, we were told, with nooses hidden in those plum-trees to obtain bear fat, which is used for medicinal purposes.

In one place, toward the end of our mountain trek, we came upon a mud hut used by wild fruit and walnut pickers, a kind of seasonal dugout in a gully slope. The hut was open, with no owner present. We could see provisions inside the hut, and ubiquitous bear tracks not far outside. We then descended into the Shirop-dara Valley, and met the first inhabitants. It was the summer camp of the wild fruit pickers whose "frontline" dugout we had seen in the mountains. With traditional Tajik hospitality, they treated us to milk, honey, pancakes and tea. Conversation was difficult because the family spoke only poor Russian, and we had only a few Tajik words - mostly names of animals - at our command; still, we understood that the grandmother of the family, who was present, had seen a gul[18] (pronounced "gool," a common

18 From the Arabic *ghul*, spelt *ghoul* in English dictionaries.

Tajik name for the supposed wildman), right in front of the hut in the mountains already known to us, when she was young. Details could not be obtained because of the language handicap. They said they knew of no recent sightings.

A Forest Service worker we interviewed later said he had seen the tracks of the gul when he was a boy. We had noticed the reluctance of most locals to discuss the subject, with the exception of educated Tajiks at the main Forest Service office in the village of Sary-Khosor. The director of the office, Saidov, and the village council chairman, Makhmat Buriev, said that from time to time they got information about wildman from hunters, shepherds, and Forest Service workers. In 1980, for example, they were surprised to see a flock of sheep being driven from the mountain pastures to the village in mid-August (usually this is done in September). An agitated shepherd told them that he had seen a big black gul near the pasture; his dogs had taken fright, and he did not have the courage to stay there any longer.

I asked whether guls are reported to steal sheep, and got a negative answer. However, shepherds sometimes report finding pelts of mice and gophers separated very nicely from the carcasses, and they believe the gul is responsible. Forked sticks are sometimes found near the entrance holes to rodents' nests; these are believed to be used by guls to catch mice.

The next leg of our journey took us to the Karatag Gorge in the Hissar Range northwest of Dushanbe, the site of a reported sighting by two Tatsl expedition members at Lake Pairon in 1980. On the way to the lake, we met and talked with Gafar Jabirov, a local Forest Service patrolman, who claimed to have seen a wildman, and even fired at him, several years before, as had been reported in the press by Igor Bourtsev. I found Jabirov to be a serious and respectable person, who had no doubt that he had seen a gul in the Karatag Gorge, and I had no doubt concerning his sincerity.

The author sitting on a boulder on the shore of Lake Pairon, mimicking a hominoid reportedly seen there the previous year.

We reached Lake Pairon and inspected the site of expedition members Geliona Siforova's and Dima Sizov's reported sighting in September 1980. Makarov and I were joined there by Igor Bourtsev and Geliona Siforova herself, who showed us the exact place and explained the details of the encounter.

She and Sizov claim to have seen a female hominoid, 10 yards from where they were spending the night, on the ground under a tree on the shore of the mountain lake. The creature sat on a boulder watching them and making munching sounds for a long period of time. Next morning, no footprints or hairs could be found where the creature had sat through its night vigil.

We spent several nights at the same spot, but no guls joined our company. One night I went and sat on the boulder, making various movements, while Bourtsev, lying 10 yards away, was telling (correctly) how I moved. We concluded that Siforova and Sizov could have at least made out the creature at that distance at night.

On the way back from the Karatag, I talked with a Forest Service man named Aslon Zakirov, at his office in Shakhrinau. He said he was much intrigued by the subject of wildman, and had interviewed his fellow-Tajiks on the matter whenever he had a chance. He told me of an encounter five years earlier of a Tajik hunter, whom he fully trusted, with "a giant hairy man, very broad in the shoulders, with the face like that of an ape." Zakirov said that, though such encounters are very rare, Forest Service rules prohibit their employees from spending the night alone in the mountains, for fear of these wild men. I then discussed the subject with an experienced local journalist in Dushanbe. For him, the existence of wildman in Tajikistan was a matter of fact, but he doubted the problem could ever be solved without forceful official involvement. He wondered where and how the creatures spend their winters; the snow is two metres deep in the Hissar mountains in the winter. He said he had observed the area during helicopter flights, and could even spot mice tracks, but never saw those of a wildman. In his opinion, the hominoids migrate for the winter to the very south of Tajikistan, where there is little snow, or often none at all.

The third and last region I visited together with Bourtsev was on the Siama River, a tributary of the Varzob River, some 50 kilometres north of Dushanbe.

This, for the last several years, has been the site of Igor Tatsl's activities, where hominoid tracks and sightings have been claimed. I found the area good from a topological perspective. Tatsl's base camp stands on a crossroads of canyons, and is partially hidden by vegetation, so that hominoids can supposedly safely approach the camp in their wanderings from one canyon to another; but how much of this really happens, and how much is just imagined by expedition members, is impossible to tell at present. Nina Grinyova, who claimed a sighting in August 1980, was present during my visit, and she reenacted the scene for us. All I can conclude is that I found her story more believable there than I had in Moscow. Attempts to repeat her claimed achievement with similar tactics (staying alone at night) have proved fruitless so far; food baits and photo traps have also been unsuccessful.

Results

Tajikistan appears to be an ecologically-suitable habitat for relic hominoids. The abundant signs I witnessed of local fauna, particularly omnivores such as bears and wild pigs, indicate enough food resources for the presumably-omnivorous hominoids the year round. Anthropogenic pressure on them is also no problem; the 93 percent of the republic's territory taken up by mountains is virtually devoid of permanent human population, so the latter poses no special danger to wild hominoids.

The long and continuing record of purported hominoid sightings in the area, supported by the new accounts discussed above, leads me to the conclusion that such creatures do exist there; but, to turn this conclusion into a scientific fact is as difficult in Tajikistan as anywhere else. Overoptimistic forecasts that appeared in the Soviet press in connection with Igor Tatsl's expeditions were based on wishful thinking, while some foreign reports exaggerated and distorted the situation out of all proportion. As a result of this expedition, I am more inclined than ever to think that relic hominoids have neither "supernatural" nor simply "animal", but what I call "superanimal" status. This is for quite evident reasons - their large brains, coupled with upright walking and free hands. These factors are responsible, perhaps, for their occasional strange behaviour, on the one hand, and their "abnormal" elusiveness on the other. The latter is largely achieved through what could be called the "guerrilla tactic of supermobility." In the words of a local hunter, the wildman "is as nimble-footed as a wild ram, as sharp-eyed as an eagle, and as good at hearing as a snow leopard. There is no one in the mountains to challenge him."

Future Plans

Tajikistan remains high on the agenda of our fieldwork. We aim to reduce the quantity, and raise the quality, of expedition members. One of our main concerns is to re-engage the scientific community in this investigation, and to raise funds for year-round fieldwork, instead of the two or three-month stints presently conducted at our own expense. [19]

---

19 Unfortunately, because of political strife and economic dislocation in Tajikistan at present, our fieldwork there has been suspended.

Part III

SIBERIA

ARCTIC OCEAN

URAL MOUNTAINS

Salekhard

Yamal Pen

Yenisei

Lena

YAKUTIA

Yakutsk

Ob

Tyumen

Novosibirsk

Irkutsk

L. Baikal

MONGOLIA

الجزء الثاني
من كتاب

مُرُوجُ الذَّهَبْ
و
مَعَادِنُ الجُوهَرْ
فى
التَّارِيخ

تأليف العَلَّامَة الإمَام
أبى الحَسَن على بن الحُسَين بن على المَسعودى الشافعى
المتوفى سنة ٣٤٦ هجرية

قال صَاحِبُ كَشْفِ الظّنُونْ

مروج الذهب ومعادن الجوهر فى التاريخ لأبى الحسن على بن الحُسَين
ابن على المسعودى المتوفى سنة ٣٤٦ هجرية من أولاد عبد الله أحد الخلفا
ومُنتوجبى الشكاء ٭ وذكر فيه أنه صنف كتابا كبيرا سماه
أخبار الزمان ثم لخّصَره ومعنا الأوسط ثم أراد أحمال
مسائله واستيار ما بسطه فى هذا الكتاب وقال ٭ ودعه لمعه
ما فى ذلك الكتابين مما ضيعنا وغيره لان من أنواع العلوم
واخبار الأمم شرحقال ٭ وسَميته بمروج الذهب لنفاسة ماحواء
وجَعَلته تحفة الأشراف ٭ ولن تزك نوعا من العُلُوم ولاخبر
من الأخبار الأ أورد ناء، مفصلا أو بجملا الى آخر ماقال ام طلبنا

الملتزم عبد الرحمن محمد بميدان الجامع الأزهر بمصر
طبع بالمطبعة البهية المصرية إدارة الملتزم
سنة ٣٢٦ هجرية

Another species of monkeys are in the northern regions, forests, and jungles, in the country of the Sclavonians and of other nations, and of which we have said they approach in appearance the figure of man.

From the book
Meadows of Gold and Mines of Gems *
(10th century A.D.)

---

* *Meadows of Gold and Mines of Gems* (in Arabic مروج الذهب ومعادن الجوهر transliteration: Muruj adh-dhahab wa ma'adin al-jawahir) is an historical account in Arabic of the beginning of the world starting with Adam and Eve up to and through the late Abbasid Caliphate by medieval Baghdadi historian Masudi (in Arabic المسعودي.).
One English version is the abridged *The Meadows of Gold: The Abbasids,* translated and edited by Paul Lunde and Caroline Stone. An 1841 translation of volume I, by Aloys Sprenger, also exists and is available at Princeton's Firestone Library. A first version of the book was allegedly completed in the year 947 AD but the author spent most of his life adding and editing the work as well.

DOES SIBERIA HAVE ITS OWN SASQUATCHSKI?

Associated Press

Moscow, February 4, 1978 - Soviet scientists say they have gathered evidence pointing to the existence in Siberia of a dark, shaggy-haired, shrill-voiced wild man resembling in some ways the legendary Snowman of the Himalayas, or Sasquatch of the Pacific coast.

The Soviet news agency TASS said specialists at the Institute of Language, Literature and History in Soviet Yakutia have been evaluating testimony of Siberians who claim they encountered the manlike creature called 'Chuchunaa.' The name means fugitive or outcast in one of the dialects of Yakutia, a vast expanse of forest, mountains and frozen tundra in northeastern Siberia. The last trustworthy sighting of the wild man was in the 1950's on the Adychi River. "Chuchunaa might have retreated still deeper into the forest, to a point which is not reached even by hunters and geologists," TASS said. The Himalayan Snowman is also known as the 'Abominable Snowman.' Large tracks in the snow are ascribed to such a creature. Some scientists believe that, if he exists, he may be a form of unclassified ape.

THE TRAIL BLAZED BY VLADIMIR PUSHKAREV

In 1958, at the time of the Snowman Commission and the Pamirs expedition, it was beyond imagination that any man-like "monkeys" or "a form of unclassified ape" might inhabit the northern regions of Russia, the country of the "Sclavonians" (Slavs) and of other nations of the North; yet the Commission did receive such information, and Porshnev published some of it in his fundamental monograph of 1963, adding that the researcher was "unexpectedly faced" with "a new, polar chapter of investigation" which would be written in due time. Death in 1972 prevented him from writing the "polar chapter," and it fell to the lot of a young geologist, Vladimir Pushkarev, to start a planned and systematic hominoid investigation in the Russian North.

By profession and character, Pushkarev was the most "roving" member of our seminar, having

**Vladimir Pushkarev
blazed the trail into
Siberia's vast wilderness
and paid with his life.**

wandered up and down the country and visited backwoods we'd never been to. Like many of us, he was apprenticed in Koffmann's expeditions to the Caucasus, but a single area was not enough for him, and he shifted attention to the boundless expanses of the Russian North. As a rule, he travelled alone or in the company of his friend, Victoria Poupko, Assistant Professor of Mathematics at a Moscow college. He regularly presented his findings to the seminar, and they never failed to fuel a very earnest and lively discussion.

Ever more engrossed in hominology, Pushkarev took an extramural course in biology at a college in Kalinin, and was preparing a thesis entitled *Current Knowledge on the Relic Hominoid in the North Eurasia.* In it he wrote that, due to the rigours of the North, the adaptive capacity of the wildman was of a level never attained by any other primate. Among the creature's physical endowments, Pushkarev noted its great capacity for swimming, and remaining underwater much longer than is possible for man. The wildman's intelligence is superior to that of any animal, while his senses are much keener than in man; this helps the wildman simply avoid perilous confrontations with man. He can be seen only rarely by the odd hunter or a reindeer breeder, but never by a "superman" breaking through the taiga on a cross-country vehicle, or blasting away at the mountains with dynamite.

The northern wildman, continued Pushkarev, hunts reindeer, catches fish, or steals it from fishermen's nets. His annual biological cycle is close to that of the brown bear.

Concluding his thesis, Pushkarev wrote the following:

The problem of relic hominoids is one of the great enigmas of Earth. Its importance is at its peak today, because in a decade or two these relics may disappear from the face of the planet, just as did the mammoth at the time of the Roman Empire and *Epiornis* (the gigantic bird of Madagascar) in the 18th century. We are the generation that finds the hominoid still alive, and that is why we are fully responsible for the solution of the problem.

In the autumn of 1978, to get more material for his thesis, Vladimir set out on yet another journey

Michael Trachtengerts, deputy chairman of the Russian Society of Cryptozoologists, Smolin seminar activist, experienced traveller and outdoorsman.

in Western Siberia. His reason for travelling alone was a hope that this increased his chances of making contact with a wildman. He went in a rubber boat down a river flowing through boggy forests in the Ob River Basin. That autumn, Western Siberia was suddenly struck by very early and severe frosts. When Vladimir failed to appear in time at a control post, a search was launched for him, in which Alya Bourtseva and Mikhail Trachtenherz of our seminar took an active and selfless part. His rubber boat was found some two hundred kilometres upstream from the post, with a note in it saying that as the river got frozen he would proceed downstream on foot. Pushkarev was a very experienced and hardy outdoorsman, so we concluded he must have suffered some fatal accident. As the ice was not yet strong, he must have fallen through and drowned. It was a very heavy blow to us, both in human and "professional" terms. The following is a translation of the last of Pushkarev's two articles published in the popular press. When this translation appeared in the monthly *Soviet Life* (March 1979), Vladimir was no longer with us.

NEW TESTIMONY
By Vladimir Pushkarev

In August 1975, I was at the lower reaches of the Ob River (Western Siberia). In one of the villages I met Luka Tynzyanov, a former taiga hunter. He told me:

> In 1960, or it might have been 1961, I was hiking one evening from Yarskogort to Vasyakovo along the bank of the Gornaya Ob. I had two dogs with me. Suddenly they bristled, began to bark, and ran ahead. They returned quickly, only to charge off again. They came running back, and this time huddled near my feet and stopped barking. Just then two *kuls* emerged from the forest. One was tall, over two metres, and the other a little shorter. I also got scared because their eyes glowed like two dark red lanterns. They came toward me and, when they were quite close, stared at me with flashing eyes. They wore no clothes. Their bodies were covered with thick short hair. Both their faces and bodies were black. Their faces jutted out, their arms were

longer than a man's, and they swung them in a strange way. Their gait was unlike a human being's. They turned their feet in when walking. When they passed us, the dogs made a beeline for the village.

What is this kul, [20] have you any idea?", I asked Luka. "Can't tell," he said, shrugging his shoulders, "I saw it four times - twice right after the war, and twice 15 years ago."

On the banks of the Synya and Voykar, at the Lower Ob, everybody knows stories of this kind, but not everyone will tell them to strangers. The Khanty (people of Northern Russia) are simple and trusting folk, very cautious about all manner of direct questions and prone to be sensitive to mockery.

The interesting thing is that it was not professional storytellers so much as the ordinary people - fishermen and reindeer breeders who had no knowledge of any other "legends of hoary antiquity" who spoke of the forest man.

I met a remarkable Russian woman in Salekhard by the name of Marfa Senkina, a former village schoolteacher who had devoted great effort to teaching the native people to read and write; therefore, it was particularly important for us to hear her account.

Before the Revolution, my father and I were constantly travelling around the northern Ob region and the Yamal Peninsula. I was 20 at the time, and our permanent residence was in Salekhard. Sometimes we stayed with an old Khanty not far from the village of Puyko. I remember that it was in September, the nights were dark, and our dogs bayed at night. Once their barking was particularly ferocious. The next night it was no less frenzied. I asked our host, the Khanty, whom they were barking at like that, and he whispered that it was at the Zemlemer (Land Surveyor).

"Zemlemer?" I was puzzled.

"I'll show you tonight," he said. "Only. watch him with caution through your fingers."

At midnight we walked out of the choom [21]. There was a large red moon. We waited for about an hour, and suddenly the dogs began to bark. Several dozen metres away I spotted a very tall man. Our chooms were surrounded by a hedge of rose willows two metres high; the man's head and shoulders rose above it. He walked fast, with long steps, pushing right through the thickets. His eyes glowed like lanterns.

---

20 The term is apparently of the same origin as gul in Tajikistan. – D B.
21 Tent of skins or bark.

I had never seen such a tall and terrible man. The dogs rushed at him, baying. One, lent courage by our presence, ran right up to him. The man bent over, picked it up and hurled it far to one side. We heard a yelp and saw the dog's body career through the air. The man left quickly and did not turn back to look at us.

"Was it a forest sprite?" I asked the old man.

"Don't say that word," he said in fright, "lest you summon him. Just call him the Zemlemer. He comes here, every year, at this time." The next morning, one of our dogs was missing.

I met dozens of people who had seen the mysterious forest creature at various times. It looked like a man, but lived a strange life hidden from our eyes. What was it?

In Salekhard there are three specialized secondary schools attended by girls and boys from the entire Yamalo-Nenets National Area, children of reindeer breeders with whom they travel all over the vast tundra. I quizzed these future teachers, doctor's assistants and zootechnicians.

To the first question, "Have you ever come across a wild man in the tundra?", 48 of the 60 asked replied in the affirmative. Twelve replied "Don't know."

To the second question, "What do the Nenets call the wild man?", all 60 replied, "Tungu."

To the third question, "Who has seen him recently?" (during the sixties and seventies), 4 replied that they had seen the Tungu with their own eyes, but at a distance and in twilight. They could not give a detailed description of him. 10 pupils said their fathers, grandfathers or brothers had seen him.

To the fourth question, "How do those who saw the Tungu describe him?", they said, "He's very tall and thin. Shaggy, most likely wearing a skin. Has a shrill whistle and runs fast." He was encountered all over the North, from the Ob to the Yenisei, in the tundra of the Gydan Peninsula, and far to the south in the forests of the Nadym and Tazu districts.

In the Nyda village of Nadym District, this time I quizzed some experienced reindeer breeders, and nobody denied his existence. Everybody said that the Tungu had often been seen 15 to 20 years ago, but not at all in the past 10 years.

"He must have left for the south-lying woods," the old folk said.

From the old reindeer breeders of Nadym District and the pupils of Salekhard, I learned that the Tungu was seen quite often in the early sixties.

If the stories about the Tungu are to be credited, encounters with him were terminated by the exploration of this area by geologists and builders. The description of the wild man proves that he could not be confused with any of the peoples of the North. His unusual, although characteristic, conduct - the absence of speech, his shrill whistling, remarkably fast running and exceptional adaption to the conditions of the North and Arctic - shows that this is a new and peculiar species, something like, and yet unlike, a human being. From where and when did the unknown wild man come to these grim Northern parts?

YAKUT TRUE STORY

L et us travel 5,000 kilometres, from the great Ob River to Yakutia (Eastern Siberia). We did comparative research there in the summer of 1974, and heard more stories about the wild forest man, called 'Chuchunaa' in those parts. Here is a typical story recorded by a reindeer-breeding team as told on the bank of Khoboyotu Creek by Tatyana Zakharova, 55, an Evenk by nationality:

> After the Revolution, in the twenties, our villagers came across a Chuchunaa while out berry picking. He was also picking berries and stuffing them into his mouth with both hands. On catching sight of us, he stood up to his full height. He was very tall and lean, over two metres, they say. Barefoot and dressed in deerskin, he had very long arms and a mop of unkempt hair. His face was as big as a human's. His forehead was small and protruded over his eyes like the peak of a cap. His chin was large and broad, far bigger than a human's. Other than being taller, he was very much like a human. The next moment he ran away. He ran very fast, leaping high after every third step.

Stories about the Chuchunaa poured down on us like rain. The more we heard them, the clearer became his image, changing from the supernatural into something almost real. He had no fantastic traits typical of fairy tale characters, but possessed the most diverse human features.

The amazing thing was the Chuchunaa's appearance on certain dates. Judging from all the stories, he had been seen most often at the turn of our century. In the twenties and thirties he was less often encountered, and in the fifties we registered only two encounters of the Chuchunaa from the Adychi River basin. Why did so many more stories about the Chuchunaa come from this area than from any other? The great-grandfathers of the present reindeer breeders had their food stolen, presumably by Chuchunaa children that they had seen swimming across the river when the ice drifted.

Everywhere, in all the stories, the description of the Chuchunaa is almost anatomically detailed, showing him as a manlike creature - strong, capable and habituated to the grim conditions of the North. The Soviet historian and ethnographer G. V. Ksenofontov wrote in his book, *Urankhai Sakhalar*:

> The Chuchunaa is a human. He feeds on wild deer and eats the meat raw. They say he tears the skin off the wild deer and wears it, just as we do the hide of a fox. He lives in a lair like a bear. His voice is unpleasant, grating and hoarse. He whistles, frightening people and

reindeer. Men come across him very rarely and often see him running away.... The Chuchunaa's face is black, and it's hard to make out the nose and the eyes. He can be seen only in summertime. In winter he is not around.

Neither in the stories we heard nor in the description given by the Soviet scholar is the Chuchunaa ascribed with any fantastic features; he is more like a creature of the Earth. It should be added that, aside from stories about the Chuchunaa, in Verkhoyansk District there are tales about rare discoveries of skeletons of giant human beings in the basin of the Adychi River.

From the above, we can establish the fact that there are true stories and new accounts of a mysterious creature resembling a human, spoken of in districts thousands of kilometres apart, and divided by natural obstacles, such as large rivers and mountains. It is too early to draw any definite conclusions, but I should like to point out that our grim expansive North conceals as many riddles and mysteries as the glamorous, snowy slopes of the Himalayas.

REPORT BY MAYA BYKOVA

Bigfoot Co-op, April 1988

In 1985, on my way back from the trip to Western Siberia, where I gathered folklore and eyewitness accounts about relic hominoids, my fellow traveller on the train happened to be a young man named Volodya, an ethnic Mansi, the indigenous people of Western Siberia. He took a deep interest in the purpose of my trip, listened to me with great attention, and asked many questions. When I said I was not one of those who dream of shooting or catching a hominoid, he suddenly avowed that he himself, his father and grandfather had seen such a creature.

Volodya told me that he had a hunting log cabin standing in an out-of-the-way cedar forest, surrounded by bogs, some seventy kilometres from his settlement. The cabin was built by his grandfather, who, about forty years ago, began to notice someone approach the dwelling after dark, and especially at dawn. Peering out of the window, Volodya's grandfather and father had glimpsed, on several occasions, a strange forest dweller who looked both like and unlike a man. He was big and bulky, without clothes, and covered from head to foot with red-brown hair, except the left forearm, which was white; for that reason, they called him Mecheny (Marked).

Surprisingly, he announced his arrival by a knock on the window. They had no idea why he did that - was it a warning or an invitation? - but the scared people would never go out of the cabin when he appeared. The hunting dog they brought along would disappear when Mecheny came, and reappear when he was gone. Having knocked on the window, Mecheny would wander for some time near the cabin, looking down as if searching for something on the ground and muttering away to himself. As a rule, he showed up in August. Some years they did not see him at all, but in 1985 he was seen twice.

I was not in a hurry to swallow the story and, seeing that, Volodya invited me to come to his cabin and see for myself that he was telling the truth.

The area in question is very far from Moscow, and in 1986 I was unable to go. In the meantime, Volodya wrote to me saying that in 1986 Mecheny had been seen three times near the cabin; then came a letter from him with an invitation for the summer of 1987. His condition - I could tell about my observation, should it take place, but withhold Volodya's surname and address from the press. Naturally, I complied. I took a bag of plaster to cast footprints, in case I found them, but did not take a camera. I was sure I would not be able to take good pictures, given the conditions of Mecheny's appearance, as described by Volodya. Besides, an attempt at photography would distract me from observation, and might frighten away the subject whose trust I needed most of all.

In August 1987, I arrived at a remote Siberian settlement in the Tyumen Region, by a tributary of the Ob. Volodya, his wife Nadya, his father and grandfather warmly welcomed me, and confirmed the information I already had from Volodya.

On Saturday, August 15, Volodya, Nadya, me, and their three-month old puppy named 'Box' (the old dog was no longer alive) set out for the cherished hunting cabin. The path was difficult, the last leg passing through bogs, so we reached our destination in the evening, pretty worn out. Before

**Encounter with Mecheny, the "marked"
wildman of Siberia. Drawn by S. Svarchevsky
under direction of Maya Bykova.**

Mecheny's portrayal based on Maya Bykova's eyewitness description. Drawing by N. Potapov.

settling down for the night, Volodya put some logs under the window and covered them with a piece of plywood used for drying cedar nuts. "Lest he surprises us," said Volodya.

His foresight was not in vain. At dawn we heard someone step on the plywood and make two quick knocks on the window. I shot out from the bed, dashed to the door, threw off the hook, and popped outdoors. Volodya and Nadya, fearing for my safety, followed suit.

It was dawning, and the first thing I saw in front of me was a white spot against a dark background of trees. After that I saw his figure. He was standing five metres away, his right shoulder leaning against the barkless trunk of a dead cedar. Sharply in view were the white forearm and brightly glowing red eyes.

It was sufficiently light and I was close enough to see him in detail. He stood two metres, give or take five centimetres. Looking down at us (Volodya is 180 centimetres tall, I am 168, and Nadya is shorter), he shifted his glance from one to another and made a sound, something like "Khe!," as if clearing his throat without parting the lips. On the whole, judging by his build, especially the lower extremities, he resembled a man, not an ape or a bear standing on the hind legs; but, like an animal, he was covered all over with fur, some six or seven centimetres long, red-brown in color, except the left forearm which, as already mentioned, was white.

I drew the creature's portrait from head to foot as it stuck in my memory. The head, when facing me, looked round, but later, when he turned, I noticed that the back of the head was elongated. The hair on the head was short, no more than three centimetres. I did not see any skin on the face - it was all covered with hair, including the ears, the nose and the nostrils. I could only see his eyes, almond-shaped like a man's, but sunken under prominent brow ridges. The jaws were slightly put forward and showed a long narrow slit of the mouth. The head sat right on the shoulders, without a neck. The shoulders were strikingly wide and strongly muscled; such musculature in humans can only be seen in body-builders. The chest was powerful and barrel-like. Hefty arms, set somewhat forward, hung loosely down. Their relative length seemed within human proportions. The hands were enormous and shaped like scoops. I could see the skin of the palms, and it was reddish. In the groin the hair was longer; the genitals were not seen. The legs were long and straight, with enormous feet. They were also covered with hair and I did not see any skin.

Compared with the sasquatch of the Patterson-Gimlin film, the similarity is obvious, considering such characteristics as size, bulk, hairiness, the barrel-like chest, and the setting of the head; the difference between them is mainly connected with the different sex of the creatures - breasts in the sasquatch and their absence in Mecheny. The latter's musculature is more developed and pronounced than in the female sasquatch; besides, he seemed devoid of the body fat that is apparent in the female. It must be remembered, though, that I saw Mecheny mainly facing me and standing still, while his American counterpart is filmed from the side and rear and on the move.

I often manage without a watch and can measure time by inwardly counting seconds. In spite of unspeakable fear and emotional shock, I inwardly counted seconds while scrutinizing the creature. My head was clear. There came a moment when I thought, *What next? Shall we approach him or he approach us? But do we need that?*

When I counted to sixty, the confrontation ended as abruptly as it began. With a hysterical barking and howling, our canine guard Box came running from behind the cabin and pressed himself against Volodya's legs, either trying to defend its master or seeking his protection. Mecheny made a quick turn to the right, stepped behind the tree, and vanished in the forest.

As if by command, we sat down on the ground and began to rub the legs, which were numb and refused to obey. Legs brought under control, we returned into the cabin and locked the door. After a while, having sufficiently recovered, we went out and walked over to the dead tree the creature had been standing by. I looked for hairs on the trunk, but it was as smooth as bone and I did not find a single hair. We then measured the height of the trunk where his head had reached.

We looked for footprints under the tree and in the direction of Mecheny's retreat, but the ground was covered with a thick mat of cedar needles which did not retain any prints. We then went round the cabin and searched for tracks at the edges of the forest where it touched the swamp, but all in vain; we never discovered any footprints.

We made sorties into the forest - the three of us together, not counting the puppy that accompanied us in the best of humour, never showing any fear. As for ourselves, we were in pretty low spirits. Volodya and Nadya said on several occasions, "Why did we go out to him?" I began to suffer from insomnia, and tried to catch sleep in the daytime.

The encounter with Mecheny took place on August 16th. We stayed there for another eight days, and then returned to the settlement because Volodya's leave was coming to an end. We took no actions to attract the forest-dweller by leaving him offerings; we figured he would come again of his own accord if he wished to, as he did the first time. There were barrels with berries standing by the cabin, as well as mushrooms drying in the yard, but Mecheny never touched them. "He is damned honest," commented Volodya. Besides mushrooms and cranberries, the place abounds in salmonberries, cowberries, and red bilberries. Game is also plentiful and includes such species as hare, squirrel, hazel grouse, wood grouse, sable and bear. Mecheny did not show up again. I returned to Moscow and the first letter from Volodya told me they felt anxiety, not knowing how Mecheny would behave the next time people visit the cabin. The letter contained the following words - "Don't know how we shall carry on." I decided to revisit them without delay and live for some time in the cabin so as to reassure them.

In mid-October, just like the first time, the three of us were on the scene, not counting Box, who had grown up and had now turned five months old. Neither the first nor subsequent nights did anyone knock on the window. Only once at night did we hear a strange plaintive cry in the forest, and thought it was a bird. In the morning we did not see Box and called him, but he did not show up. We searched in the forest and some hundred metres from the cabin found his body ripped apart from the tail to the clavicles. The skull under the skin on the right side was crushed, the jaws clamped tight, the tongue sticking out on one side and pierced by the teeth. We were shocked by this sight. "Mecheny's job," said Volodya. Indeed, no other known animal can treat its victim in that manner - it takes hands and tremendous strength.

We surmised that Mecheny had stalked Box, grabbed him by the hind legs and smashed him against a tree, breaking the skull. Before his death the dog made the cry we heard at night, and bit the tongue, then Mecheny may have stepped on one hind leg of the dog, pulled at the other, and ripped the body apart.

The frozen ground revealed just a puddle of frozen blood, but no tracks of the killer. We buried Box in the swamp under a heap of moss - that was on October 22nd. A fearless woodsman, hunting bears, Volodya was seriously worried by what had come to pass and started to pack up. That very day we left the place.

That's the story in a nutshell. The main result is that Mecheny, for me, is now a real zoological specimen. I could not have been mistaken because I was prepared for such an encounter. Many years of active interest in relic hominoids gives me the right to say so. My experience testifies to the recurrence of encounters. Sightings of the specimen in question go back over forty years.

The continuation of the relationship depends on two factors; first, on the behaviour of Volodya and his family, who feel the strongest fear of Mecheny, and an anxiety after the killing of their dog and no need for a closer contact than the one they've had for years; and, second, on the behaviour of the hominoid himself, who is advanced in age and probably not inclined to change his habits. As for me, I'll do my best to give this contact a happy ending.

REPORT BY DMITRI BAYANOV
Bigfoot Coop, June 1988

This is to bring the reader up to date on the situation here and comment on Maya Bykova's adventure, but first be advised there was no need to get excited over agency reports about Igor Tatsl's sighting in the Hissar Range (see p.77). Having learned of fresh events up north in Siberia, Tatsl lost no time in reminding the world of his own efforts in the south - just that and nothing more. Media reports on our problem should be taken with a grain of salt, while tabloid stories are pure inventions, as you know.

As you may remember, Nikolai Avdeyev was expected to return to Komi in 1987, where he had been fired on in 1986. It is little wonder that he changed his mind and went instead to Western Siberia, to an area first reconnoitred by Maya Bykova. As Avdeyev and Bykova adhere to different philosophies and methods in hominology (he carries a gun and dreams of producing a specimen, dead or alive, while she is against any violence), a sharp conflict of interest ensues between them. Unfortunately, my peacemaking efforts failed to reconcile the sides, and the conflict is still with us.

Avdeyev claims to have come into contact with a hominoid at night - he saw its glowing eyes in the light of his bonfire. According to him, the creature mimicked his whistles the same number of times -twice and thrice - but with a different sound, very sharp and unpleasant, making Avdeyev's skin creep. This reminds me of a similar story from America, in *Bigfoot* by B. Ann Slate and Alan Berry, 1976, of which Avdeyev is unaware. Despite Bykova's protests, Avdeyev intends to return to the place this year.

Now, we get to Bykova's own sighting in a place she keeps secret from Avdeyev and the rest of mankind, but first some light on the researcher herself. In the words of a British reporter who interviewed her, "Mrs. Bykova is a lady of 55, possessing that determination one associates with those elderly gentlewomen of English legend, who would travel without qualms in the scruffier regions of the Near East, like Rose Macaulay's Aunt Dot, undeterred by whatever the natives might try on them. More important, though, she has been in the "snowman" business for more than 25 years." (Rupert Cornwell, "Nothing trivial about the pursuit of Soviet Snowman," *The Independent*, January 15, 1988, p. 10)

Yes, Maya was an assistant of the late Prof. Porshnev, the father of hominoid research in this country, and she is a veteran activist of our seminar, and an old friend and colleague of mine. By

education she is an agronomist, and before retirement was a science editor of an agricultural magazine. By character, she is independent and unpredictable, the pussycat that walks by herself.

Her story got a lot of publicity in the Soviet media, and about the same amount of disbelief, because she has no photographic evidence to support her words. Here, I must tell a secret - she has never used a camera in her life. Even if she had, I doubt that under the circumstances she could have produced convincing results. Incidentally, note that the Patterson-Gimlin film is yet to be recognized by science. "There is little doubt that the scientific evidence taken collectively points to a hoax of some kind," wrote John Napier about the film in 1973; yet he endorsed the Wooldridge "yeti" photograph, even though many investigators,

Maya Bykova, whose fieldwork experience in hominology is second to none.

myself included, took it for a rock from the very beginning.

That said, Bykova did herself and our cause a disservice by failing to take a camera with her a second time (she has a camera at home used by another member of her family), and not photographing the mutilated dead dog as very interesting and important evidence; privately, she admits as much. Avdeyev claims Bykova made up the story to steal attention from his results. Others think she fell for a hoax perpetrated by the local people. To the best of my knowledge, Bykova's story is true, no matter how difficult to believe. My confidence comes not only from knowledge of her personality, but also from the evidence I was privileged to inspect - her correspondence with Volodya, both before and after the sighting – but more of that later.

Before I try to evaluate the significance of Bykova's sighting, let me comment on some details. Mecheny's knock on the window is most impressive and disturbing with regard to the implications of his near-human nature. It confirms my view on relic hominoids, but still makes me hold my breath. (In case somebody's curious, the distance between the window and the tree Mecheny stood by is about eight metres.)

Regarding Mecheny's glowing eyes, John Green asked me whether there was any light for the eyes to reflect, or whether these were "internally-illuminated" red eyes. Certainly the former is the case, for it was at daybreak and Mecheny, according to Bykova, was facing eastwards.

The extreme hairiness of his face must be of an adaptive nature, taking into account the Siberian climate. One of the names for wildman in Komi folklore is "gyona pel" ("hairy eared"), in contrast to humans who are called "kush pel" ("bare-eared"). Mecheny's white forearm, which earned him his name, seems incongruous at first sight, but in actual fact it's a potent sign of his reality. From a genetic point of view, there just must be piebald hominoids, as there are piebald individuals among other mammalian species, including man. Due to a presumed high rate of inbreeding in dwindling populations of relic hominoids, such phenomena among them may be of a more frequent occurrence than among humans. John Green mentions a Sasquatch that had "brown hair all over it except for a white spot on the throat," and on another one, "its head was kind of yellow, and the rest of it was black like a bear."

Puzzled by her failure to find the tracks of the wildman she observed, Bykova was relieved to learn of wildlife biologist Hewkin's words, "I feel confident that Sasquatch seldom leave tracks to be looked at" (*Cryptozoology,* Vol.6, p.83). Folklore, both in Eurasia and the Americas, ascribes magic ("hypnotic") powers to wildmen. Some people here make much of the fact that Bykova and her two Mansi friends felt numbness in the legs after facing the wildman. I do not rule out the possibility of interesting discoveries in this respect in the future, but feel it is impossible to say at present whether the said numbness was not simply a result of a very strong and sudden fear. "Damned honest" Mecheny never touched berries and mushrooms gathered by humans, perhaps because he had lots in the forest and probably in his stomach. More significantly, he spurned the meat of a still-young dog. Does it mean he opts for more palatable squirrels and hares, or does the mere sight of a dog spoil his appetite?

It was suggested at the seminar that Mecheny ripped the dog in a customary fashion; perhaps it's wildmen's usual way of disembowelling game. During a spate of news about Bigfoot in Northern California thirty years ago, *The Humboldt Times* came up on October 19, 1958, with the piece *New Bluff Creek Mystery Puzzles Indian: 4 Dogs Found Ripped To Pieces*, which said, in part:

> The Indian told Goodwin that all of the dogs had been torn apart and one of them had apparently been slammed against a tree... The construction worker said the discovery of the dogs had changed the minds of many skeptics working in the area. "This," he said, "is when all of us old-timers start to believe."

Until recently this information was known only to me, and Bykova was much impressed by it when I showed and translated the piece to her after we reassembled in Moscow at the end of October, 1987.

According to Bykova's Mansi friends, Mecheny always appeared alone, and usually in August. They think their cabin stands on his migration route; if so, then, to my mind, his knocking on the window may have been learned elsewhere, and with different results for Mecheny. Perhaps in some other place he received nice offerings after knocking on the window, while at Bykova's place he always wonders (muttering to himself) what dull people inhabit Volodya's cabin. Pity they did not offer him something special – say, honey or roast beef - after he knocked on the window.

An artist made two drawings of Mecheny from Bykova's description. She approved one drawing (the one printed in the *Co-op*), but was not happy with the other. Both were sent to Volodya, along with a copy of Bykova's newspaper article describing Mecheny. In his reply, dated February 26, 1988, Volodya criticizes the second drawing almost in the same words that Bykova did ("not enough muscles on the neck and shoulders," etc.), and praises her description - "No one could describe him better than you did. We would not be able to." - by which he implies their Russian vocabulary is not as rich as Maya's. There are also these lines in the letter - "It is quite unusual that he (Mecheny - *D.B.*) visited us in October. As my grandfather said, at this time of year he usually sleeps. He is an animal, after all, not an evil spirit. It is cold (in October.- *D.B.*)."

Well, what does this sighting mean? Where do we stand now? Where do we go from here? It's the first time a veteran hominologist set her eyes on a hominoid - a breakthrough in itself - and it's a third time, to my knowledge, that local people offered this chance to an outsider; first in China in 1950, second in the Caucasus in 1959, and now in Siberia. No doubt left any longer - it's the local people that hold the key to the problem. If we want them to share that key with us, we must win their trust. It is not by chance that an unassuming folklore collector, devoid on her expeditions not only of weapons but even a photo camera and tape-recorder, proved successful in winning such trust.

Now she is under constant pressure from the media, especially TV people, asking her to take them to Volodya's cabin to photograph Mecheny. No go; that is no priority at all. The priority is to habituate a hominoid, and then photograph to your soul's content - it seems we were offered that golden chance at last. Accordingly, at my suggestion, Maya wrote to Volodya, asking him either to let our people make an attempt at habituating Mecheny, or to try it himself with our advice and financial assistance. While we waited for his reply, all sorts of wild ideas crossed my mind, including sending an invitation to my pen-friend, Jane Goodall,[23] to come from Africa to Siberia to observe the Wildman - that would be something to pique the scientific community with.

Volodya's reply to Maya came in a letter of February 20, 1988, and said, in part,

> "It is too bad that all people, just as I thought, want more. At first you also wanted just to see. So you did. Now everybody wants at least the same. Besides they want to bring Mecheny to Moscow or come all together to our place to immobilize him, photograph him, take samples for analysis. And those people will be followed by killers...."

Quite reminiscent, I must say, of Margaret Atwood's *Oratorio for Sasquatch, Man, and Two Androids* in *Manlike Monsters on Trial.*

The letter continued,

> "I ask you not to try this kind of propaganda on me... I understand everything. If things turn out too bad for us, we shall call for help. But none of us wants the occupation of our forest plot, nor seeing cross-country vehicles, forest fires and strangers here. If they want to investigate, let them go to other places, let them "solve the problem" with other animals, not Mecheny. He is not the only one in the world. And drop that talk of the seriousness of the problem. My folks don't want to hear that either. And as for you, you are always welcome."

What an anticlimax! Now, let me change the subject somewhat. In December 1987, availing ourselves of the new situation in the country, we officially established the Association of Cryptozoologists (with a charter and budget of our own) under the auspices of the Darwin Museum.

It's a public organization, not connected with nor recognized by the Academy of Sciences, the majority of whose members are still very strongly opposed to us, saying we spread pseudo-science. The chairperson of our Board is Marie-Jeanne Koffmann; also on the Board are Igor Bourtsev, Alexandra Bourtseva, Maya Bykova, Dmitri Bayanov, and some others. Bayanov is chairman of the seminar. As our parent organization is the Darwin Museum, which is under the Ministry of Culture, some media reports put our Association also under that ministry.

Simultaneously, a group of enthusiasts in Leningrad established the "Snowman" Association, made up mainly of young people bent on a mix of hominology, UFO-logy, parapsychology, etc. Ours, to the contrary, follows strictly biological lines, in keeping with the ISC[24] principles. But there is a difference from the ISC, too – no-one can become an acting member of the Soviet Association of Cryptozoologists without giving a written pledge not to use any methods endangering the life of a

23 The famous British primatologist studying chimpanzees in the wild.

relic hominoid. At a recent Board meeting, I came up with a proposal that we should make a serious effort to habituate a relic hominoid. In my opinion, this can be done by means of a "mobile animal farm," having, on the one hand, such attractions for the subject of our research as a horse, a donkey, a sheep or a she-goat, and, on the other, rabbits, guinea pigs, ducklings and chicks - let the hominoid come and take whatever he likes. No matter what makes science recognize the existence of relic hominoids, I believe there is no way of studying them in the wild other than through habituating a number of specimens.

I reminded those present of the fact that man-powered flight, considered by some people impossible, did become possible after an attractive prize was offered for the achievement; so, with our problem, an attractive prize will no doubt speed up the solution. The prize should be offered to anyone who habituates a hominoid in such a way that it becomes possible for invited researchers to repeatedly observe and photograph the creature. The offer should guarantee, if desired, the anonymity of the prizewinner and the secrecy of the location. It is noteworthy that in Bykova's case, her friend Volodya is mainly worried by the threat of an invasion of their forest; it is not yet certain what his reply would be if we could guarantee him, along with a big prize, the safety of Mecheny and the undisturbed ecology of that forest spot.

Everybody approved the idea, but realized with regret that our present financial situation precludes any prize offering, so I am writing this with a hope that someone in the world may find it possible to offer a prize to a Wildman tamer, wherever he or she may turn up - in China, Nepal, Siberia, or America. Perhaps such an offer could discreetly be made through the good offices of the International Society of Cryptozoology.

THE SECOND ENCOUNTER WITH MECHENY
By Maya Bykova
Bigfoot Co-op, December 1988

I n August 1988, I made another trip to the place in Western Siberia where I saw Mecheny last year. This time I took a camera along, at least as far as Volodya's settlement. I had planned everything in advance and had a hard time persuading Volodya to accept my plan. When he finally did, I had no strength left to contradict him when he said, pointing to the camera, "And this thing we leave here."

Nadya, Volodya's wife, was still very fearful, and did not feel well enough to accompany us to the cabin, so her place was taken by Volodya's grandfather. In keeping with my plan, from August 10 to 15th, Volodya and I spent the nights in concealment on the edge of the forest surrounding the clearing in which the cabin stands. We lay on the ground, using a tent as a sleeping bag. The moon was bright and visibility was good. On two occasions we observed two foxes apparently hunting mice, and that reassured us that we were well concealed. From August 16th to 20th we remained in the cabin, staying awake at night. We had fixed roasted meat on poles outside the cabin, prepared the ground around for possible tracks, and stretched threads between the nearby trees. None of

---

24 The International Society of Cryptozoology, founded in 1982.

these devices were disturbed, and we concluded that Mecheny had not approached the cabin.

From August 21st to 25th, we spent the nights on the edge of the forest and swamp, some 800 metres from the cabin, a place which we suspected last year to be on the way of Mecheny's comings and goings. We lay in a depression, peering in the direction of the swamp, which was much drier than usual on account of a drought. On the night of the 22nd the sky was overcast, and it would have been pitch dark if not for odd flashes of summer lightning which now and again illuminated the swamp in front of us like a theatre stage. During such an illumination, Volodya and I simultaneously noticed a dark hunched figure at a distance of about seventy metres away. We took hands like children and I began shivering. During another illumination, the figure straightened up and we clearly saw the white forearm. That was Mecheny! He moved in an irregular jumpy manner, falling on the ground from time to time. Getting up, he would hold his right hand to his mouth, as if eating something. Was he catching frogs, lizards, or mice?

We watched him busily engaged in this pursuit for more than an hour, from midnight to one-fifteen. He moved in different directions, sometimes heading towards us, sometimes moving away. Surprisingly, we followed his whereabouts even in the darkness, for his movements were marked by sparks whenever his hairy legs rubbed against the grass; there must have been lots of electricity in the air that night. Once he came as close to us as 25 metres, and the pressure of fear was overwhelming. There was a moment when I could no longer control myself, and made an attempt to get up. Volodya pulled me down with both hands, whispering, "If you don't want my death, stay still!"

Mecheny made his exit as suddenly as he had appeared. We stayed put some time longer, unable to stop shivering, then furtively we returned to the cabin and slept. Early in the morning we went back to the sighting place. The trampled grass and moss confirmed what we had seen during the night. There were narrow trails where Mecheny walked and huge spots where he fell on the ground, but we did not find a single remnant of his food, nor a single hair.

We spent two more nights in the same place, but Mecheny did not return. Volodya's leave came to an end and we wound up the expedition. I find it important that I saw Mecheny for a second time, and in the place that we expected him to visit, and also that we watched him for over an hour behaving freely and normally in the wild, without seeing us. That is explained, I believe, not only by our good concealment, but also by his total concentration on the hunting.

The emotional impact of watching this creature defies description. The nearest I can say is that it is a blend of wonder and numbing fear. Proceeding from this season's result, I intend to continue fieldwork in that place next year.

While I was in Western Siberia, the media news mentioned a hominoid sighting in the Kola Peninsula in the Northwest of the USSR. In September, three members of the Soviet Association of Cryptozoologists - Victor Rogov, Mikhail Gavrilov, and myself - made a reconnaissance trip to the Kola Peninsula to check the reported sighting.

The events there had also unfolded around a cabin in a remote forest, but, unlike the Mecheny case, the cabin was built not too long ago by a group of local teenagers who used to go there to fish, pick berries and deafen the surrounding area with tape-recorded pop music. That was too much for a quiet family of local hominoids, and they attempted to evict the noisy intruders from the cabin and drive them away altogether. First they acted rather gently, but, when the boys resisted, the hominoids put on more pressure. The boys invited local hunters, who also saw one of the creatures, but failed to find any when combing the forest.

I am glad that this time I was not a lone researcher and did not have the constraint of the hosts, as in the case in Western Siberia. We interviewed the boys and the hunters, found suspicious lairs among the rocks, and collected hair samples from them (now being analyzed by specialists in Moscow). So far the main result is a most interesting story of hominoid bluff behavior, as it transpires from the boys' testimony, but that will be the subject of a separate report.

FOLLOW-UP
By Dmitri Bayanov
Bigfoot Co-op, June 1989

Sorry to convey sad news. In her last report (Co-op, December 1988), Maya Bykova wrote that "Nadya, Volodya's wife, was still very fearful and did not feel well enough to accompany us to the cabin, so her place was taken by Volodya's grandfather." Nadya and the grandfather are no longer alive. She died last September, and he in the spring of this year. She had kidney trouble and he - well, he was old - but imagine the impact of these deaths on Volodya. He suspects they are connected with Mecheny. Superstition aside, if Nadya and the grandfather sincerely believed that they would be punished for showing Mecheny to Bykova, that could fatally influence their health.

In November and December I addressed, via Bykova, two letters to Volodya, thanking him for all he had done for Maya and our research, and expressing my deep sorrow over Nadya's passing. I also described the situation created by Bykova's stories, which fascinated some and irritated others because she could produce neither any evidence nor a witness to support her claims. I asked Volodya if he would care to support Bykova's story in a letter to me.

I received Volodya's reply letter, dated January 12, 1989, saying, in part,

> Thank you for understanding my grief. I haven't made up my mind yet as to Mecheny's role in the life of my family.
>
> I was right in demanding that Maya Henrikhovna (Bykova's patronymic. - *D.B.*) would not give Mecheny away... Let my pseudonym stand. (In her published articles, Bykova refers to Volodya as Volodya Veikin, the latter word being the nickname of his grandfather. – *D.B.*) I would hate appearing at your seminar or making my family name well-known. Suffice it is for me to watch the general treatment against Maya Henrikhovna just because she was willing to share her knowledge. I told and warned her, but she did not believe me. I have seen what she had. Her description of Mecheny is

correct. I am not venturesome. You can't lure me out of my backwoods. I have your address and hope I can apply to you if I remain all alone....

Respectfully, Volodya.

I wrote back right away, saying that, to my mind, if Mecheny is "an honest comrade," he ought to be grateful to Volodya's family for the deference they have shown to him. I also asked Volodya what animals he thought Mecheny had been hunting in the swamp, but there has been no more word to me from him.

Thus the Mecheny adventure is suddenly and indefinitely suspended. The focus is shifted this summer to the Kola Peninsula. I hope to provide the background material based on last year's data in my next message.

Part IV **EUROPEAN RUSSIA**

One of the oldest known symbolic portrayals of the hominoid from an illustration of the Gilgamesh epic: Babylonian King Gilgamesh fighting a bull with the help of Enkidu, according to the epic, a tamed hairy Wildman depicted here as half man, half beast, by using the attributes of horns, hoofs and a tail. The symbolic character of these appendages is suggested by the fact that none of them are referred to in the epic's text. Imprint of a Babylonian cylinder seal, 3rd millennium B.C.

VOICES AND PICTURES FROM THE PAST

S tep by step we were giving in to the strange idea that snowmen inhabit not only the Himalayas, but also the Caucasus, the Pamirs, and even Siberia. The more forbidding or distant the land, the easier it was to accept it as a habitat of relic hominoids, but when it came to territories west of the Vrals, well.... Remember the learned opinion of Professor Vereshchagin?

> ...While legends about trolls, demons and witches have lost their credibility with modern Europeans, travelers and mountain climbers have probably fallen hook, line and sinker for similar legends and myths current among the peoples of the Himalayas and the Pamirs, giving enthusiasts the fuel they desire.

Desire or not, in the 1980s we were getting plenty of fuel for hominoid sightings direct from European Russia, places not far distant from Moscow and St. Petersburg! In this connection, Professor Vereshchagin is quoted in the press advising the eyewitnesses to go see a psychiatrist.

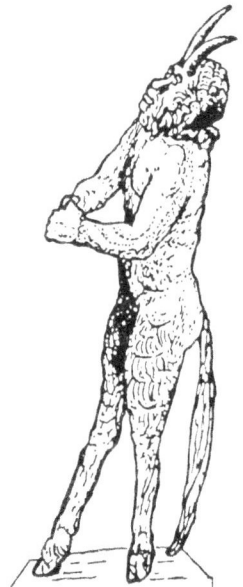

As nimbuses serve to identify divine persons in Christian art, so horns, hoofs and tails indicate heathen gods of hominoid origin in ancient art. Here is an image of the ancient Greek god Pan, patron of herdsmen, hunters, beekeepers and fishermen (circa 100 B.C.). The word 'panic' originates from the great fear experienced by people stumbling on this 'god.' When heathen gods were turned into demons, their distinguishing features were also transferred to the latter.

We are of a different opinion. If today we accept Europe as a land of snowmen as well - Western Europe in the past, Eastern Europe (i.e., Western Russia) at present - that is due in large measure to the fact that, in keeping with Boris Porshnev's ideas, we have given our research not only a special, but also temporal, i.e., historical, dimension. If Bourtsev did a tremendous amount of spade work in Abkhazia searching for Zana's bones, then I did quite a bit of "spade work" in the Lenin Library in Moscow, one of the richest in the world, digging up historical evidence of relic hominoids in different lands, Western Europe included. Those findings were quite revolutionary - first of all in my own mind, changing radically and irrevocably my views on certain aspects of the history of art, folklore, and religion, not to speak of anthropology.

To make our views on snowmen in Russia more acceptable to the reader, we should first give him or her a taste of that historical evidence in Western Europe. Some of it we published in the scientific journal *Current Anthropology* (June 1976), as follows:

SOME ANCIENT AND MEDIEVAL EVIDENCE

A celebrated source of information on hominoids is Titus Lucretius Carus (1st century B.C.), who in Book 5 of his *De Rerum Natura* describes a race of "earthborn" men which

> …was built up on larger and more solid bones within, fastened with strong sinews traversing the flesh; not easily to be harmed by heat or cold or strange food or any taint of the body.... nor as yet did they know how to serve their purposes with fire, nor to use skins and clothe their body in the spoils of wild beasts, but dwelt in woods and the caves of mountains and forests, and amid brushwood would hide their rough limbs, when constrained to shun the shock of winds and the rainshowers… and like bristly boars, these woodland men would lay their limbs naked on the ground, when overtaken by night time, wrapping themselves up around with leaves and foliage.

Modern naturalists and historians of science have praised Lucretius for his foresight (or is it hindsight?) in portraying what one specialist called "for his time, a surprisingly accurate picture of the appearance and life of prehistoric man;" yet, nobody has ever wondered out loud how Lucretius succeeded in fathoming things which science only learned some two millennia later, thanks to Darwin and modern archaeology. That Lucretius did not rely on clairvoyance or on knowledge confided by Martians is evident from his fantastic description of the origin of these very woodland men. Let it also be noted that Lucretius's prehistoric man did not have the power of speech, did not make tools or use fire, and did not wear clothes or build houses.

For the hominologist, there is only one answer to the secret of the ancient philosophers' insight into this matter - they used relic hominoids as models for their portraits of prehistoric man.

From contemporary reality, they were aware of the hairy hominoid, the skin-clad barbarian, and their own civilized selves, and, on the basis of these three points in man's development, they traced

Lifelike presentations of the hominoid on a bowl of Carthaginian or Phoenician origin, dated 7th century B.C., found among the treasures of a Roman villa in Palestrina, Italy. Hominoid in attack. Note the low cranium, prognathism, the nose with deeply sunken bridge, and considerable knee flexure in locomotion. The use of the left arm for stone throwing is also significant for the researcher.

The difference between human and hominoid is well illustrated here.

Hominoid and human depicted on a Greek vase, suggesting that the ancients had ways of making friends with hominoids. Note the lack of hair on the hands and feet of the creature called "Silenopappos" by art specialists, and the more-than-normal human knee-bending in locomotion. The presence of a tail is purely symbolic. Other scenes in Greco-Roman art show hominoids making love, drinking wine, sleeping, carrying loads, stealing fruit from orchards, and pulling thorns from the soles of each other's feet.

Silenus. Note the lack of hair on the hands, knees and feet.

in their imaginations a curve of man's historic rise. It was not much more difficult than looking at the "bristly boars," surmising the origin of domestic pigs, and describing the life of their wild ancestors.

We do not know why Lucretius did not name his models, but we guess that he did not feel like mixing natural history with the names of satyrs, fauns, etc., for such were the popular appellations of hominoids in the Greco-Roman world of his day; yet ancient authors did use these names from time to time, in a rather down-to-earth manner. According to Plutarch, when the Roman general Sulla (old spelling Sylla), having sacked Athens in 86 B.C., was returning with his army to Italy, he came to Dyrrachium (modern Durres in Albania):

> In that neigbourhood stands Apollonia, near which is a remarkable spot of ground called 'Nymphaeum.' The lawns and meadows are of incomparable verdure... In this place, we are told, a satyr was taken asleep, exactly such as statuaries and painters represent to us. He was brought to Sylla, and interrogated in many languages as to who he was; but he uttered nothing intelligible, his accent being harsh and inarticulate, something between the neighing of a horse and the bleating of a goat. Sylla was shocked with his appearance and ordered him to be taken out of his presence.

This gem of ancient evidence is corroborated in certain details by reports of modern sightings; we have two reports, for example - one from Central Asia, the other from the Caucasus - of people stumbling on a sleeping hominoid. Capture or killing of hominoids during sapiens' military activities in various epochs is also quite well represented in our files.

Geographer Pausanias (2nd century A.D.), in his *Descriptions of Greece*, says that the Silenus race must be mortal, since their graves are known. He also says that when satyrs grow old, they are called 'sileni,' and when we read in Pliny the Elder's *Natural History* that "… the Satyrs have nothing of ordinary humanity about them except human shape," we know exactly what he means. As a matter of fact, there are both realistic and 'surrealistic,' or symbolic, representations of the hominoid in ancient art. Those students who, mindful of the satyrs' and others' traditional beastly attributes such as hoofs, horns, and tails, are prone to think of them in purely mythological terms, seem to do no better than those of tender age who take the fairy-tale attributes of a Santa Claus too much to heart, failing to see a biological reality behind his mask. The symbolic signs of the

Another case of peaceful co-existence between human and hominoid: a tamed wildman and his 'showman' counting the returns of their lucrative business. North portal, NotreDame, Semur-en-Auxois, Burgundy, France, 13th century.

This is one of the most valuable presentations of the hominoid in medieval art, for it shows most accurately his difference from man - hairy body, "absence" of the neck, low cranium, big face with high cheekbones, wide nose, large mouth and heavy jaw. The sculptor must have modelled from life.

hominoid in art and folklore initially served the purpose of identifying the creature and distinguishing him from both humans and animals. Besides, symbolism, like euphemism, tends to sprout under the influence of emotion and mystery, and these have always been part and parcel of man's relationship with the hominoid; this is, however, another vast theme, which for lack of space,

No love lost between dog and 'devil'. Another most realistic scene of hominoid life. Drollery from *Queen Mary's Psalter*, English, 14th century. British Museum, London.

This is one proof among many that the inhabitants of Britain, in the Middle Ages, had no need to go to the Himalayas to look for the 'abominable snowman'.

we dare not pursue.

Besides a fair number of mythological images, which have played not a small part in European culture, we owe to the 'classic' hominoids of the Greco-Roman epoch such notions as 'satyriasis' and 'nymphomania,' which reflect certain traits of hominoid theology, and hint at the problems of man's relationship with creatures endowed with such patterns of behaviour, and even one or two anatomical terms which seem to reflect certain peculiarities of hominoid physique (this is not to forget, of course, the term 'fauna' and the erroneous shifting of the names 'Pan' and 'Satyrus' to give zoological terms to apes).

The hominoid's presence in medieval Europe is amply documented in Richard Bemheimer's *Wild Men in the Middle Ages* (1952). Here's just a sample quote from the book:

> About the wild man's habitat and manner of life, medieval authorities are articulate and communicative. It was agreed that he shunned human contact, settling, if possible, in the most remote and inaccessible parts of the forest, and making his bed in crevices, caves, or the deep shadow of overhanging branches. In this remote and lonely sylvan home he eked out a living without benefit of metallurgy or even the simplest agricultural lore, reduced to the plain fare of berries and acorns or the raw flesh of animals. (p. 9)

We should also mention Albertus Magnus (1193-1280), who is characterized in encyclopaedias as a philosopher deeply interested in natural science. In *De Animalibus*, he cites the recent capture in Saxony of two (male and female) forest-dwelling, hairy monsters much resembling human beings in shape. The female died of blood poisoning caused by dog bites, while the male lived on in captivity and even learned the use, albeit very imperfectly, of a few words. The creature's lack of reason, concludes Albertus, is evidenced by, among other things, his ever trying to accost women and exhibit lustfulness.

Eighteenth Century

In 18th century Europe, hominoids became akin to "the last of the Mohicans" in the West of the continent. Here a good source of information in English is *Wolf-Children and Feral Man* (Singh and Zingg, 1942). For example, they report the following case from Spain:

> According to Le Roy, in the Pyrenees, shepherds who herded their flocks in the wood of Ivary saw a wild man in the year 1774 who lived in clefts in the rocks. He appeared to be about thirty years of age, and was very tall, with hair like that of a bear, who could jump and run as quickly as a chamois. He appeared to be bright and happy and, according to all appearances, was not ungentle in character. He never had anything to do with anyone, and had no apparent interest in so doing. He often came near to the huts of the shepherds without making any attempt to take anything. Milk, bread, and cheese appeared to be unknown things to him, for he would not even take them when they were placed in his way. His greatest pleasure was to frighten the sheep, and break up the herds. When the shepherds put dogs on him, as they often

A wildman family at leisure. Drawing by Hans Dürer (1478-1538)

Fight in the Forest by Hans Burgkmair (1473-1531). Judging by this picture,
a burly European wildman could be a match for American bigfoot.

did, he would disappear as quickly as an arrow shot from a bow, and he allowed no one to come near him. One morning he approached one of the huts, and as one of the people who lived there approached him to catch him by the foot, he laughed and fled... No one knows what became of him.

Turning to Eastern Europe, we learn that in 1767 the inhabitants of Fraumark in lower Hungary, pursuing a bear in the mountains, "came to a cave in the rocks in which a completely naked wild girl was found. She was tall, robust, and seemed to be about eighteen years old. Her skin was brown and she looked frightened. Her behaviour was very crude. They had to use violence to make her leave the cave, but she did not cry out and did not shed any tears. Finally they succeeded in bringing her to Karpfen, a small town of the county of Atlsohl, where she was locked in an Asylum. She would only eat raw meat...

A very detailed description of a hominoid's appearance and his behaviour in captivity (which contrasts dramatically with the creature's state in the wild) is given as follows (italics added. *D.B.*):

Here you have information about the wild boy who was found a few years ago in the Siebenburgen-Wallachischen border (Romania) and was brought to Kronstadt (now Brasov), where in 1784 he is still alive. How the poor boy was saved from the forests... I cannot tell. However, one must preserve the facts, as they are, in the sad gallery of pictures of this kind.

This unfortunate youth was of the male sex and was of medium size. He had an extremely wild glance. *His eyes lay deep in his head*, and rolled around in a wild fashion. *His forehead was strongly bent inwards*, and his hair of ash-gray colour grew out short and rough. He had heavy brown eyebrows, *which projected out far over his eyes*, and a small *flat-pressed nose*. His neck appeared puffy, and at the windpipe he appeared goitrous. *His mouth stood somewhat out* when he held it half open as he generally did since he breathed through his mouth. His tongue was almost motionless, and his cheeks appeared more hollow than full, and, like his face, were covered with a dirty yellowish skin. On the first glance at this face, from which a wildness and a sort of animal-being shone forth, one felt that it belonged to no rational creature... *The other parts of the wild boy's body, especially the back and the chest, were very hairy; the muscles on his arms and legs were stronger and more visible than on ordinary people.* The hands were marked with callouses (which supposedly were caused by different uses), and the skin of the hands was dirty yellow and thick throughout, as his face was. On the fingers he had very long nails; and, on the elbows and knees, he had knobby hardenings. The toes were longer than ordinary. He walked erect, but a little heavily. It seemed as if he would throw himself from one foot to the other. *He carried his head and chest forward...* He walked bare-footed and did not like shoes on his feet. He was completely lacking in speech, even in the slightest articulation of sounds. The sounds which he uttered were ununderstandable murmuring, which he would give when his guard drove him ahead of him. This murmuring was increased to a howling when he saw woods or even a tree. He seemed to express the wish for his accustomed abode; for once when he was in my room from which a mountain could be seen, the sight of the trees caused him to howl wretchedly. When I saw him the first time, he had no sense of possession. Probably it was his complete unfamiliarity with his new condition, and the longing for his earlier life in the wilds, which he displayed when he saw a garden or a wood. Similarly I explain why, at the beginning, he showed not the slightest emotion at the sight of women. When I saw him again after three years, this apathy and disrespect had disappeared. As soon as he saw a woman, he broke out into violent cries of joy, and tried to express his awakened desires also through gestures... Yet he showed anger and unwillingness when he was hungry and thirsty; and in that case would have very much liked to attack man, though on other occasions he would do no harm to men or animals. Aside from the original human body which usually caused a pitiful impression in this state of wildness, and aside from walking erect, one missed in him all the characteristic traits through which human beings are distinguished from the animals; it was rather a much more pitiful sight to see how this helpless creature would waddle around in front of his keeper growling and glaring wildly, and longing for the presence of animals of prey, insensible to everything which appeared before him. In order to control this wild urge, as soon as he came near to the gates of the city, and approached the gardens and woods, they used to tie him up in the beginning. He had to be accompanied by several persons, because he would have forced himself free and would have run away to his former dwelling. In the beginning his food consisted only of all kinds of tree leaves, grass, roots, and raw meat. Only very slowly did he accustom himself to cooked food; and, according to the saying of the person who took care of him, a whole year passed before he learned to eat cooked food, when very obviously his animal wildness had diminished.

I am unable to say how old he was. Outwardly he could have been from twenty-three to twenty-five years old.

Probably he will never learn how to speak. When I saw him again after three years, I still found him speechless, though changed very obviously in many other respects. His face still expressed something animal-like but had become softer... The desire for food, of which he now liked all kinds (particularly legumes), he would show by intelligible sounds. He showed his visible contentment when one brought him something to eat, and sometimes he would use a spoon. He had become used to wearing shoes and other clothes; but he was careless about how much they were torn. Slowly he was able to find a way to his house without a leader; the only work for which he could be used consisted of giving him a water jug which he would fill at the well and bring it to the house. This was the only service which he could perform for his guardian. He also knew how to provide himself with food by diligently visiting the houses where people had given him food. The instinct of imitation was shown on many occasions; but nothing made a permanent impression on him. Even if he imitated a thing several times, he soon forgot it again, except the custom which had to do with his natural needs, such as eating, drinking, sleeping, etc., and everything which had connection with these. He found his home in the evening, and at noon, the house where he expected food, led only by his habits. He never learned to know the value of money. He did accept it but only with the intention of playing with it, and did not care when he lost it again. Chiefly he was in every respect like a child whose capacities had begun to develop, only with this difference that he was unable to show any progress in that regard. He showed his likeness with a child in the fact that he would gape at everything which one showed to him; but, with the same lack of concentration, he would change his glance from the old objects to new ones. If one showed him a mirror, he would look behind it for the image before him. But he was completely indifferent when he did not find it, and would allow the mirror to get out of his range of vision. The tunes from musical instruments seemed to interest him a little, but it was a very slight interest which did not leave any impression. When I led him in front of the piano in my room, he listened to the tunes with an apparent pleasure, but did not dare to touch the keys. He showed great fear when I tried to force him to do so. Since 1784, the year he left Kronstadl, I never had a chance to receive any more reports about him *(Wolf-Children and Feral Man, pp.237-240).*

If only all observers of unusual phenomena recorded them as thoroughly as the author of this report!

Unlike scholars of ancient and medieval times, who knew full well that wildmen, even if called "satyrs" or "fauns," were an integral part of Nature, educated Europeans of the enlightened 18th century usually took them for "feral men," i.e., humans who had gone wild as a result of some misfortune. The words in the last report, "How the poor boy was saved from the forests... I cannot tell," indicate that the author was of the same opinion. Such a misidentification of relic hominoids has also contributed a great deal to their remaining beyond the grasp of science for so long.

It is clear to us now why the "boy of Kronstadt" must be classified as a "natural wildman," and not a human gone wild. That is testified to by his hirsute and muscular body, his facial features, his walk, and many other characteristics. And how similar was his taming and behaviour to those of Zana, the wild woman in Abkhazia. I am especially touched by the words in the report, "When I led him in front of the piano in my room, he listened to the tunes with an apparent pleasure…." A 'snowman' listening with pleasure to piano music two centuries ago in a room in Europe! Shall we ever be able to replicate this marvellous experiment?

Classic novelist Ivan Turgenev (1818-1883)
whose testimony is one of the best in the
snowman saga.

FROM THE STORY FEAR
By Guy de Maupassant

W e are truly afraid", he repeated, "only of what we do not understand."

A sudden memory woke in my mind, the memory of a story told us one Sunday by Turgenev, in Gustave Flaubert's house. I don't know whether he had written it in any of his books.

The great Russian novelist was supremely able to thrill us with this shudder of the veiled, unknown world, to reveal, in the half-light of a strange tale, a world full of uncertain, disturbing, threatening things.

That day he also said to us, "We are truly afraid only of what we do not understand."

Arms hanging down, legs stretched out and relaxed, hair quite white, he was sitting, or rather lounging, in a large arm chair, drowned in that flowing tide of beard and silvery hair that gave him the air of an Eternal Father or a river-god from Ovid.

He spoke slowly, with a certain indolence which lent a charm to his phrases, and a rather hesitating and awkward manner of speaking which emphasised the vivid rightness of his words. His wide, pale eyes, like the eyes of a child, reflected all the changing fancies of his mind. This is what he told us:

> He was hunting, as a young man, in a Russian forest. He had tramped all day, and towards the end of the afternoon he reached the edge of a quiet river. It ran under the trees, and among the trees, filled with floating grasses, cold and clear. An overmastering desire seized the hunter to fling himself into this transparent water. He stripped and dived into the stream. He was very tall and very strong, active, and a splendid swimmer. He let himself float gently in great content of mind; grasses and roots brushed past him and tendrils of creeping plants trailed lightly over his skin, thrilling him.

> Suddenly a hand touched his shoulder. He turned round in startled wonder and saw a frightful creature staring hungrily at him. It was like a woman or a monkey. A vast, wrinkled, grimacing face smiled at him. Two nameless things, which must have been two breasts, floated in front of it, and its mass of tangled hair, burnt by the sun, hung round its face and fell down its back.
> Turgenev felt a piercing and appalling fear, the icy fear of the supernatural. Without pausing to reflect, without thinking or understanding, he began to swim frantically towards the bank. But the monster swam quicker still, and touched his neck, his back and his legs with little cacklings of delight. Mad with terror, the young man reached the bank at last, and tore at full speed through the wood, with never a thought of recovering his clothes and his gun.

The frightful creature followed him, running as quickly as he did and growling all the time. Spent and sick with fear, the fugitive was ready to drop to the ground, when a boy who was watching his goats ran up, armed with a whip; he laid it about the fearsome human beast, who ran away howling with pain. And Turgenev saw her disappear among the leaves of the trees, like a female gorilla.

It was a madwoman, who had lived in this wood for thirty years, on the charity of the shepherds, and spent half her days swimming in the river.

The great Russian writer added: "I have never felt such fear in my life, because I could not imagine what this monster could be." I related this adventure to my companion, and he replied: "Yes, we are afraid only of what we do not understand." [25]

COMMENT ON TURGENEV'S TESTIMONY

In some respects, this is the best story in the whole snowman saga, but first let's take our bearings. We are already on Russian soil proper, right in the heart of the country's European part. The great Russian novelist Ivan Turgenev (1818-1883) was born at Orel, a town south of Moscow, and used to hunt in the dense forests along the Desna River (a tributary of the Dnieper). As the encounter took place when he was "a young man," we conclude that it happened sometime in the 1830's or 1840's.

Turgenev's testimony, as rendered by Guy de Maupassant (for Turgenev never published it), is crucial for at least two reasons - first, the witness being such a respectable figure, nobody holds his words in question; and second, his words provide ample proof that the "frightful creature" he encountered, far from being a madwoman, was not a human at all - it's another famous case of mistaken identity. In my book, published in 1991, I devoted a whole chapter to arguing this point.

The heart of the argument is this - the most salient trait of the "madwoman" is her semi-aquatic nature; now, that is out of the question for any madwoman, a Russian madwoman in particular. Russian peasants called up to the army in tsarist times had to learn to swim, while nobody ever taught Russian peasant women to swim.

On the other hand, from many sources, we know that wildmen and wildwomen are excellent swimmers, and are attracted by rivers, lakes, and sea beaches. We have already mentioned the aquatic proclivity and capacity of hominoids in Asia and as for Europe, Richard Bernheimer writes in his book of "the wild men and women who inhabit not the woods, but the water." That is an exaggeration, of course, explained by the fact that Bernheimer based his information on literary and folkloric rather than biological sources. Still, his word is worth listening to:

The creature in question is an ogre who dispatches people by pulling them

---

25 Guy de Maupassant. *The Complete Short Stories.* Cassell, London, 1970, Vol. 3, pp. 192-195.

under the surface of the water. Significantly, the pond is located in the midst of a wild wood, and the wild man is caught and imprisoned in a manner that reminds one of the capture of his sylvan brother. But aquatic wild men are not always limited to a habitat in stagnant ponds, and one, described as tailless and hairy but bald, is supposed to have been caught in 1161 in the sea near Orford on the English coast, and to have been dumped back again, when it turned out that nobody could make him talk.... The writers of medieval epics, when they consign their creatures to an aquatic life, make sure that their kinship to creatures on land is well understood.

As for the New World, John Green devotes a whole chapter to *Apes Under Water*, which begins as follows:

Would an animal built like an upright gorilla be at home in the water? Obviously not. If you were making up a semi-aquatic monster, an ape should be the last thing you would think of. They can't even swim. And if you were dreaming up a way of life for a monster ape, about the last place you would put it would be in the water. Why, then, does water figure so prominently in so many sasquatch stories?

The chapter does not give an answer, but the book does. Relic hominoids of both the Old and New World, especially their northern regions, are attracted by the natural bodies of water because the latter provide more stable and reliable sources of vegetable and animal food than the land does. Water plants, fish, crawfish, clams - all these are available in rivers, lakes and seas the year round. Sighting reports give us enough evidence of hominoids actually getting and eating those foods from the water. For example, Green writes of a 10-year-old boy who phoned him from West Linn, Oregon, recently:

...to say that he and his aunt and uncle had seen a big hairy animal standing upright in the Detroit Reservoir in Oregon, and had watched it reach down and catch a fish, which it ate after biting off the head. When it noticed them it ran off and left 16-inch footprints in the mud. A logger in northern Oregon saw one standing in a small lake. There are dozens of such stories.

He also writes of a witness who saw two female sasquatches in November, with snow on the ground, standing in a creek, pulling up water plants and eating them.

Two of the reports involve the sasquatch either disappearing under water or appearing from it, and the Indians I spoke to said that the creatures could not only swim a long way under water, but could do so at tremendous speed. Perhaps the most startling account of aquatic activity was contained in a publication called *The Yeti Newsletter*, that was put out for some time by Gordon Prescott and Frank Hudson at St. Petersburg, Florida. It stated that a shrimp boat crew from Placida told of seeing such a creature swimming in the Gulf of Mexico 20 miles from shore, and said a captain had seen one swimming under water.

'Beast' turned beauty - an embellished image of rusalka, an ancient Russian name for hominoid females. The embellishment of female hominoids in the popular mind, on account of their amorous behaviour towards human males, is also evident in Greco-Roman nymphs and Persian peris. Drawing by Ivan Bilibin (1876-1942).

The last account seems to lend credibility to the report of a wildman caught in 1161 in the sea near Orford on the English coast. Green is right; in their aquatic prowess, wildmen are totally different from the great apes, but not from monkeys in general, some species of which are good swimmers and divers, nor from humans, some of whom are capable of swimming over from England to France. Considering the evolutionary links between apes, wildmen and humans, there is nothing unusual that some characteristics are shared by all three (e.g., tree-climbing), others only by wildmen and humans (e.g., erect locomotion and swimming), and still others only by wildmen and apes (hairy bodies, lack of speech, etc.).

But, to return to Russia, semi-aquatic hominoid creatures are part and parcel of Russian folklore and demonology. The common name for the female creatures of this kind is *rusalka*. There are two trends of describing rusalka in Russian and Slavic folklore; one trend is realistic and portrays rusalka as an ugly apelike woman with enormous breasts - a copy of the creature encountered by Turgenev. The image of rusalka in poetic tales is more like that of Western mermaids and water-nymphs, bent on beguiling human males. The latter kind of rusalka is a common character in the writings of Russian national authors, such as Pushkin, Gogol, and Turgenev himself.

On the one hand, rusalka is supremely adapted to the water, being encountered in rivers, ponds and lakes, on the other, to the wonder of schoolchildren studying Russian classics and learning Pushkin's verses about rusalka by heart, she likes to climb trees and swing on the branches (now we understand why). According to Pushkin, who draws his knowledge from folklore, rusalkas can also laugh and whistle.

But the most characteristic trait of rusalkas, known from folklore and poetry to all Russians, is their habit of accosting a young man bathing in a lake or a river, and, with much delight and merriment, "tickling him to death" (i.e., until he drowns). And that is exactly what the "madwoman" in the case of Turgenev was prepared to do - "...touched his neck, his back and his legs with little cacklings of delight." Had Turgenev not been "a splendid swimmer," Russian and world literature would have suffered a heavy loss from the hands of a rusalka.

The business of tickling, as part of lovemaking, is ascribed not only to Russian rusalkas, but also to their counterparts in the folklore of Tartars, Bashkirs, Kazakhs, etc., and what is most interesting and important is that it is also typical of anthropoid apes, as observed by the famous English primatologist Jane Goodall. Here's how she describes a tickling bout in chimpanzees:

> Presently Mike reached out toward Flo's hand and began almost imperceptibly to play with her fingers. Soon she responded, gently grasping his hand, twisting and pulling away only to reach out and grasp it again. After a few minutes Mike sat up and leaned over Flo, tickling her neck and her ticklish groin until, protecting Flint with one hand and parrying Mike with the other, Flo started to shake with panting gasps of chimpanzee laughter.
>
> After a while she could stand it no longer and rolled away from him. But she was roused, this ancient female with her stumps of teeth, and soon she was tickling Mike in the ribs with her bony fingers. Then it was Mike's turn

to laugh and reach to grab her hands and tickle her again himself. [26]

Returning to rusalkas, the danger of drowning from their caresses was once so real for Russian countrymen that people invented a very simple but potent means of defence - just a pin or a needle held at ready while bathing. Folklore has it that it is enough to give rusalka a pin-prick or show her a needle to make her flee. The whip is also mentioned by folklore as a means of defence against rusalkas, and it was probably well known to the peasant boy who saved Turgenev from the "madwoman."

Now let's look anew at Turgenev's description of that woman - "like a woman or a monkey," "a frightful creature," "the fearful human beast," "like a female gorilla," "the monster." She uttered not a word during the whole encounter, making only such sounds as "little cacklings of delight," "growling all the time," "howling with pain." I leave it to the reader now to decide whether it was a madwoman, or an authentic and natural wildwoman.

Why, after all, that notion of a madwoman in Turgenev's narration? My theory is this - there is a Slavic incantation against the rusalka which begins with the words, "Water-girl, forestgirl, 'shalnaya' girl!" "Shalnaya" is the Russian for "crazy, mad, foolish, wild, unruly, whimsical, odd." I suppose that when Turgenev made inquiries about the creature which nearly drowned him, it was described to him by his peasant interlocutor with the word 'shalnaya' or a synonym, which Turgenev rendered in French as 'folle,' which means, in English, "mad, insane, senseless, foolish, wild, frolicsome, excessive." Of course, it makes a world of difference which meaning of the word we, or translators, apply to the creature in this case.

One more point should be made here. I suppose that Turgenev's informants did not avow to him that it was indeed a rusalka for one of the following reasons, or a combination of them - the Orthodox Church is known to have viewed any contact with such 'pagan creatures' as a great sin; in fact, in the incantation that I mentioned a young peasant asks a rusalka to go away and leave him alone because he is a Christian. He advises her to seek the company of the 'forest lord,' who has prepared for her 'a bed of moss and grass.'

Another reason is that educated and free-thinking Russians among the higher classes, like Turgenev, tended to mock and dismiss popular superstitions, in which they included peasant beliefs in wood and water creatures. The great irony of it all is that Turgenev himself, by one of his well-known stories *Bezhin lug*, has instilled in generations of Russian people the conviction that the rusalka is nothing but a mythological figure. So great was the difference in his mind between the romantic image of rusalka in folk tales and its simian prototype that accosted him, that he never made connection between the two.

I have paid so much attention to this case because I think it is of a special significance in the 'court of history.' It is not simply a story or an episode of a writer's biography. It is simultaneously a document of paramount importance in the science of anthropology, throwing light in several

---

26 *In the Shadow of Man*, Boston, 1972, p.127

directions and on several aspects of that science. The Zana case tells us of interbreeding between humans and a wildwoman held in captivity. The Turgenev case suggests the possibility of such interbreeding with free-ranging wildmen. It gives veracity to the age-old reputation of 'water-nymphs' and helps us understand the origin of the ancient term of 'nymphomania.' It vindicates the reports of medieval Arab travellers who populated 'the northern regions,' the lands of the Slavs and their neighbours, with 'monkeys' that greatly resemble man.

Lastly, having accepted the existence of relic hominoids in Russia in the 19th century (the Turgenev case gives us no other choice), we find our minds open enough to the possibility of their survival into the 20th century. The following materials are to show that this really is the case.

LETTER FROM MOSCOW
By Dmitri Bayanov
Bigfoot Co-op, August 1991

Last year Maya Bykova, who wrote a remarkable contribution for the *Bigfoot Co-op* (April 1988, December 1988), had her first book published, titled *A legend for Grown-ups Thoughts on Secretive Animals*. The book is about various subjects of cryptozoology ('cryptids' in my terminology), which Maya happened to learn about from reading, as well as her own field expeditions. Most attention is devoted to relic hominoids (wild men), but whatever cryptids the author deals with, she strongly pleads for a humane, non-violent way of tackling the problem. The chapters on relic hominoids include the materials already published by Bykova in newspapers and magazines, one chapter being devoted to letters received from the readers of those accounts. The following is my translation of a letter published in Bykova's book, the author of which is a woman identified as A. M. Mitina, of the city of Kaluga. She refers to a time in her childhood.

> My grandfather was one of the first to join a collective farm in the early 1930s and worked at an apiary. At the time the Ryazan Region *(southeast of Moscow - D.B.)* still had large tracks of forest broken by swamps and ravines. One day grandfather came home from the apiary in low spirits and grandma asked him what had happened. When he answered her in a low voice she threw up her hands uttering, "Oh! Oh!". I wanted to know what they were talking about, but only overheard the word 'he,' used in a strange way, as if applied to a snake or something.

> In the morning, grandma prepared some food which grandfather carried for his lunch and then accompanied him to the outskirts of the village. I noticed that her anxiety did not subside and pleaded that she tell me what was the matter, but she refused. At the weekend, there was a similar scene and then grandma said she must visit the apiary. With much difficulty, I talked her into taking me along.

> The sun was setting beyond the horizon when we saw the familiar site: the beehives, the cabin, a bonfire.... As the soup was cooking over the bonfire,

grandfather put some potatoes to bake amongst the fire's embers, and we went into the cabin. It was getting dark, but they didn't light the lamp. I heard grandfather say to grandma, "Just watch him come over." They put their faces to a little window and told me to play on the floor with our dog. Some moments later, the dog sprang to his feet, his coat bristling as he began to howl plaintively. I became very frightened. Presently grandfather whispered, "Look there, under the hazel to the right." I could no longer stay behind, and joined them at the little window, looking in the direction pointed out by grandfather. Although it was dark, from the even greater darkness in the cabin I could discern outside a tall man with wide shoulders stepping out slowly and heavily. We held our breath. I started crying. Grandfather stroked my head and said, "There, there, he won't come here." My teeth now chattering with fear, I continued to watch. He made straight for the bonfire, dropped on all fours and started scattering the embers of the fire. When they flared up, the whole figure of the stranger became lit up. I well remember his hands and face covered with hair, as was the whole of his body. He snatched the potatoes from the embers and threw them to one side. Then he grabbed several, tossed them into the other hand, pressed them against his belly and marched off in the direction he'd come from.

When we had calmed down, grandfather explained that it was the lord of the forest. As food was scarce in the forest, he would come to the apiary in the evening and stand in the hazel-grove until grandfather had eaten. When grandfather left the bonfire, he would come over and take away the baked potatoes which grandfather had left in the embers. Once, on a visit to the apiary, I fell asleep in grandma's lap and, upon waking up, overheard grandfather tell grandma the following: "The horse got lost the other day. He was wearing a little bell, but I still couldn't find him for quite some time. I first thought that he'd fallen into the ravine, so I climbed down there, clutching at the shrubs as I descended. I heard someone moaning and thought the horse must have broken a leg. Heading in the general direction from where the sounds appeared to be coming, I moved through the bushes. God almighty, what a sight! Under a roof of tree roots, a lair of sorts, with a mattress of grass, and lying on it is the "mistress," her belly enormous and in birth throes. He was squatting at her side, the elbows on the knees, the head on the hands, and mooing. That's why they didn't hear me. Surprisingly, they're just like people; even birth pangs the same."

That same year I had an encounter with the lord of the forest under quite unusual circumstances. Our whole family went to the forest to gather bast. While the adults collected the lime branches, my brother and I stayed with the horse in a clearing. I noticed a gadfly on the horse's hind leg and took a stick to drive the gadfly away, but the moment I touched the horse's leg with the stick, the animal involuntarily kicked and hit me. I fell to the ground. I remember hearing my brother yell loudly in panic, calling for mother and granny. At that moment I can recall the sensation of being lifted up and carried quickly away. Next I felt cool water running over my head. I opened my eyes. Bending over me was a horrible human face. It was covered with hair, like the rest of the body. I screamed. Back came granny's desperate cry. The next thing I remember is granny taking me in her arms and shouting at mother for her lack of adroitness.

Later grandma told me they'd found me, not on the clearing, but on the edge of a pond called Wolf's Hole. The creature had fetched handfuls of water and poured it onto my head, looking around all the time. When mother spotted him, she yelled and he immediately ran off into the bushes.

Grandfather did not see him again during the whole of that autumn, the only sighting after that being at dusk one day during the next spring, when he walked past without looking back, just uttering mumbling sounds.

Let me comment that the above testimony is remarkable for its graphic description of the wildman's humanlike; nay, simply humane behaviour, which makes me even doubt whether the term 'superanimals' does sufficient justice to their intelligence. It is also a reminder that the way to the wildman's heart lies through his stomach, especially when food is 'scarce in the forest.'

Also I take this opportunity to inform Co-op readers that the French popular science journal *Archeologia* (June 1991) carries Marie-Jeanne Koffmann's extensive materials on the wildmen of the Caucasus, entitled *L 'Almasty - Yeti du Caucase.*

I warmly support Mike Pincher's idea of an International Sasquatch Society, and hope *Bigfoot Co-op* readers across the world share my feeling on this. The International Society of Cryptozoology and the proposed Sasquatch Society may well complement one another. The scientific, cultural, and undoubted human-interest potential of the theme of relic hominoids is enormous; it is necessary to find the right way of tapping it.

#|

THE URALS

W e had received reports from this area back in Porshnev's days and later. In July 1978, I received a letter from a young soldier in the army named Alexander Katayev. He had read our article in a youth magazine, and wanted to share his experiences. An exchange of letters ensued, from which transpired the following. In August 1974, fourteen-year-old Katayev, who lived in a village on the Chusovaya River in the Urals, was walking at night along the riverbank when he overheard splashes in the water and voices; one low, as of a male, the other a high-pitched, 'metallic' (as, Katayev put it) laughter, apparently of a female. Curious, he moved through the brush to the edge of the water to see who it was, and saw (the moonlight was bright) two humanlike figures standing in the water. Presently they came out of the water onto the bank and sat down on the ground some five metres from the boy. "That allowed me to see them very well," Katayev writes. Yes, one was male, the other female, both covered all over with grey hair. The male was over two metres tall, the female shorter. He had very long and hefty arms, she had very big breasts,

Eyewitness Alexander Katayev (left) with researcher Mikhail Trachtenherz, 1980.

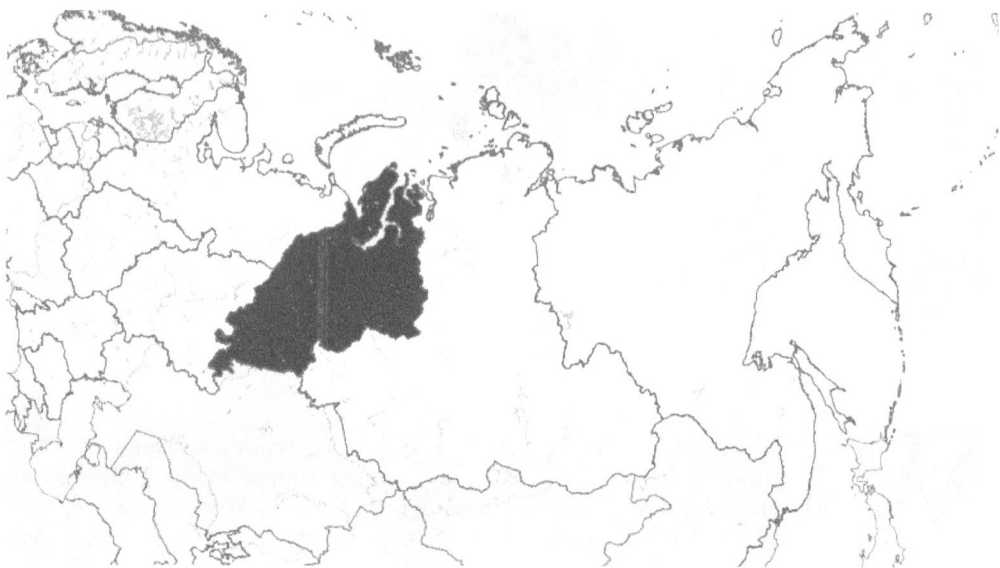

and an outstanding belly indicating pregnancy. They sat for some time, then the male got up, stepped aside, and picked up from a bush a receptacle which Katayev calls "a box made of birchbark." To quote from his letter:

> He said something to her, she answered and they began to eat from the box." They ate for a long time, but I could not make out what it was. Then they threw the box away into the water. They talked again and she laughed. He got up and helped her to get up. They moved to one side. I stopped breathing - I thought they detected me, but no. He stopped and I heard a splashing; he was urinating. She did the same. They talked some more and then walked into the river again. They swam across the river, swimming quickly, he helping her all the time. When they got onto the other bank they shook the water off themselves and climbed a very steep rockface, a face which is very difficult for man to climb, but they made it to the top very quickly. A stone fell back into the water and there was no trace of them anymore. I remained where I was for probably a further 10 minutes. I was shaking. To prevent my teeth from chattering, I had to bite on my cap. My hair felt like it was standing on end. When my legs eventually managed to move, I got up and ran for my life the three kilometres back to the village. It seemed to me like they were following me all the way back. I could not sleep that night.

When Alexander told the story to his friends they did not believe him:

> I stopped telling it anymore. But now, reading your article, I recalled it all anew. I remember them so clearly, as if they were standing in front of me right now. A lot more could be written about them. They did all sorts of other things besides those I described, including attempting to make fire

by pounding stones together, but it didn't work.

The geographical data in Katayev's story checked out clearly and precisely. The high and steep rockface on the bank of the river that the creatures climbed (Katayev gave me its name) is a famous wall of rock called Giant Stone - over a kilometre long and 125 metres high, which is mentioned in all the guidebooks on the Chusovaya River. The following are some of my follow-up questions and Katayev's answers:

Q. Can you tell me about the stone-pounding bout?

A. The male searched out the stones on the bank and was striking them for a short time before the creatures began to eat. I did not see what size the stones were. It seems to me they were white. There were many sparks flying from them. He held the stones in both hands. Then he threw them away on the bank.

Q. What were their other doings? Did they kiss or embrace?

A. They waved the hands, lifted the legs; their habits resembled those of apes. No, they did not make love.

Q. How did they sit on the ground?

A. They sat on the buttocks, with legs extended, about a metre from one another.

Q. What did the birchbark box look like?

A. Like a rolled-up piece of birchbark. It was well visible because of its whiteness.

Q. What about their 'talking' and vocalization?

A. The sounds they made were very strange, resembling those of humans but dumb humans: "Kh-Kh-Kh, M-M-M, No-No." The female made both high and low sounds, and he too, but she also laughed like a girl, only with a metallic sound. They talked in turn. After saying something, one would be silent for maybe a minute, then would speak again, waving the hands. The sound phrases were short.

Q. How did they swim? Were their arms visible when they swam?

A. They swam like animals, with only the heads above the water. They swam without a sound.
Q. How did he help her while swimming? Did he pull her?

A. When they started to swim. he dashed ahead very fast and she lagged behind. He then returned and they swam on together. No, he did not pull her.

Q. How wide is the river there?

A. About 40-50 metres.

Q. How did they shake off the water when they got onto the other bank?

A. They did it with their hands; he helped her and she helped him.

Q. Why do you think they climbed the rock wall in that difficult place?

A. Because to bypass it by walking along the bank takes a long time and is difficult.

Katayev did not smell the creatures, nor did he see their eyes glow. He was armed with a shotgun. Why didn't the hominoids detect an eavesdropping human at such close range? Presumably because they were much preoccupied with one another and with having a good time, as is clear from her laughter.

What I like, among other things, about Katayev's story is the way he sticks to his own scenario no matter what the 'specialists' say. The 'specialists' say hominoids cannot talk, while Katayev, after Albert Ostman [27], of whom he never heard, asserts the contrary. It's a different matter, of course, whether the creatures have a human or 'monkey' language, a kind of exchange in emotions, not ideas. Why didn't he see their eyes glow (about which he read in our article)? Can it be because they never looked in his direction?

LETTER FROM DMITRI BAYANOV
Bigfoot Co-op, May 1987

Y ou must have noticed that the bulk of information about relic hominoids in Russia comes from the southern mountainous regions of the country. One notable exception is the contribution by Vladimir Pushkarev, who made expeditions to the northern and eastern areas.

During the 1980s, another field researcher came to the fore through his explorations in some of the areas formerly visited by Pushkarev - he is Nikolai Avdeyev of the city of Chelyabinsk in the Urals. His following report was compiled from two long letters he sent me in recent months. It shows the kind of dangers and problems confronting the hominologist, in what seems rather promising country. You will probably have many questions, as I do, after reading Avdeyev's report. I hope to have them answered when Avdeyev comes to Moscow to speak at our seminar and is interviewed in person.

---

27 A Canadian who claims to have been kidnapped, and held prisoner for a time by a sasquatch.

REPORT BY NIKOLAI AVDEYEV

First a few words to introduce myself. I am a biologist, a graduate of the Urals State University. In 1961 I received, as a gift, the book *On the Trail of Unknown Animals* by Bernard Heuvelmans, in an adapted Russian edition. The book made a very strong impression on a twelve-year-old boy, and eventually led me into the field of cryptozoology. I began by investigating the problem of a possible recent survival of the mammoth, a goal I am still pursuing.

In 1975, on a visit to Moscow, I met and had a long talk with the late general M. S. Topilsky, who claimed to have seen a slain wildman in Soviet Central Asia in 1925. Topilsky struck me as a very earnest and straightforward person. He asked us young researchers to do all we could to resolve the problem and restore his reputation as a sober-minded person, not a fanciful dreamer, as some people claimed. As a result of that meeting, I became what we call a 'hominologist,' and have since been engaged in fieldwork in the Urals and the Komi Autonomous Republic, lying west of the North Urals.

In August 1986, I led a group of associates in an expedition to the Timansky Ridge in the Komi Republic. The area is still wilderness with a fauna of reindeer, elk, bear, lynx and a host of smaller animals. The local Komi name for the wildman is *yagmort* (*yag* - 'pine forest,' *mort* – 'man'), a creature well known to the Komi people, but not readily discussed with outsiders. Despite this, we managed to collect three eyewitness accounts. One event took place in December 1985, when two men went to the taiga to cut down a New Year fir tree. Having encountered a yagmort, they took fright and hurried home, while the 'woodsman' was trailing them from a distance for quite a while, following a parallel course through the taiga.

Another local witness, Valentin Lytkin, told us that in early August 1986, while haymaking, he was frightened by a yagmort who opened the door of a hut in which the witness was spending the night with his fellow mowers. Shortly before the appearance of the 'woodsman,' the dogs were barking furiously, then stopped and disappeared. The creature opened the door, stood for a moment in the doorway, then turned and went away. It was covered all over with light grey hair and its eyes were glowing. The dogs reappeared only the next day.

A third witness, a hunter of 31, some three years earlier had encountered a "forest old woman who was hairy all over and with breasts hanging almost to her knees." He said he had seen her when returning to his home from a neighbouring village. Mustering all his courage, he tried to follow her, but she quickly left him behind.

The last witness was the most cooperative of all, and promised to inform me if he got any fresh information on the subject. In September, back in Chelyabinsk, after the expedition, I received a letter from him saying that while hunting that month in the upper reaches of the Belaya Kedva, he sighted what appeared to be a family of yagmort: father, mother and child. Their hair was greyish, the male was over two metres tall, the female smaller, with long hanging breasts. Their arms appeared longer than in humans and their gait differed from human. The hunter sighted them across the river, near a cave in the bank which they soon entered, disappearing from view.

Having read the letter, I decided to fly back to the area and, with the help of the hunter, locate and inspect that cave. I had much difficulty raising the money for this unexpected trip and getting extra leave from my place of work. However, within a few days I had managed to reach the settlement of Kedva and make contact with my hunter-guide. Next morning we set out by motorboat up the Kedva and then its tributary, the Belaya Kedva, covering about 80 kilometres in the day. Next day we hid the boat and trekked some 20 kilometres through the taiga. At day's end, as we set up camp for the night, my guide said we had to walk another four kilometres to reach the cave. As it was not yet dark, I went round the camp, looking for tracks. I did find a set of human-like footprints on sandy soil alongside a nearby brook. One track was especially clear, and so I photographed and made a plaster cast of it. It was 32 centimetres long and 14 centimetres wide in the ball area. The toes seemed to have scraped the ground before taking a firm hold. The tracks looked quite fresh. That was on October 1, 1986.

Next morning, as we prepared breakfast before the last leg of our trek, we were in buoyant mood. Suddenly a gunshot rang out, and we realized that the bullet had hit the pot over the fire in which our breakfast was cooking. The shot took us so much by surprise that I started to pick up the pierced pot to place it back over the fire, when a second bullet struck near the tent. We realized we were being attacked. The guide snatched his hunting gun and took a defensive stand. Then we heard a man shouting to us from a thicket on the hillside across the brook, "Don't you go any further! You have no business in that cave. Turn round and go home right away!"

I made an attempt to negotiate with the unseen gunman, but the only response was another bullet, which hit a tree-trunk close by. As I had no wish to tempt fate any more, the guide shouted to the attacker, "Stop shooting. We won't go there. We're going home."

So we did, with the greatest regret and disappointment of my life. On the way back to Kedva, I asked my guide what all that meant. He replied that his Komi people, especially old men, believe that any meddling with yagmorts would bring misfortune to the Komi people - "Yagmorts are not meddling with us, and we must not meddle with them." Apparently, the young hunter had hoped to avoid the protective vigilance of the old men, but was not successful in his efforts. That poses a serious problem for fieldwork in the Komi Republic.

In conclusion, I must add that the Kedva area had not previously been visited by hominologists, and the information we had received seemed to be free of any 'outside influences.' As for hominoids' 'denning' in the winter, the question remains unresolved, as there are reports, though rather rare, of winter sightings, too.

SECOND LETTER FROM DMITRI BAYANOV
Bigfoot Co-op, May 1987

Nikolai Avdeyev has recently visited us in Moscow, and I got answers to my questions regarding his story. He showed us the cast and we studied it. By my measurement it is 32 centimetres long, 13 (not 14) centimetres wide in the ball area, and 10 centimetres in the heel (which is relatively very wide). The print is almost completely flatfooted. The toes, relatively long, show the same characteristic stance that is seen in many sasquatch footprints - pressed together, their tips inclined downward - which makes one think the creature walks as if grasping the earth with its feet.

Very regrettably, Avdeyev has no photos or casts of the other tracks in the set. Since it was getting dark, he concentrated his attention and work on the best track, and left the rest for the next day; but next day they were fired on, and speedily retreated from the place - so what we are left with is just his word. He says the weather was overcast but there was no rain, the temperature being about five degrees centigrade above zero. The tracks looked no more than one or two days old. They were pigeon-toed, with almost a metre-long stride. Their depth was 4.5 centimetres, whereas his boots left only slight marks (in full gear Avdeyev weighs 80 kilos).

Whoever fired on Avdeyev and the guide knew only too well what they were up to; this means he was from Kedva, had seen Avdeyev there, and knew about his intention. It is possible the attacker caught up with them on horseback. His warning first came in Russian, then he shouted to the guide in Komi and Avdeyev made out the word "yagmort." After the incident the guide told Nikolai, "Let us agree I have told you nothing, and never use my name in this connection." That is why the key witness must remain anonymous.

According to Avdeyev's informants, yagmorts can mimic human voices, are fond of horses and visit stables. All the information came from younger men, and whenever he asked older men they would promptly ask back in surprise, "Who told you that?" When he named his informants, the old men would retort with responses such as, "Oh, he made that up. There is nothing of the sort. Young men drink too much nowadays." Avdeyev plans to return to the target area in August with a solid group, bypassing Kedva and leaving local guides aside.

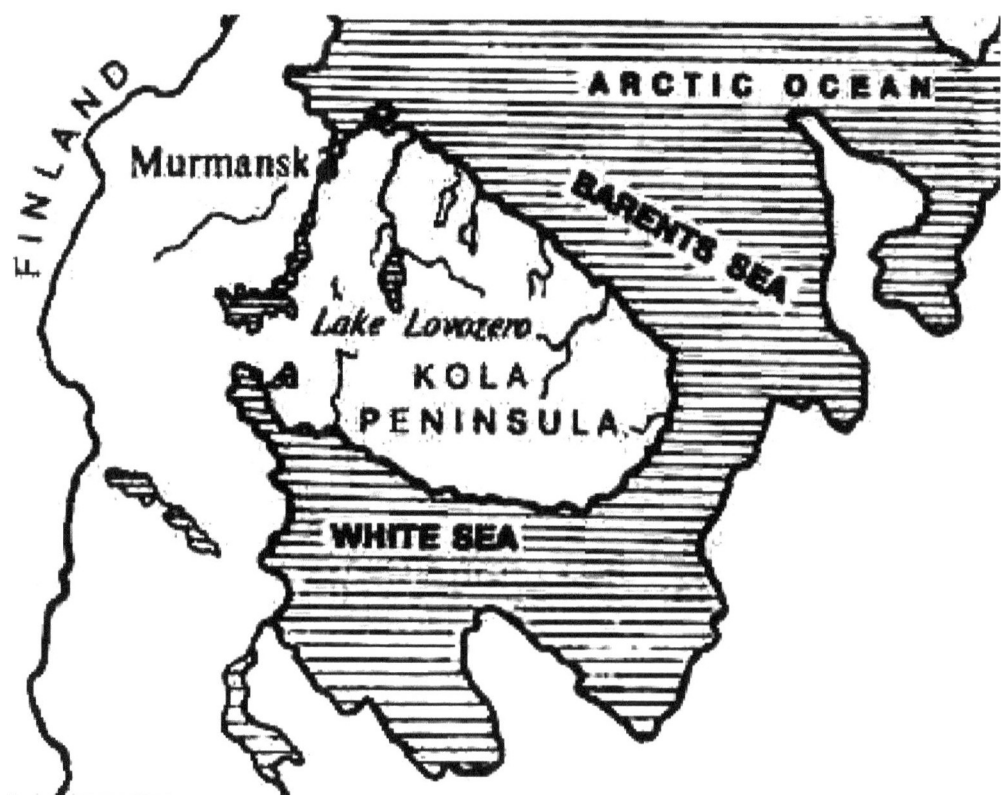

REPORT BY LEONID YERSHOV

Bigfoot Co-op, August 1989

I n the centre of the Kola Peninsula (in the northwestern corner of Russia) is a lake, 60 kilometres long, called Lovozero. There is a settlement of the same name on its shore. In August 1988, six Lovozero boys aged 15-18 fished in the lake and picked berries and mushrooms around a cabin they had built for themselves in the forest some 40 kilometres from the settlement. The cabin stood by a mountain creek, a short distance from the lake. To protect the cabin from flooding in the spring, they had built it on pillars of standing fir trees cut high from the ground.

Lovozero Lake in the Kola Peninsula. Photo by Ivan Perminov.

The cabin on the shore of the lake the scene of repeated sightings. September 1988. Photo by Leonid Yershov.

In the summer of 1987 and July 1988, life had been as usual; only in August did things begin to happen. There was an unaccounted for disappearance of their three-month-old puppy. For several nights it had stayed in the cabin with the boys, some of whom, for lack of space slept on the floor. The puppy kept wetting their bedding, so one night they tied it to a tree outside. In the morning, they found the puppy gone, together with its leash.

August 11 - As the boys sat round a fire in the evening, they had the feeling that someone was lurking around in the bush. Five of them went into the cabin and a sixth, Sasha Prikhodchenko, lay down by the fire, peeping from under a blanket. Suddenly he saw, through the open space under the cabin, what seemed to be enormous hairy legs approaching the cabin from the opposite side. He dashed into the cabin and told the others what he saw. The boys looked out and saw a giant of a man, covered with light-grey hair, stooped over, his head and hump almost at one level, walking round the cabin with long strides in a peculiarly fluid manner without either jerking or swaying. The boys took fright and bolted the door with a stick (there was no lock on the door). None of the boys could sleep during the night as they discussed the event. Could it be a 'snowman?' They nicknamed him Afonya.

August 12 - In the daytime all was quiet. As evening approached, to forestall Afonya and scare him away, the boys raised a lot of noise. A tape recorder blared pop music at full volume and the boys yelled and threw rocks into the bush. As dusk set in. they sat down again around the fire. Suddenly a big rock fell into the fire and another struck the cabin. The boys took shelter and, as the bombardment continued, one boy put a metal pot on his head and looked out to see where the projectiles were coming from. He discerned the light-coloured figure of Afonya moving against the dark backdrop of the forest. Later the intruder came up to the cabin and repeatedly made 2-3 knocks on the wall and the window. The boys decided he had lived in the cabin during their absence and was now trying to evict them.

August 13 - In the morning, the boys made off in their outboard runabouts, headed for the settlement to tell the world what had happened at their fishing spot. They had closed the door and lodged a short stick leaning against it to indicate if anyone entered the cabin during their absence. Back in the settlement, nobody believed them, and they proposed to those who laughed the loudest that they come along and see for themselves that 'little monkey.' Nobody was interested. In the evening the boys returned to the cabin, the stick remained in its place, the boys kept quiet and the night was peaceful. They even felt a little disappointed. Someone suggested that they raise a noise again, and as soon as Afonya appeared, attack him from all sides and kill him with axes to prove that they had seen a snowman. But when others argued that they themselves could become victims, the plan was turned down and the opposite idea was suggested - make friends with Afonya.

August 14 - The boys laid the table outside the cabin with all kinds of food they had, and retreated to their boats on the lake. From there they shouted to Afonya to come and taste their food. In the evening they spotted him on the shore some 50 yards away. When they started their motors, he became startled but did not leave. He was also startled when they struck metal with a hammer.

When he had gone, they went ashore and returned to the cabin. The offerings on the table lay untouched. Before going to bed, Slava Kovalev went out to satisfy his need and, standing by a corner of the cabin, saw Afonya two yards away. The boy rushed in and they bolted the door with a stick pushed through clamps. Afonya came up to the door and gave it a push. The stick broke and the door was flung open. A cry of horror ensued, and some boys ducked under the plank-bed; but he didn't enter, just banged on the door and stepped back. The boys did not sleep throughout the entire night and heard his steps on the roof, the thick boards bending and squeaking under his feet, though they never heard him climb onto the roof. The door remained open since they were afraid to even approach it. As morning came, Afonya left and the boys fell asleep.

August 15 - Three more boys arrived from the settlement. In the evening, as they sat around the fire, they felt scared, but the new arrivals wanted to see Afonya, and the original six boys braced themselves up. When they noticed him, he was crouching in juniper bushes across the creek, some 15 yards away. His stance was ape-like, legs bent, hands on the ground, eyes shining brightly. As soon as all the boys turned and stared at him, he made a long jump in their direction, a jump backward, a jump forward again and then made for them. Commotion followed as the boys scrambled into the cabin, each trying to hide some place. Only Slava Kovalev snatched the clamp off the door, put his foot on the doorframe and shouted, "You fools, lock the door!"

Roman Leonov leapt to his assistance, axe in hand, and Slava commanded, "Thrust the handle through the clamps!" As Roman started doing so, Afonya pulled the door half open and Roman saw his hand. It was like a man's, only bigger, its back sparsely covered with hair, the sinews and dark skin showing through. The boys pulled the door back and tried again to bolt it, and then Afonya pulled in earnest.

Roman Leonov said, "I saw his face right in front of mine. Mind you, he was standing on the ground and I was on the floor, which is raised high above the ground. His face is brown and wrinkled. Somehow I did not notice his nose and mouth, I just remember the eyes - glittering, angry and reddish. They are set wide apart, like a horse's, sort of looking sideways. The forehead is wide and polished, the head is round like a ball. I can't remember how I got under the plank-bed and dropped the axe. I came to my senses because of a strong knocking on the wall and the boys yelling like mad. The knock was so strong that I dashed back to the door. It was open and I saw Slava Kovalev crouching by the fire and moaning in pain. As I learned later, when Afonya pulled the door sharply, Slava was thrown out of the cabin and hit his shoulder against the doorframe. He was so angry that when he returned to the cabin he said he would go out again and face up to our adversary, but we asked him to stay inside the cabin.

Afonya again turned up on the roof. It seemed he would fall through and the boys again were gripped with fear. By the noise he was making, they realized he had pushed at the chimney. As the stove was burning, he must have burned his hands. He made a mooing sound, jumped from the roof and took off.

August 16 - Six boys went to the settlement; three, including Roman Leonov, remained on site. In the daytime they fished in the lake. In the evening, heading for the cabin, when they had almost reached its corner, they spotted Afonya. Seeing that he would beat them to the door, they climbed onto the roof with the aid of a nearby ladder. Once on the roof, they yelled like crazy with fear, but then changed the tune and Roman pleaded, "Afonya, darling, please go beyond the creek! And we will go back to the boats!" Strangely enough, having circled the cabin two or three times, the wildman did as Roman had asked. As soon as he had vanished behind the trees, the boys jumped from the roof, rushed to the boats and motored off to the settlement.

August 17 - Meanwhile, the six boys that were already in the settlement had related once again, to all who cared to listen, what was going on around their cabin. Nobody believed them except some mothers. Svetlana Podgayetskaya, Roman Leonov's former school teacher, said, "On August 17 I met with Roman's mother. She was crying. She said the boys had come from the forest and told what was going on there. Nobody believed them. Some people even accused them of taking drugs. The boys were very annoyed and intended to go back to the cabin. 'What will happen to them?' cried Roman's mother."

August 18 - Twelve boys arrived at the site. Three new arrivals among them, after sighting Afonya on the shore, changed their minds and headed for the opposite bank. In the evening, the nine remaining boys watched Afonya running along the shore following their boats. Trying to get a better view of him, they attempted to come closer, but he did not like that and threw rocks when they approached. Once he picked up a birch pole and threw it in their direction. The pole flew over a fir tree, which must have been 40 metres high, landing near one of the boats.

August 19 – The boys were at the water's edge preparing to go fishing. Sasha Prikhodchenko stayed home because he had hurt a knee against a rock. He was standing outside the cabin, sweeping leftovers from the dining table with a branch. Someone sighted Afonya and shouted a warning to Sasha. The latter called back, "Stop kidding. He doesn't show up in the daytime." But then Sasha turned and saw Afonya standing five yards away and watching him sweep the table. Sasha hid in the cabin and bolted the door with an axe. The others jumped into their boats and took off from shore. Later they returned to see how Sasha was doing and went back to fish from the boats.

In the evening, returning to the cabin, they spotted Afonya on the shore. Again he was following the boats. They saw that they could not attempt a landing because he was standing in the way. They decided to motor off again and then, if he followed, quickly turn back and beat him to the landing place to pick up Sasha, who was stranded in the cabin. The stratagem did not work. Although the boats motored at full speed, 45 kilometres per hour, Afonya kept pace with ease and was first at the landing spot. They had to wait. At last he disappeared. They quietly rowed to shore and three of them dared to land - Slava Kovalev, Sasha Sveilis, and Roman Leonov. They had hardly made a few steps forward when Afonya jumped on them. The boys turned back; Slava and Roman leapt into a boat and took off, while Sasha's boat stuck and its motor fell into the water. Afonya ran up to Sasha from behind. The others shouted to Sasha to run along his boat and jump onto theirs, but he, paralyzed with fear, just gripped the edge of his boat and turned deathly white. Afonya did not touch him; he just crouched down and then straightened up again, trying to see what Sasha was up to. Seeing that he was doing no harm to Sasha, Roman and Slava took heart and rowed their boat up to Sasha's, telling him to jump into theirs. Trying to do so, Sasha turned, looked at Afonya and fainted. Roman and Slava dragged him into their boat and made off from shore as fast as the motor would take them. They slapped Sasha's cheeks, splashed water on his face, and he came to.

They again waited. When Afonya disappeared behind the trees, Sasha Prikhodchenko shouted from the cabin that Afonya had gone beyond the creek. This time there was a general landing. Armed with axes, hammers and rocks, they ganged up and headed for the cabin to retrieve their friend. Charging again, Afonya cut into the middle of the group, splitting it into two. Slava Surodin, holding a rock at ready, almost automatically threw it at the assailant and hit him on the shoulder. The assailant just mooed. Two of the group ran to the cabin; the others ran back to the boats. Afonya chased those who headed for the cabin. Ivan Dyba said, "As I felt him literally breathing down the back of my neck, my legs failed me. I snatched at Zhenya Trofimov, running in front of me, and we both fell to the ground. We crawled and scrambled forward and into the cabin."

Now there were three boys in the cabin. Afonya pounded on the wall and, bending down, peered in the window. Ivan Dyba could hardly move his legs, while Zhenya Trofimov lost his voice for a time and could not speak; yet, when Afonya seemed no longer around, they risked leaving the cabin and headed for the lake. They reached it when Afonya made for them. Sasha Prikhodchenko and Zhenya Trofimov ran back to the cabin, while Ivan Dyba jumped into the water fully clothed

**Senior game warden Igor Pavlov discussing the event with eyewitnesses
Slava Kovalev (left) and Sasha Prikhodchenko (right).
Photo by Mikhail Gavrilov.**

and swam to a boat. Those aboard helped him out. The water was very cold and they motored to the opposite shore to dry Ivan's clothes.

Three boys sped off to the settlement to seek help from the authorities. They arrived at 2 a.m. and went to the settlement's executive committee. A woman on duty called a patrolling militiaman. The latter listened attentively to the boys' story. He could not believe it, and constantly asked for more and more details. At last he telephoned senior game warden Kuznetsov, who arrived at 3 a.m., listened to the story, 'giggling' from time to time, and concluded, "I am not going to alert anybody in the dead of night. I don't want to become a laughingstock on account of your 'snowman.' I'll send someone over in the daytime."

August 20 - Help to those in the cabin arrived in the persons of senior game warden Igor Pavlov and his two assistants. They listened to the story and followed the boys' usual procedure - motoring along the shore and yelling in the evening. They stepped ashore at 23 hours (visibility is still good in the Kola Peninsula at 11 p.m. in August). They headed for the cabin, the boys leading the way, when they cried, "There he is! There he is!"

Senior game warden Pavlov stated,

Rifles at the ready, we headed in the direction pointed out by the boys. When we saw someone standing behind a fir-tree, about 20 metres away, we stopped. My first impression was that it was a man, although we had expected to see a bear. When being given the assignment, we had been told that the boys must have been frightened by an old bear and that we had better shoot it. But what stood in front of us was not a bear. We made three more steps in his direction and I shouted, "Now I am going to shoot!" I figured that, if that was a man, he would call back, "Stop it! Let's call it off!", or something. To tell the truth, I was not quite sure the boys were not pulling my leg, but what we saw next removed my suspicions. In a split second we saw the creature, fully 25 metres away from the fir-tree it had stood behind just a moment before. It was running fast into the forest. That greatly surprised us, and I realized it was not a human. We could not observe it further because it vanished among the brush. We came up to the fir tree and tried to reach the branch that gave a good indication of the creature's height. It was about two and a half metres high. What did I notice when observing the specimen? When it stood behind the tree, what especially struck me was its big, round, light-colored buttocks. On the whole, it was light gray or white in colour, but in some places the hair was a shade darker. Its arms hung to the knees. It ran very fast, but very smoothly, taking great strides.

We did not sleep that night; there was not enough space in the cabin, so we kept talking. I was standing by the wall when it received such a powerful knock from outside that the whole cabin trembled. I wanted to go out, but the boys insisted that I stay in. For a while we kept silent, and all was quiet, but when we resumed talking loudly, the cabin was pelted with rocks. In the morning the boys left for the settlement and I, in the company of my assistants, inspected the area around the cabin. In one place I discovered three tracks on a rotten birch log. In those spots the log was pressed to the ground, whereas I could press it just a little. We were not disturbed at night and left the site the next day.

For a whole week the cabin was unattended by humans.

August 27-28 - Several adults from the settlement, accompanied by the boys, came to the site for the weekend. They experienced a night rock bombardment. For the first time there were photographers among those present and, using flashlights, they searched for Afonya around the cabin at night and made snapshots at random, but neither saw nor photographed him. Sunday evening they all left.

August 29-30 - A great influx of visitors on the site - two TV crews (from Murmansk and Leningrad), plus 25 hunters with four dogs. They combed the area around the cabin and along the shore, but without result. The TV crews interviewed and filmed the boys, subsequently shown on the program *Up to 16 and Older*. After that, the situation calmed down.

A task requiring patience and perseverance: looking for snowman hairs in the grass, On the left: Maya Bykova. Photo by Anatoly Yegorov.

I arrived at the settlement on August 30. On the way, I talked on the bus with an old woman who lived in the village. She told me that local fishermen and reindeer breeders had long talked of such creatures. In the settlement I met and interviewed the eyewitnesses - the boys and game wardens and other people.

September 1 - I visited the site in the company of six local hunters and a dog. As the ground around the cabin and along the shore had been trampled on by the previous parties, we searched for evidence on the hillside. Half a kilometre from the cabin, we found three indistinct tracks with a stride of 120-130 centimetres. Later we found two more tracks in one place and a print of the right foot in another place. Its approximate length was 39 centimetres. Also found were three sizeable piles of excrement, which the hunters failed to identify. Nearby we discovered what could have been Afonya's bed in the grass on the edge of a clearing. I collected 13 hairs from the bed, coloured from white to fawn with dark spots, and filmed all possible evidence with a movie camera. We did not stay for the night, as all were pressed for time.

As I learned later, the same day, September 1, a couple named the Popovs were picking mushrooms in that very area. Having collected mushrooms, they were having lunch on the shore beside their boat, and, to their surprise, noticed what they first took for three spots of snow on a hillside in the distance. They were surprised because the summer was hot and the snow had melted. "Look, exclaimed the husband, the spots are moving!" The spots began to move very quickly along the hillside, and then they saw a fourth little spot some distance from the three others, moving parallel with them, until they eventually vanished from view. To my question whether what they had seen could have been wild reindeer, the Popovs answered that there are no reindeer in those parts in summer, and besides, the creatures were of a different shape; they were vertical like people, not horizontal like animals.

Later in September, the site was visited by Maya Bykova and some others from Moscow. They found more tracks, excrement, two suspicious little caves - or, rather, holes, in the hillside - and collected more hair samples. Such, in short, were the results of the 1988 season. Hopes are pinned now on the summer of 1989.

COMMENT BY DMITRI BAYANOV
Bigfoot Co-op, August 1989

Dear friends,

I hope you enjoyed Leonid Yershov's report as much as I did, some inevitable regrets notwithstanding. Residing in Murmansk, Leonid is a member of our Association of Cryptozoologists, based in Moscow, and until 1988 he had conducted field investigations in

Tajikistan, the southernmost corner of the country, thousands of kilometres from Murmansk; but last year prompted him to do fieldwork in his own back yard. Now, it takes Leonid a weekend ride on the bus to reach very promising hominoid country, even though it lies beyond the Arctic Circle, i.e., as far north as the northern part of Alaska. True, the climate there is much milder than in Alaska on account of the warm Gulf Stream currents reaching the Barents Sea. The Kola Peninsula is the only place in Russia where forests grow beyond the Arctic Circle.

As to inevitable regrets, they are as follows. Again and again, in this country and elsewhere, we are confronted with the fact that people don't know how "best" to behave in the presence of a hominoid and what to expect of him. It clearly indicates that serious, non-sensational hominological information is

Leonid Yershov, a leading hominologist of the Kola Peninsula.

unknown to the general public. Again and again hominologists come onto the scene after a troop of hunters and curious onlookers have scared the creature far away. Also regrettable is that, in keeping with a general pattern here, there was no photographer among those country boys. Even so, one would expect a fuller description of Afonya's appearance, given the amount of observation they had; but, of course, it was his behaviour, not appearance, that they were mostly concerned with, and in this respect the young eyewitnesses give us plenty of food for thought and comparison. The Lovozero boys have never heard of John Green, nor has Leonid Yershov ever read Green's book *Sasquatch: The Apes Among Us*; yet, the story under discussion seems to have been specially designed to illustrate a chapter of that book, headed *Gentle Giants*. Green's conclusion is that in encounters with humans, sasquatches exercise "remarkable self-restraint," being "deliberately very gentle." Amazingly, Afonya, a sasquatch counterpart on the other side of the globe, takes a leaf out of Green's book. I have the impression that at first he was 'bluffing in earnest,' but then almost became amused by the boys' reaction and started playing cat and mouse with them.

I skip numerous other parallels between North European and North American evidence, both in the hominoid's appearance and behaviour, but I want to draw your attention to the distinction Afonya clearly made between the scared teenagers and the adults armed with rifles. As soon as the latter came on the scene, he chose to keep out of sight.

As is the rule with other primates, including man, and as was the case with Albert Ostman's "Old Man," Afonya, being a strong adult male, is probably the reconnoiterer and guardian of his family. It was his duty to drive the boys away from the place chosen for the family, and that may be why he, alone, confronted the humans. That the other members were around, though concealed, is strongly suggested by the evidence of the Popov couple. While hunting parties searched round the cabin and along the shore, Afonya and family stayed in the hills, but when Yershov and the hunters headed in that direction, the hominoids had to quickly move on in broad daylight, as witnessed by the Popovs, who happened to be on the scene at the time.

Pinning all my hopes on befriending a hominoid, I took special note of the fact that Afonya, like Mecheny, did not take food offerings. Two thoughts occur in this connection; first, those at the receiving end must of necessity be in the 'right mood' to accept offerings from their 'adversaries' - apparently that was not yet the case with Afonya. The confrontation stage was not yet over, and, under the circumstances, it would have been beyond his 'dignity' to accept inducements. Second, let us remember that it was August, the time when food is most available in those parts; however, the instances of hominoids taking or stealing food from humans, both in Eurasia and North America, are so numerous and compelling that I do not lose hope. It is the tamer, not the animal, who has to be persistent, inventive, and flexible in such situations.

Let me also discuss one very interesting detail which I have left for dessert: the disappearance of a three-month-old puppy mentioned by Yershov - so it looks like Afonya did take some thing from humans. What did he do with the puppy? Ripped it apart, like Mecheny did? I doubt it - first, because there is usually quite a difference between puppies of three months and five months (in Mecheny's case). My second reason calls for a little digression.
Over the last two centuries, ethnographers in this country have collected and published volumes of folklore on wood and mountain 'ghosts' and 'spirits,' known under various local names, which

ethnographers take for fantasies, and I take for relic hominoids. On the basis of these volumes, which I read carefully, I wrote my own manuscript of a book on hominoids in folklore, which friends and colleagues find fascinating; and, one of the most intriguing and surprising things I learned from folklore concerns the dog-hominoid relationship. Yes, folklore fully confirms what we already know from eyewitness accounts - dog and hominoid are bitter enemies. But then I came across something else which amazed and baffled me. A folklore source in the north of European Russia says that the "lord of the forest" has "faithful dogs" of his own which "follow him everywhere, but which are difficult to see." A source in Soviet Central Asia confides that wildman "may have a dog of his own." A source in the Caucases says that the "wood ghost" has "his own dogs but is afraid of dogs belonging to humans." Could such a marvel be true?

Then came *A Message to Soviel Hominologists for 1989,* from Eric Beckjord, founder of the Cryptozoology Museum in the U.S., saying, in part,

> I have experienced very strange dogs appearing in Bigfoot areas, coming near my camp, walking by, acting for all the world like spies. Others have reported dogs running with Bigfoot in a pack.

Yes, I know what some of you may be thinking, and hasten to cite another source:

> Russ had talked to a man at Orofino who was the night watchman at a small sawmill in the forest 20 miles north of the town. The animal was described as being about six feet tall, completely covered with shiny dark hair except for its face, hands and the nipple areas of its very large breasts. All visible skin was pink. He thinks it may have been nursing a baby.… He and several other employees had seen many tracks in and around O Mill all during the summer of 1969.… They (*sasquatches – D.B.*) played in the sawdust pile and ate sandwiches he had put near the carriage.… They were in and around the mill most of the summer, and he once saw a very large dog which he believed was running with them.

> (John Green. *Sasquatch: The Apes Among Us*, pp. 288-289).

Now I can safely leave it to you to guess what was the fate of that puppy, and whose best friend it may be now.

Lastly, if hominoids are present in the Kola Peninsula, why not in other parts of northern Scandinavia? Surprisingly, John Green is helpful here too.

> One would think that there might be reports from the forests of Scandinavia, and Norwegian friends of mine have told me that they have heard of giant footprints in the snow in the mountains there.

The fearless foursome that grabbed a snowman and bundled it into a car boot. Against a backdrop of the now famous apple orchard on the bank of the Volga, from left to right are: Alexander Zhemchuzhnikov, Anatoly Yashenko, Sergei Pirozhenko (an amateur boxer) and Oleg Degtyarev. Behind them the unique passenger car that had the distinction of transporting a snowman. Photo by Sergei Maslov.

INCREDIBLE CASE IN SARATOV REGION
By Dmitri Bayanov
Bigfoot Co-op, August 1990

Last summer we had for the first time a spate of sighting reports from the Saratov Region (see the city of Saratov on the Volga River southeast of Moscow). They were the usual kind of hominoid sightings, made by farmers, shepherds, and a number of children. We had the impression the area was visited by a family or a group of hominoids of different ages. Most reports mentioned sightings in cropfields, once even in a greenhouse. One explanation put forward at our seminar was that the hominoids invaded the crop-growing Saratov Region because of the drought in some neighbouring forested regions. Except for the area itself, there was nothing new for us in the information, not counting, perhaps, one case of rather small footprints reportedly left by a two-metre tall wildman.

But a truly unique case was claimed in September on the Progress State Farm in the south of the Saratov Region. The state farm owns a big apple orchard (2 km x 1.5 km) along side the Volga River. The farm director hires guards to protect the apple crop from thieves. The guards are paid in kind, so the more apples they safeguard, the more they get as a percentage of the crop, which they then take to neighbouring towns to sell at the markets; I mention these details to show that the guards have every reason to do their job diligently. Last summer the job was taken on by four young men from the Ukrainian city of Kharkov. Unarmed, they patrolled the vast orchard in their *Zhiguli* car, making sure they catch a thief on the spot to avoid arguments that might otherwise arise if the malefactor got outside the orchard.

Thursday, 21 September, 1989, was a hectic day for the guards. In the afternoon they detained two men with a shotgun, and, as the intruders claimed they were local managers and had the right to hunt in the orchard, the guards took them to the local militia (i.e., police) station, where the two men continued to argue their right to hunt in the orchard; meanwhile, the guards had to argue back with the militiamen that they had no such right. Annoyed, the guards drove back and reached the orchard at about 6 p.m. Driving down one of the orchard's many lanes, they glimpsed the dark outline of yet another intruder, half-hidden by apple trees and tall weeds. The guards pulled up and quickly got out of the car. The strongest of them, amateur boxer Sergei, made straight for the intruder, while the other three performed a pincer movement; to surround the presumed thief, in keeping with their usual tactics.

Running with difficulty through the tall weeds, Sergei reached the intruder and grabbed him before seeing clearly who it was. Here he got the shock of his life. The subject was naked and hairy all over, about as tall as Sergei; the mouth of his dark face was open in a kind of grin, and showed big yellow teeth. In addition, the stranger emitted a foul smell. Instinctively Sergei recoiled, but it was too late; the captive had already embraced his captor in a rather affectionate manner.

Trying to free himself, the amateur boxer punched the stranger in the ribs, but that didn't have the slightest impact on the wildman, whose body felt as hard as wood. By that time, Sergei's colleagues had zeroed in and promptly used their usual ploy - one pulled the stranger backward with a stick put from behind across his throat, another obstructed his feet, and a third pulled his arms. They threw the subject, which offered little or no resistance, to the ground, and bound his arms at the elbows with a rope. No more rope was available for the legs.

It then dawned on the guards that something very strange had fallen into their possession. What to do next? They lifted the heavy body, which made inarticulate sounds and which hardly offered any resistance, carried it to the car, bundled it into the boot and slammed the lid shut. After that, Sergei had a fit of vomiting.

They drove to the state farm central office and telephoned the militia station they'd been to earlier in the day. What had they to do with a hairy wildman they captured in the apple orchard? The militiamen had apparently had too much trouble from the guards on a single day and the answer was, "Hold him overnight. We'll come in the morning." The state farm had a huge fruit refrigerator storeroom partly loaded with apples. It was turned off and the guards asked permission to put their trophy into the storeroom for the night, but the person in charge flatly refused to "mix ape with apples."

It was already dark when they returned to the orchard. By then, the captive had become very lively, and his stirrings in the boot shook the car wildly. The guards wondered how long the vehicle could withstand such a shaking. Sergei went to check out whether the boot was locked with a key. Inadvertently, he pressed the button of the lock, with the result that the lid sprang open, allowing the wildman to pop out like the proverbial genie from the bottle. His arms were free (he must have broken the rope while still in the boot), he remained motionless for a moment, then straightened up and disappeared into the darkness. He had been in the boot for three hours.

That happened on the very night our seminar had its monthly session in Moscow, but we learned of the event about a week later. Progress State Farm was visited and the orchard guards were interviewed and videotaped by hominologists Vadim Basov and Sergei Maslov, both of Saratov, who reached the place three days after the event, and later by Mikhail Trachtenherz, deputy chairman of the Association of Cryptozoologists (based in Moscow). The following account is a summary of the information collected by these researchers, reported at the October session of the seminar, and published in the press.

The first thing the researchers did was look for hairs in the boot, but, to their disappointment, the guards said they had thoroughly washed the compartment to clean it of the foul smell. Secondly, the researchers wondered how the wildman could have been placed and shut in the boot, and the guards successfully demonstrated the action with one of them playing wildman. The subject was about 180 centimetres (6 feet) tall, weighing 100-120 kilograms, hairy all over except the face, the palms, and the soles (the latter showed evidence of many cuts). The skin of the face was dark, the nose was flat, the teeth were yellow, the forehead very slanting. The male organ was not prominent. As they thought more thoroughly of the encounter, the guards recalled some suspicious things they had noticed before the event, such as tracks left by bare feet, which is not typical for the locals, or half an apple hanging from a branch, the other half having been bitten off.

A heated discussion took place at our seminar over the presumed hominoid's 'spineless' behaviour during and after capture. Some argued the wildman had suffered a shock, a phenomenon known in wild animals as a result of capture. Others recalled the testimony by military doctor, Karapetian, who, in 1941 in the Caucasus, examined a captured wildman who also offered no resistance to people.

It seems that every instance which offers the potential of a final solution of the "wildman" question appears inevitably and almost mystically marked by bad luck. On the other hand, the prosaic explanation is that the rewards of keeping a specimen, dead or alive, are unknown or doubtful to the people concerned, whereas the bother and hardships are only too evident; again, this reinforces my view that friendly contact with a free-ranging hominoid would be the best solution.

Thus ends yet another incredible hominoid case, the like of which will probably never happen again.

Herald Sun
Melbourne, Australia
February 1, 1992

Two abominable snowmen were seen breaking into a military builders' barracks in a northern Russian town. Moscow Radio said about 30 people watched them enter. "One was about two metres tall and the second was probably a young one, approximately a metre tall.", according to the broadcast. Tufts of fur were found on the barbed wire fence. There were no other details.

Sun
Vancouver, B.C.
February 3, 1992

Reuter's wire service reported the story of 30 people watching two abominable snowmen breaking into a barracks in the town of Kargupol. One was seven feet tall and the second was approximately three feet tall. Fur was later found on the barbed wire fence.

REPORT FROM MOSCOW
By Dmitri Bayanov
Bigfoot Co-op, February 1993

Dear friends, seeing in the October 1992 Co-op wire service reports of two snowmen breaking into a military barracks in northern Russian, I realized that I owe you that story in full.

The sighting happened on the night of January 24, 1992, at a military roadbuilders' barracks near the town of Kargopol (not Kargupol), some 600 kilometres north of Moscow. The case was investigated on the spot, first by the local authorities and later by two Moscow members of our cryptozoological society, Vadim Makarov and Mikhail Trachtenherz. Their report was discussed at our seminar.

Two hominoids, one an adult male and the other much younger, entered one of the barrack buildings at night (the door was not locked) and were seen in the corridor by the soldier on duty, who took fright, rushed into the dormitory where his comrades were sleeping, and raised the alarm. Surprisingly, the adult hominoid also entered the room, and seemed to try to convey some message or request to the people there. He waved his arms, squatted and straightened up, all the time uttering vocal sounds like "hook, hook." Confronted by the staggered and terrified soldiers, the hominoid left the dormitory, followed by two soldiers who noticed the young hominoid perched on a bedside table that stood in the corridor, whimpering like a human child. Apparently the young hominoid was frightened by the commotion; the adult took it into its arms and left the barrack.

In the morning, footprints in the snow showed that the hominoids had entered the barrack, having come down from the loft where they had probably stayed for several days (which happened to be very cold - minus 30 degrees Centigrade; by January 24 the cold spell had ended). Leaving the barracks compound (fenced by barbed wire) the adult, carrying the young one, got onto the roof of the canteen, walked over to the edge that touched a pine tree growing outside the compound, and thus got out into an adjacent wood. The adult was two and a half metres (8 feet) tall, stooping, covered all over with light coloured hair, long hair on the head, big ears, big nostrils, reddish eyes, long arms with big fingers, plus a distinct and unpleasant smell of rotten meat. The young hominoid was about 90 centimetres (3 feet) high, covered with darkish hair. Other details were not supplied. The footprints in the snow measured 38 x 14 cm for the adult and 14 x (?) for the child (the latter, carried by the adult for the most part, happened to walk a short distance at one place in the wood). The sighting was made by nearly 30 people, who gave identical evidence in separate interviews. The reported presence of a young hominoid is most important, showing that the creatures still multiply. There are no answers to the questions: Why was the hominoid mother missing? Why did the creature enter the barrack and face the people in such a daring way? Did he want something of them, or was it just wishing to say "Thanks for letting us stay in the loft during the cold spell."?

The tufts of "fur" found on the barbed wire fence proved to be bird down. Samples of hair picked up on the bedside table in the corridor and in the loft haven't yet been analyzed in a laboratory (due to exorbitant charges at present). Also found in the loft were faeces thought to have been left by the young hominoid. A sample has been analyzed in a lab, with the conclusion that the coprolite contained only remains of plants, such as sedge and wild cereals growing in marshy places.

Other and earlier sighting reports were collected by Makarov and Trachtenherz in villages around Kargopol during their trip to the area in February 1992.

But a word of caution - yes, Dahinden is quite right, there is no lack of storytellers here either. Beware of another recent report from Russia, that of Dr. Nikolai Aleutsky, who claims to have seen a female hominoid tear up a she-bear. So far we have every reason to suspect that the story is untrue.

In the April/June 1992 *Co-op,* I wrote of a pending Russian-French expedition in Kabarda, in the Northern Caucasus, under Marie-Jeanne Koffmann's leadership. It did take place, but after a delay and on a much more modest scale than had been expected due to funding problems. By the time useful feedback from the locals had appeared, winter had set in in the mountains and fieldwork was suspended. Koffmann has returned to Paris to acquire more equipment and is expected to return to Kabarda in a couple of months, accompanied by her Russian and French assistants. Also this news from France - first results of two expeditions (1988 and 1990) in search of wildmen in northwestern Pakistan (not far from Tajikistan border) led by Jordi Magraner, a zoologist at the Museum National d' Histoire Naturelle (Paris), have been published by him in a solid report entitled *Notes sur les hominides reliques d'Asie Centrale* - 84 pages of very interesting reading, with tables, drawings, photographs. I have a copy from Koffmann and am advised that reprints can be obtained from *Troglodytes*, 69, rue Fouques Duparc, 26000 Valence, France (price 40 francs).

Our latest - on November 6, 1992, a giant wildman was seen by a reliable witness in a wood 37 kilometres north of Moscow! That is the nearest sighting so far to the seat of our seminar. Now we keep our fingers crossed and look forward to the subject of our studies appearing live at our next seminar session!

Part V   **THE RUSSIAN FAR EAST**

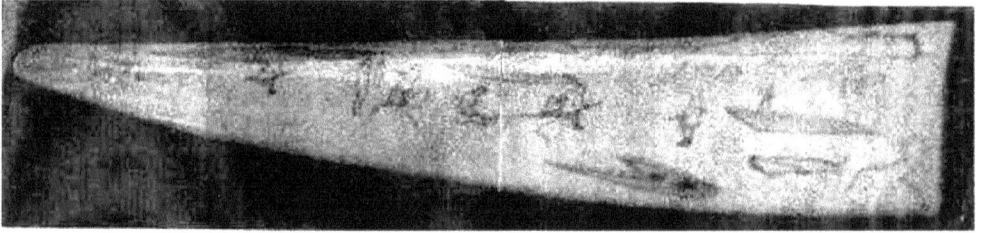

TOP: A walrus tusk depicting the scene of a dramatic encounter between man and snowman chiselled by a native artist.

BELOW: Reproduction of the events depicted on the walrus tusk: A) a hunter armed with a hunting gun is fleeing from a snowman (marked by the absence of clothes) defending his hunting ground; B) having climbed an Ice-hummock, the hunter turns and fires almost point-blank at the snowman who is about twice as tall as the hunter; C) the bullet-hit snowman sags to the ground, blood gushing from the wound; the hunter, still in fear, turns and runs again; D) the snowman lying prostrate, the hunter returns to the scene and stands on the alert.

As shown by works of art reproduced in this book, bloody clashes between man and snowman have been recorded throughout history. No wonder man's hairy relative is not too eager to show up.

REUTER REPORT
August 16, 1990

Soviet KGB border guards were put on a state of maximum alert after a patrol sighted a creature 2 metres tall with brilliant eyes. The beast, which surprised the guards of the Red Flag border post in the Soviet Far East, resembled the mythical Abominable Snowman, or Yeti. Soon afterwards, it was seen trying to climb up to a roof, but eventually retreated to the forest.

REPORT BY DMITRI BAYANOV
Bigfoot Co-op, February 1991

The *Bigfoot Co-op*, October 1990, carried a Reuter report regarding an alleged snowman which surprised the guards of a border post in the Soviet Far East. Our attempts to check the story and obtain more information proved fruitless, as border posts in this country are still shrouded in secrecy; but we have an earlier report of a wildman sighting in the Soviet Far East supplied by a former border guard named Constantine Shembarev, now living in Ukraine. The sighting took place in the winter of 1983, and this is how it was described to me in a letter from Constantine dated March 27, 1988.

This happened not far from the city of Birobidzhan, in a forest on the Chinese border. My driver, an ethnic Uzbek, and I were spending a night outdoors. It was very cold and we made a fire. I left him looking after the fire and went to collect firewood. As there was much snow, it took me about half an hour to collect an armful of brush. Suddenly there was a blood-curdling cry from the fire pit. A cry like that on the border is especially alarming. I dropped the firewood, took my tommygun at the ready, and ran to the campsite.

Suddenly I stopped, seeing a beast heading in my direction. It was very big, and I was taken aback. As for the beast, it showed little fear. When there was only about three metres remaining between us, it straightened up and I saw that it was a man. He was very shaggy, and in some places the hair was matted into plaits. The eyes were humanlike and he stared at me. I thought that if he made another step I would shoot; but he made a sound like a chuckle and went aside. Walking away, he turned around a couple of times as if to make sure I was not following.

He was stooping very much, but the arms were not hanging down like those of an ape. Then I remembered my driver and ran toward the vehicle. The driver was hiding behind the bonnet and was very glad to see me. He was trembling excessively and it took me about an hour to calm him down. He told me the following story - he was tending to the fire when that thing stepped out of the forest. The driver became petrified with fear and could not make a step. The shaggy man approached the fire and started throwing snow onto it. The driver noticed his very long fingers. Suddenly the 'man' heard the crunching of snow under my feet, and turned in my direction. At that moment, the driver let out a piercing cry and dashed toward the automobile, while the 'man' headed in my direction. In brief, that's the whole story.

Answering my queries in two subsequent letters, Constantine added some details. He did not remember exactly the month and day of this encounter, but thought it had occurred in late January 1983. It was night, but visibility was good because of the moon and snow. The wildman was about two metres tall, very wide in the shoulders, dark-coloured, with long head hair. The forehead 'stuck out', the nose was wide and flat, the chin was covered with hair, and the neck was not visible. The arms were long, bent in at the elbows and pressed against the body as if he was feeling cold. The border guard took the creature for a male although he did not see the sex organ. When walking away, the wildman looked back, turning the whole upper part of the body. Engraved in the driver's memory were the wildman's big eyes and long, thin fingers. He took handfuls of snow and threw them onto the fire, growling in the meantime. The driver was standing not more than two steps away - that is why he received, as Constantine put it, such a "dose of fright".

The terrain there is wooded and hilly. Constantine and his driver were not of one mind regarding the creature they had encountered. The border guard thought of apes and feral man, while the driver, being an Uzbek and Muslim, thought they had met a shaitan (devil). They spent the rest of the night in the vehicle. Constantine's border guard colleagues did not take the story seriously, and soon the episode was forgotten. Constantine did not have the driver's address (otherwise I would have also tried to get the driver's own testimony). The most interesting thing here is the wildman's attitude toward fire. In North America, there is a report, presented by John Green, telling of a Bigfoot amusing himself with a hunter's fire. From Mongolia we have a report of almastys warming themselves by a fire left by humans. In folklore collected and published in this country during the last century there is mention, on the one hand, of wildmen approaching fires to warm themselves, and, on the other, of wildmen destroying fires by scattering them or even putting them out with water. The specimen encountered by the border guard apparently belonged to the "fire brigade" category. Such behaviour of our hairy friends clearly shows their difference from animals and resemblance to humans. Jim McClarin called them 'manimals,' and I call them superanimals.

BIGFOOT PLAYING WITH FIRE

Here is, for comparison, a report of 1870 from California, cited in John Green's book (slightly abridged):

A correspondent of the *Antioch Ledger*, writing from Grayson under the date of October l6th says:

> I saw in your paper a short time since an item concerning the 'gorilla' which was said to have been seen in Crow Canyon and shortly after in the mountains at Orestimba Creek. You sneered at the idea of there being any such a 'critter' in these hills, and, were I not better informed, I should sneer too... I know that it exists, and that there are at least two of them, having seen them both at once not a year ago. Their existence has been reported at times over the past twenty years....
>
> Last fall I was hunting in the mountains about 20 miles south of here, and camped for five or six days in one place, as I have done every season for the past fifteen years. Several times I returned to my camp after a hunt, and saw that the ashes and charred sticks from the fireplace had been scattered about. An old hunter notices such things and very soon gets curious to know the cause. Although my bedding and traps and little stores were not disturbed, so far as I could see, I was anxious to learn who or what it was that so regularly visited my camp, for clearly the half-burnt sticks and cinders could not scatter themselves about. I saw no tracks near the camp, as the hard ground covered with leaves would show none. So I started in a circle around the place, and, three hundred yards off, in damp sand, I struck the track of a man's feet, as I supposed - bare and of immense size. Now I was curious, sure, and I resolved to lay in wait for the barefooted visitor. I accordingly took a position on a hillside, about sixty or seventy feet from the fire, and securely hid in the brush. I waited and watched. Two hours and more I sat there and wondered if the owner of the feet would come again, and whether he imagined what an interest he had created in my enquiring mind, and finally what possessed him to be prowling about there with no shoes on. The campfire was on my right, and the spot where I saw the track was on my left, hid by the bushes. It was in this direction that my attention was mostly directed, thinking the visitor would appear there, and besides, it was easier to sit and face that way. Suddenly I was surprised by a shrill whistle, such as boys produce with two fingers under their tongue, and turning quickly I ejaculated, "Good God!" as I saw the object of my solicitude standing beside my fire, erect and looking suspiciously around. It was in the image of a man, but it

could not have been human.

I was never before so benumbed with astonishment. The creature, whatever it was, stood fully five feet high, and was disproportionately broad and square at the foreshoulders, with arms of great length. The legs were very short and the body long. The head was small compared to the rest of the creature, and appeared to be set upon his shoulders without a neck. The whole was covered with dark brown and cinnamon-colored hair, quite long on some parts, that on the head standing in a shock and growing close down to the eyes, like a Digger Indian's. As I looked, he threw his head back and whistled again, and then stopped and grabbed a stick from the fire. This he swung round until the fire on the end had gone out, when he repeated the manoeuver. I was virtually dumbfounded and could only gaze upon his activities. Fifteen minutes I sat and watched him as he whistled and scattered my fire about. I could easily have put a bullet through his head, but why should I kill him? Having apparently amused himself with my fire, he started to walk off, but, having gone a short distance, he returned, and was joined by another - a female, unmistakably - when both turned and walked past me, within twenty yards of where I sat, and disappeared in the brush. I could not have had a better opportunity for observing them, as they were unconscious of my presence. Their only object in visiting my camp seemed to be to amuse themselves by swinging lighted sticks around.

I have related this story many times since, and it has often raised an incredulous smile; but I have met one person who has seen the mysterious creature, and a dozen of whom have come across their tracks at various places between here and Pacheco Pass.

(John Green, *Year of the Sasquatch*, 1970, pp. 14,15)

MORE INFORMATION ON SNOWMEN IN THE FAR EAST AND BEYOND

Time and again we see the same reaction of people who suddenly come across a hominoid - they can hardly believe their eyes. Turgenev said, "... I could not imagine what this monster could be." The Californian witness says, "I was never so benumbed with astonishment before." What's the cause of all the wonder and astonishment? The author of the last report puts it succinctly - "It was in the image of a man, but it could not have been human."

This brings to mind Nizami's dictum - "The highest animal is the Nasnas, a creature... of erect carriage and vertical stature, with wide, flat nails."

A bone figurine presenting the traditional image of pikelian (and similar popular images) in the native art of the people of Russia's North East. Note the creature's very large mouth and lefthandedness.

In the image of a man, but not human.... The dolphin is in the image of a fish, but phylogenetically it is very distant from fishes - so the question arises, how close, or distant, a relative of ours is this highest animal which is in the image of a man? If Nizami's information is correct and the Nasnas can really conceive by man, and also, if Zana was truly a wildwoman and gave birth to humans, then undoubtedly the creatures under discussion, at least those of Eurasia, are phylogenetically our closest kinsfolk.

Why and when did our ancestors part company in evolution with our hairy cousins "of erect carriage and vertical stature?" Boris Porshnev's unequivocal answer is this - our ancestors evolved into humans and parted company with the highest manlike animals because they (our ancestors) 'invented' the most useful tool of human life - language. On the scale of evolution, that happened so rapidly and so recently that our whistling-but-speechless kinsmen, those who did not share in the 'invention,' are still around, being genetically so close to humans that the two kinds of primates can interbreed.

Language made it possible for man to start and continue a technological evolution whose initial instruments were stone tools and fire. Now, looking at the relic hominoids of the present day, can we detect a hint of similar creatures of yore beginning to turn stones into handy tools and fire into a means of technology? I think we can. Remember the rather spontaneous 'experiments' with stones by Zana of the Caucasus and the wildman of the Orals. As for fire, the Californian report provides a most eloquent example.

This raises the question of Bigfoot and Sasquatch, the wild men of North America. After a showing of the Patterson-Gimlin film in Moscow, an anthropologist told the audience that the film could not be genuine because apes and monkeys are not part of North American wildlife. The latter statement is true and makes us conclude that relic hominoids did not evolve in North America, but came there from Asia - as did many other animal species, and as did the ancestors of American Indians as well.

Migration must have taken place during the Ice Age, when the sea level dropped and a land bridge, called Beringia by scientists, linked the northeastern corner of Asia with the northwestern corner of America.

In hominoid habitats rural urchins like these stand a good chance of seeing snowmen. Photo by Alexandra Bourtseva

It is remarkable that sighting reports of wildmen are still reaching us from those regions of Asia and North America. In 1988, my contacts in the northern Russian city of Magadan, on the coast of the Sea of Okhotsk, sent me a copy of *Magadanskaya Pravda* with an article by S. Kozlovsky, a student of local lore. He writes that in 1979, as part of an educational programme, he lectured to local Even reindeer herders on the origin and evolution of man. The lectures were accompanied by slide showings of reconstructions of prehistoric men. Audiences of herders, often with their families, would listen, stone-faced and in solemn silence, to the interpreter, rendering from Russian into Even what Kozlovsky had to say. But the moment a reconstruction of apeman (*Homo erectus*) appeared on the screen, old Evens started whispering to each other, "Erek pikelian!" ("That's pikelian!"). This reaction was repeated with every new audience, and Kozlovsky became increasingly interested in the question of pikelian. He collected stories about it and presented some of them in his article.

The pikelian is a manlike creature covered with grey-brown hair. According to one story, a hunter named Mikundya observed a female pikelian in the mountains. She dug up a root, cleansed it and started eating it. Mikundya was a brave man, and decided to catch the creature. He jumped from behind a rock and grabbed her; she gave out a raucous scream, and dragged him some distance until he bumped heavily against a rock, when he let her go. After that the hunter is said to have found a cave with a bed of grass and moss, and lots of bones of

Alexandra (Alya) Bourtseva, Smolin seminar activist, amateur artist, dare devil motorist, the only hominologist to reach and explore the 'End-of-the-Earth' Chukchi Peninsula.

animals presumably eaten by pikelians.

Other stories cited by Kozlovsky mention pikelians stealing reindeer meat from herders and "storing it in cold puddles," a thing never done by animals. Also, a hunter claims to have seen a pikelian steal a wild ram which he had shot and which had rolled down a slope.

Another of my Far Eastern correspondents, Alexander Gumennik, a journalist in the city of Khabarovsk, also gathered sighting accounts among reindeer breeders living on the mountainous coast of the Sea of Okhotsk. The wildman's name he heard is *kheyak*, a creature two and more metres tall, capable of running very fast, making great leaps, whistling and yelling very loudly. A team leader of reindeer herders told Gumennik that as a child he witnessed a huge hairy kheyak enter, on all fours (because of his size), the tent in which the boy slept with his parents. The wildman approached the boy, caressed and kissed him, and then, still on all fours, backed out of the tent. The parents never woke up and the boy was not a bit afraid "because the kheyak has hypnotic powers." When the boy told his parents what had happened, they became terribly frightened and left that place in a hurry.

The northeastern tip of Asia, jutting out into the Bering Sea vis-a-vis Alaska, called the Chukchi Peninsula, is likewise not devoid of hominoid sightings. This remote corner of Russia was visited by Alexandra Bourtseva in 1971, and the information gathered published in a popular-science magazine. Her informants were the natives of the peninsula, the Chukchi and the Lamut. The Lamut name for large manlike creature is *mirygdy* ('broadshoulders'); other names translate as 'goggle-eye,' 'swift-runner,' and 'sharphead.' The creature is very tall, with no visible neck, hairy, and secretive. If a hunter should leave part of his kill to be retrieved the next day, he will return to find it gone, and big footprints surrounding the location. Inevitably, stories gathered among the indigenous people have a mythological ring; so we always aim to get a 'control account' from a person not belonging to the local population.

For the Chukchi Peninsula, such an account - a sighting report, in fact - was received by us from an ethnic Russian, Victor Chebotarev, now a resident of Moscow. In August 1970, when he worked in the Chukchi Peninsula, during a hunt on the Amguema River, he and two of his fellow-hunters sighted a gigantic hairy figure, both apelike and manlike, with wide shoulders, hefty arms and legs, and a small head. The creature stood motionless for some time, then turned and disappeared behind a rock. When the witness showed us how the wildman moved

we thought, 'just like the Bigfoot of the Patterson film.' When Chebotarev saw the film, he said, "The creature I saw walked exactly like that."

The wildman migrants from Asia to America must first have reached Alaska, which is just across the Bering Strait, from the Chukchi Peninsula. John Green presents several accounts of wildmen from along the Yukon River, mentioning belief in a giant hairy 'Nakentlia,' or 'Bushman,' which is spread among the Indians of the area. The physical description of the Bushman is very much like the Sasquatch of British Columbia. It is manlike in form, walking erect and leaving manlike tracks. It is covered with hair and has a large stature and great strength. These creatures are generally nocturnal, they are good swimmers, they steal dried salmon from the fishing camps, they throw rocks and sticks at people, and they make a loud, high-pitched whistling noise. Mothers are afraid they will steal children, and the Bushman is often used as a threat to keep the children from wandering.

Another source on wildmen in Alaska is a book by anthropologist Richard K. Nelson, *Make Prayers to the Raven: A Koyukon View of the Northern Forest, 1983*. The author writes of "a human creature that occupies the wildlands and remains almost totally alien from society." This is *nik 'inla 'eena (obviously a different transcription of "Nakentlia" mentioned by John Green - .D.B.)*, 'the sneaker,' called 'woodsman' in English. "Woodsmen are as real as any other inhabitant of the Koyukon environment, but they are extremely shy and quick to vanish when people come near.... Occasionally they harass people or steal from them, but they are not a great danger. People tell countless stories about encounters with woodsmen, and regard them as regular inhabitants of the environment." (p. 21)

In addition to information supplied by Green, Nelson reports that the woodsman, besides whistling, makes a sound similar to human laughter; it retires to a den during the winter, like bears; it, or at least its den, has a nauseating odour; it sometimes teases people out in the bush by throwing sticks or messing up nets or other equipment; it runs incredibly fast; it sometimes steals human children; some who have encountered one report a hypnotic power which made it difficult for the percipient to move or react; it is very bad luck to see or kill one; and seeing one can result in insanity.

What is very bad luck for Indians is extremely good luck for us hominologists, and for our overseas counterparts. John Green reports of his 'control sighting' in Alaska, as follows:

> Bob Titmus, of New Hazelton, an active Sasquatch investigator
> in California and then British Columbia since 1958, reports that
> while going to Alaska on a small ship during World War II, he
> went outside in the late evening and saw on the beach, close at

OPPOSITE: Rodents form the staple of the snowman diet. As seen in this picture, the item is readily available even in the 'barren' North. Photo by Alexandra Bourtseva.

hand, an erect creature about seven feet high, covered with dark hair and very heavy. (*The Sasquatch File*, p. 17)

However, the best single piece of evidence coming from North America so far is the Patterson-Gimlin filmstrip - but that's a different story.

AFTERWORD

There is no conclusion offered by this book; only the Afterword, for the research described in it is just beginning in earnest. First, some additional information on two cases already known to the reader - Leonid Yershov, whom I introduced as a leading hominologist of the Kola Peninsula, in subsequent meetings with the boys involved in the Lovozero sighting learned a detail of the hominoid's behaviour which rather impressed him, and he passed on the information to me. According to the boys, when Afonya ran at full speed along the bank, he sometimes suddenly climbed a tree at a single bound and disappeared from view.

The arboreal habits of hominoids are presented consistently enough in our files both by sighting reports and literary sources. Various ethnic traditions mention hominoids of both sexes sitting in a tree or swinging on branches. The Slavic rusalka is usually seen in water or in a tree, the latter posture having been depicted by artist I. Bilibin. From the epic *Iskander Namah* by Nizami, it transpires that shepherds used to capture divs sleeping soundly in trees. But it was from the young Lovozero observers that we learned, for the first time, about the hominoid's acrobatic way of climbing trees; this can explain some cases of the hitherto-inexplicable disappearance of hominoid footprints reported from time to time in different areas. In the case of Afonya, being an adult and a heavily-built individual, such agility on his part is truly surprising.

The other piece of information concerns the guards at the apple orchard who claim to have captured a snowman by mistake. Frankly speaking, it seemed strange to me that the release of the captive had also occurred inadvertently. Though the last word from the guards was different, I have retained the initial report in the book for the sake of objectivity. According to the present version, the hairy captive held in the car's boot, having regained self-control, started such a violent commotion that the owner of the car became very apprehensive for the safety of his most treasured possession. As a result, the hominoid was freed not unwillingly, but deliberately, in order to save the car.

This version makes more sense to me. Besides, one can read on the boys' faces, as seen in the photograph, that they were brave guards and artless storytellers. When first interviewed by the excited hominologists, they just had no heart to avow that the hominoid had slipped away of their own accord. The truth came out only in later interviews when the excitement had subsided.

Let us recall another episode in the book which could have resolved the problem - I mean the case of a Kabardian farmer who found newborn almasty twins in a field of sunflowers. Had he collected those pretty babes and handed them over to Marie-Jeanne Koffmann, the state (and status) of hominology today would be quite different. Why didn't the farmer do that? His explanation - "Who knew that it was important! Never in my life have I heard it said that such a thing could be of interest to anyone." Or, take the case of the Lovozero sighting in the Kola Peninsula. The boys had certainly heard about the snowman and realized they were facing one, but the adults, including experienced hunters, didn't take the matter seriously and, as a result, the hominoid wasn't even photographed. Speaking elliptically, the situation can be described like this: those who can, don't care; those who do care, can't. To interest the first and enable the second, it is necessary to bring about a psychological change, a change of awareness, both in the scientific community and the public at large. We need to make people 'snow man conscious' in a proper way, especially in the countries, regions and continents where the creatures still exist and are being sought, such as Russia, China and North America. To achieve recognition of relic hominoids by science is necessary not only for the growth of knowledge, but for their very protection and preservation. As the numbers and influence of those who do care are too small in each country, logic demands that hominologists unite their voices and efforts in a single international organization. It may be called the International Institute of Hominology; may this book help its formation.

January 1996

BIBLIOGRAPHY

Bayanov, Dmitri
A Hominologist's View from Moscow, USSR. *Northwest Anthro- pological Research Notes*, 1977, 11(1), pp.128-134.
Why It Is Not Right to Kill a Gentle Giant. *Pursuit*, 4, 1980, pp.140-141.
A Note on Folklore in Hominology. *Cryptozoology*, 1, 1982, pp.46-48.
The Case for the Australian Hominoids. In *The Sasquatch and Other Unknown Hominoids* (edited by Vladimir Markotic and Grover Krantz), Western Publishers, Calgary, 1984, pp.101-126.
On the Trail of Yeren. *Asia and Africa Today*, 2, 1985, pp.61-63. Why Cryptozoology? *Cryptozoology*, 6, 1987, pp.I-7.
Bayanov, Dmitri, and Igor Bourtsev
On Neanderthal vs. *Paranthropus. Current Anthropology*, 17(2), 1976, pp.312-318.
Big Foot Lands on the Screen. *Soviet Life*, 3, 1979, pp.57-58.
Bayanov, Dmitri, Igor Bourtsev, and Rene Dahinen
Analysis of the Patterson -Girnlin Film: Why We Find It Authentic. In *The Sasquatch and Other Unknown Hominoids*, Western Publishers, Calgary, 1984, pp.219-234.
Bernheimer, Richard
Wild Men in the Middle Ages. Harvard University Press, Cambridge, 1952.
Bourtsev, Igor
The Abominable Snowman: The Riddle Persists. *Asia and Africa Today*, 2, 1982, pp. 58-61.
Green, John
On the Track of the Sasquatch. Cheam Publishing, Agassiz, 1968.
The Year of the Sasquatch. Cheam Publishing, Agassiz, 1970.
The Sasquatch File. Cheam Publishing, Agassiz, 1973.
Sasquatch: The Apes Among Us. Hancock House, Seattle, 1978. Heuvelmans, Bernard
On the Track of Unknknown Animals. Rupert Hart-Davis, London, 1963.
Les Betes Humaines d'Afrique. Pion, Paris, 1980.

Heuvelmans, Bernard, and Boris Porshnev
L'Homme de Neanderthal est toujours vivant: Pion, Paris, 1974.

Hew kin, James A.
Sasquatch Investigations in the Pacific Northwest, 1990. *Cryptozoology*; 9, 1990, pp.82-84.
Sasquatch Investigations in the Pacific Northwest, 1991. *Cryptozoology*, 10, 1991, pp.76-78.
Sasquatch Investigations in the Pacific Northwest, 1992. *Cryptozoology*, 11, 1992, pp.109-112.

Hunter, Don, with Rene Dahinden
Sasquatch/Bigfoot. McClelland and Stewart, Toronto, 1973.

Koffman, Marie-Jeanne
Brief Ecological Description of the Caucasus Relic Hominoid. In *The Sasquatch and Other lInknown Hominoids*. Western Publishers, Calgary, 1984, pp.76-85.
L'Almasty, yeti du Caucase. *Archeologia*, Juin 1991, pp.24-43. L'Almasty du Caucase, mode de vie d'un hominide. *Archeologia*, Fevrier 1992, pp.52-65.
Les hominoides reliques dans l'antiquite. *Archeologia*, Decembre 1994, pp.33-43; Archeologia, Janvier 1995, pp.56-66.

Krantz, Grover S.
Big Footprints: A Scientific Inquiry into the Reality of Sasquatch. Johnson Books, Boulder, 1992.

Lara Palmeros, R.A.
Ukumar Zupai: Yeti argentin. *Cryptzoologia*, Juillet 1995, pp.7-8. Magraner, Jordi *Les hominoides reliques d'Asie Centrale*. Valence, Editions Association Troglodytes, 1992.

Martyr, Deborah
An Investigation of the *orang-pendek*, the "Short Man" of Sumatra. *Cryptozoology*, 9, 1990, pp.57-65.

Mayor, Adrienne, and Michael Heaney
Griffins and Arimaspeans. *Folklore* (London), Volume 104, 1993, pp.40-66.

Poirier, Frank E., and J. Richard Greenwell
Is There a Large, Unknown Primate in China? The Chinese Yeren or Wildman. *Cryptozoology*, 11, 1992, pp.70-82.

Porshnev, Boris
The Troglodytidae and the Hominidae in the Taxonomy and Evolution of Higher Primates. *Current Anthropology*, 15(4), 1974, pp.449-450.

Rayna I, Michel
L'Homme Sauvage dans Ies pyrenees. *Cryptozoologia*, Juillet 1994, pp.1-8.

Sanborne, Marc
An Investigation of the Duende and Sisimite of Belize: Hominoids or Myth? *Cryptozoology*, 11, 1992, pp.90-97.

Sanderson, Ivan
Abominable Snowmen: Legend Come to Life. Chilton, Philadelphia, 1961.

Shackley, Myra
The case for Neanderthal survival; fact, fiction or faction? *Antiquity*, 56 (216), 1982,

pp.31-41.

Singh, J.A.L., and Robert M. Zingg

Wolf-children and Feral Man. Harper, New York and London, 1942.   Zeligman, Evelina

The Puzzle of the "Iceman". *Asia and Africa Today*, 1, 1983, pp.58-61.

Zhou, Guoxing

The Status of Wildman Research in China. *Cryptozoology*, 1, 1982, pp.13-23.

INDEX OF NAMES

Updates for the 2015 Edition

URAL MOUNTAINS

Yamal Pen.

Ob

Yenisei

Salekhard

YAKUTIA

Yakutsk

Tyumen

Novosibirsk

Irkutsk

L. Baikal

MONGOLIA

SNOWMEN AROUND LAKE BAIKAL

A Russian translation of Charles Stoner's book *The Sherpa and the Snowman* was published in Moscow in 1958 - the peak of general interest in the problem, spurred by the Himalayan expeditions in search of the Yeti. In a foreword to the book, Dr. G. D. Debets, a noted Soviet anthropologist, I asked the question "Can the stories told by the Sherpas be taken as indisputable evidence of the Yeti's existence?" and answered:

No, they cannot. This author happened to visit the upper reaches of the Ilim River in the Irkutsk Region [adjoining Lake Baikal], in 1929. Today the area is crossed by a railroad but at the time it could not boast a single school or a literate person among the local population. The author was often told stories about the Leshy, and with details not in the least inferior to the Sherpa stories about the Yeti. Leshy (from the Russian word "les" - wood, forest) used to be, and still remains, a sign of popular "ignorance" and "superstition" in the eyes of educated Russians. Russian-English dictionaries translate "Leshy" as "wood-goblin," "goblin of the woods," with the mark "folklore." By comparing Yeti to Leshy, Dr. Debets implied that the belief in both was the result of a superstition.

Professor K.K. Platonov, in his book *The Psychology of Religion* (Moscow 1967), has this to say: "I had occasion to converse with an old Transbaikal [i.e., east of Baikal] hunter who said: 'I don't know if apes exist or just imagined, but I saw the Leshy with my own eyes, and more than once." Again, the professor cites this example as a clear case of the superstition, shared and supported by a so-called "eyewitness."

Taking the Leshy for a goblin, a figment of the imagination, ethnographers have collected and published volumes of folklore on the subject. The information covers and reveals all real biological traits of relict hominids, known to us from eyewitnesses, and even some previously unknown from the latter source, as, for example, the wildman's friendship with wild dogs. Folklorists find some of the Leshy's traits paradoxical, while a hominologist finds them quite normal and familiar. As, for example, this: "The Leshy is dumb but vociferous." Or this: "You must not whistle in the wood - the Leshy can be offended." "Don't whistle in the home or in the wood - it's only the Leshy who whistles."

Leshy is the main character of many Russian proverbs and sayings, being interchangeable in them with the devil. When a person appears after a long absence, Russians sometimes say "Where has the leshy (the devil) been carrying you?" (Remember Albert Ostman!) In my Baikal region file I have a reference to an eyewitness who said that in the 1920s he happened to encounter a "hornless devil." This helps to explain the proverb "The devil is not as ugly (terrible, scary) as he is painted." In Russian icons the devil is usually painted with horns. It turns out that in reality the horns are absent.

Another item in the file says that the leshy can strike a friendship with a hunter and bring him squirrels in exchange for vodka refreshments. It sounds like a joke and fable, but folklore (and not only folklore!) about "joint ventures" of hunters and wildmen, from the Gilgamesh epic onward, is so abundant that we should not reject it out of hand.

"According to Transbaikal Cossack stories, water devils come out of the water to play with bathing children." Wildman's love of human children is a ubiquitous feature of folklore. One unfortunate result of this love is that children happen to be kidnapped by wildmen.

One more item from Transbaikal Cossacks: "Sometimes a she-devil falls in love with hunters in the wood and becomes pregnant therefrom, but the child conceived by man is torn apart by her at the very moment of birth."

But enough of folklore. One of my correspondents in the region, Victor Lushnikov, wrote that his father, Innokenty Lushnikov (1871–1920), was Editor of the newspaper *Baikal*. As a boy, Victor used to hear eyewitness accounts about "forest people" told to his father by local hunters. According to his great-grandmother, when she was young, her girlfriend was kidnapped by a Tungu (the Even name for wildman).

Another correspondent, Victor Cherepakhin, a resident of the city of Chita (east of Baikal), an artist by profession, wrote me of what he witnessed in June 1968 in the northern part of the Chita Region, where he was painting landscapes. At a certain moment, during his work in the mountains, he felt "a kind of uneasiness."

"It felt like I was being watched. I turned cautiously and began to scrutinize the surroundings. At first I did not notice anything, but then, continuing to peer, I suddenly saw a manlike creature standing by a tree. It was dark, darker than the pine trunks, rather tall, 190–195 cm, maybe even taller. It looked bulky, despite its height. Trying to see better, I was standing still. The creature also stood motionless. Then it turned to one side, bent down, as if picking up something from the ground, and disappeared in the wood."

The artist hastened to leave the place.

Later, recollecting what I saw, I concluded that the way the creature moved indicated it was devoid of clothes. The movements were neither slow nor hurried, very natural and resembling those of man. And at the same time they were somewhat different from human. I had then, and retain now, after so many years, the feeling that I happened to touch an innermost secret of Nature.

Now one of the last letters from the Chita Region, received in May 1996 from Yuri Lagunov, 46. It begins with the story about Yuri's friend, "Uncle Vasia," who flatly declined Yuri's plan to go hunting in a certain place rife with hares. The reason was divulged only after they emptied a bottle of vodka. It turned out that in 1969, Uncle Vasia had an encounter there with a huge, wild, "hairy muzhik." In the evening, the latter entered half of his body into the hunter's hut and eyed the stunned owner of the hut for a minute, and then quietly departed. (Did he want to strike a "deal" with the hunter?) Uncle Vasia snatched his gun and remained seated with it through the night, unable even to shut the door. That's why he declined Yuri's proposal to go hunting in that place. The letter goes on as follows:

"At 46 I have understood: a man opens up only in a moment of drunken sincerity. Hunters may see and shoot and even kill a snowman but keep silent. If you talk, people will laugh and mock, say it was a bear, you just imagined it, etc. I didn't believe that story either, until my own incident.

"This happened in 1975, when I was 25. I worked as a film projectionist in the settlement and was at the time on leave. It was haymaking time, the 16th of August. My father and I, we had mowed some grass and waited for it to dry. Everybody who has been hunting or fishing know what a great appetite you get there, and haymaking whets your appetite even more. So father says to me 'Why don't you go hunting on the salines? Maybe you'll kill something.' So off I go to the salines, about two kilometers from the settlement. I had only four buck-shot cartridges. I was seated on a small platform, raised two meters from the ground. That way mosquitoes and midges are less annoying. Hell, I had forgotten to bring anti-mosquito ointment. So I was smoking to get the mosquitoes away. The gun was charged, the cock raised. The sun had set down behind the hill. Just the right time for gurans (wild goats) to show up. Suddenly I hear a guran cry some 100–150 meters from the salines, and then run away. I smoked again to check the wind direction. It was all right.

"What could have frightened the goat? So I sit and wait; the dusk is getting thicker, no sound is heard. Now I begin to feel sort of scared. I'd been hunting goats on the salines many times without a problem. Why this fear now? So I am trying to reassure myself, saying inwardly there's nothing to fear, I've got a gun with me, the settlement is not far, the bears don't attack in the summer.

"Suddenly I hear a growling on the hill. Must be wild dogs. The growling stops and my fear subsides a bit. A full moon is rising from behind the hill. Visibility is good now. Not a whiff of air, not a leaf moving on the shrubs and trees. Then I feel being watched. I turn the head - Oh, terror! There he is, the snowman, standing 5–7 meters away, half-turned to me. Broad face, wide shoulders, the chest like that of a boxer, the height about two and a half metres. Mine is 180 centimetres and I reached the platform from the ground with a fully outstretched hand. He was taller by half a metre or more than the platform.

"When I saw him, fear gripped me in earnest. I thought: am I asleep and dreaming? But the cigarette burned my hand and I dropped it. Slowly I moved the gun and pointed at him. If he attacks, I fire. But what's the use? It's like shooting at an elephant with buck-shot. At 25 you want to live. I was in love and hoped for a better life. Today I would shoot without a second thought, just to prove the snowman exists. But at that time, aiming at him and trembling with terror, I began to pray to all gods that they make him disappear. Mind you, I am not a believer, but, as the saying goes, a muzhik would remember God only when it thunders. Having crossed myself and the snowman, I whisper 'Jesus Christ, and the Son*, and the Holy Spirit, I entreat you, do make him disappear!' Nothing happens. He is there. I pray 'Great and Holy Allah, I entreat you, do make him disappear!'

"No go. He is there. I pray 'Great and Holy Buddha, I entreat you, do make him disappear!' Nothing happens. He is there. Now the moon is high in the sky and sheds enough light on him. His eyes are burning, I see his hairy face, his developed torso, the chest, the muscles on the arm. How long we eyed one another, I don't know, I had no watch. At last I saw him raise the hand, move a branch slowly, and disappear in the brush.

"Some minutes later I heard a cry I never heard before. And a similar cry far away. I thought it was an echo. But no, some time later I hear a far cry again and a cry in response quite near. I realize there are two of them, and pray to all gods again that daybreak come sooner. As day was breaking I see a guran approach. I don't shoot, just watch it moving. I figure, if the goat is startled and cries, it means the snowman is nearby. The goat passed by without fear. It means the way out is free for me. I lighted a cigarette and headed towards the road, carrying the gun at the ready and bypassing dense clusters of shrubs.

* The witness's belief that Jesus Christ and the Son are not the same shows him to be truly an unbeliever (when it does not "thunder").

"When I reached the road I heard the snowman growl on the other side of the gully. The growling was uninterrupted. A dog growls with breaks, when it inhales the air; a bear roars abruptly, letting the steam out in one blow. This thing was growling without a letup while I was running away along the road to the settlement. In the morning sounds are heard afar. When I reached home mother had already milked the cow and, seeing my eyes almost out of their orbits, asked what's the matter? I then stammered out what had happened."

Two remarks in conclusion. Firstly, I am sorry that my translation has failed to reproduce the folksy flavor of this "confession." Secondly, I am very glad that Yuri Lagunov did not resort to the gun in his confrontation with the Leshy. Every gun shot at our hairy woodland cousin only postpones, not brings closer, the hour of their recognition by science. It is only by establishing friendly contact with them that researchers will be able to study them in earnest and take protection and preservation measures. (First published in *Bigfoot Co-op*, June 1999, pp. 7-11)

LATEST FROM SIDEROV

Sighting in the Far North: Back in Tomsk after his expedition, Georgy Sidorov learned of a homin sighting in the far north of Siberia, in July 1999. Following his field report, he informed me of the event by letter. A party of geologists, three men and two women, engaged in prospecting, pitched camp at the foot of a low hill, near a nameless lake in the tundra, 45 km from the Byrrang Mountains in the Taimyr Peninsula, which is the northernmost projection of Siberia. Their two tents stood on dry ground on the bank of a brook flowing into the lake.

That day, four expedition members had gone off prospecting, while one woman (who insists on remaining incognito) stayed at camp. Sitting by the brook she was sorting out and classifying the collected rock samples. As she told Sidorov, she was feeling warm and fine. It was about noon, July 10th. Suddenly she felt she was being watched. She turned and became stupefied. From the northern side of the hill, which was still covered with ice, a huge hairy man was marching towards her. For some time she was unable to collect her wits. Then she realized who it was but was unable to budge. Her carbine was by her side but she forgot about it. So she stayed put when the "snowman" came up to her.

The witness said his eyes looked human despite his overall beastly appearance. In her estimate, he stood about three metres in height and was covered with thick brown hair, almost black on the chest and back. His neck seemed non-existent, his arms and legs very strong. She also remembered a flat nose with straight nostrils on a gorilla-like face, with a powerful lower jaw. But in spite of his frightening looks his eyes were not malicious.

He looked at her and chuckled. Then he circled her but never touched. "Had he touched me, I'd have died right away," she said. Then he squatted and started "talking" to her. She insists she heard sounds resembling human speech. "The voice was low and even pleasant." But mostly he "was signalling" her not vocally but "with lips" (!?). Having finished his short "speech", the snowman stood up, looked in the tents, touched the hanging linen, and went off on his way. The witness was unable to stand up from her collapsible stool until the arrival of her colleagues. Her legs simply failed her. Stammering, she told them of the event and, although the tracks were clearly in view around the tents, she was immediately ridiculed.

"That's all there is to this regrettable story," concludes Georgy. "The hominoid himself attempted contact but the human failed to respond and show him hospitality ... If we'd ever had such a fluke!" The story gives the hominologist a feeling of déjà vu. As if programmed, the humans behaved in the usual way: the witness first stupefied, then ridiculed; others distrustful, ignoring the footprints .... The homin's character and behavior are also familiar: self-confident, inquisitive, not devoid of a sense of humour (judging by his chuckling), non-aggressive when unprovoked. Of great interest and importance is additional information (to already existing) on the subject of vocalization resembling human speech. It touches on the crucial aspect of hominology and the origin of man. His "signalling with lips" seems apelike (has to be checked with primatologists).

What, to my knowledge, is unprecedented, is the region of the encounter. The Taimyr Peninsula is as far north as the middle part of Greenland, it's more northerly than the Kola Peninsula, the Chukchi Peninsula, and the whole of Alaska. That our hairy cousins survive at such inhospitable and chilly latitudes is reassuring enough. Stories like that will be repeated over and over again, until hominology turns from a Cinderella of science into a princess of primatology.

(First published in *Bigfoot Co-op*, June 2000, pp. 3–4)

A STORY THAT RANG THE BELL AND A MYSTERY

As economic conditions in Russia are slowly improving, old members of our seminar begin again to attend its sessions, Yuri Krashnikov (opposite) and Yakov Polyakov among them. At a recent session they recalled an episode of their expedition to Tajikistan in July-August 1984. It happened not far from Lake Pairon, visited by me in 1982 (see *In the Footsteps of the Russian Snowman*, p. 116). At the end, Yuri Krashnikov mentioned something that sat me straight up and brought to mind my contributions to the *Bigfoot Co-op* two decades ago.

In 1981, Warren Thompson of The Bay Area Research Group (California) sent me Archie Buckley's "Report on Sasquatch Field Findings," from which I quoted as follows: They (sasquatches) are excellent mimics. In order to communicate and conceal their presence, they will at times employ the mimicking of other animals, birds, and natural sounds. We have heard them bark like dogs and coyotes, whistle, and pound rocks. I have even had them repeat my voice. Another sound they occasionally use when your presence is near - is one which has the phonetics of a small brass bell; as if one were to tinkle a bell softly four or five times, then stop for several seconds and repeat (*Bigfoot Co-op*, October 1981).

We had ample confirmation of the homins' mimicking ability in Eurasia, both by folklore and witnesses, but I had never heard of their making bell sounds. So when in the same year (1981) I came across mention of bell sounds while reading *A Note on the 'Wild People' of Tibet* by Johan van Manen, I hastened to share that point with colleagues through the Co-op. The relevant text is offered in the above mentioned work as an appendix entitled "Strange Phenomena in the Himalayas," one passage of which reads as follows:

"But even stranger than the musical sounds made by eddies and gusts of winds whistling up glens and ravines, is the beautiful clear tinkle of a bell heard sometimes on lonely nights. The sound has been heard in Switzerland, and in the Andes, and in the Himalayas by travelers and mountaineers. A missionary once heard it in Western China and his letter, I think I am right in saying, produces one or two [testimonies] from people who said they had heard it in remote parts of Scotland. Naturally some will say that the bell must have been round the neck."

Software developer Yury Krashnikov, Smolin Seminar member, who heard mysterious sounds in the mountains of Tadjikistan in August 1984 of some concealed cow or sheep, but if that explanation were acceptable to the men who have described the phenomenon there would be no mystery at all. The whole point is that the tinkle of the bell has been heard in places where,

according to those who tell the tale, there was no possibility of cattle or sheep being present. The sound, too, is described as indescribably beautiful and as persisting only for a few seconds. It is heard and is gone (*Bigfoot Co-op*, April 1982). Now I return to Yuri Krashnikov's story. During a hike he and Yakov Polyakov, overtaken by darkness, had to spend the night on a mountain slope, away from camp. The moonless night was pitch-dark. They went to sleep and then woke to the sounds of someone walking nearby. They heard stones rolling and the crackling of twigs in rhythm with the steps. They were approaching. Yuri Kraskhnikov: When the distance between us and the source of the sounds equaled several meters, the sounds stopped. There was silence. We also kept silent and did not budge. Suddenly, from the place where the movement stopped, came sounds resembling the tinkle of a small bell. [Hearing that I almost jumped from my chair!—D.B.] The sounds repeated periodically, once or twice a second. And their source began to move around us, counterclockwise, at a distance of several meters. No other sounds, those of steps, for example, were heard. Taking into account that we were far away from the stream and silence was complete, we must have heard all sounds that were produced. But we heard nothing but the tinkling of a bell. What's more the tinkling seemed to come from the air above us. Having circled us and returned to the starting point, it stopped. Then we heard the sounds of retreating steps.

In the morning we detected indistinct marks of big tracks on the ground strewn with fine-grained rock.... The 'bell sounds' we heard were very peculiar. The description is only approximate, referring to something familiar. They were TOO clear, so clear they seemed almost unreal. If I heard them now, and not 17 years ago, I'd sooner describe them as 'computer-made' or 'synthesized.' Yakov and I compared our impressions and they coincided in minutest detail.

Both witnesses had never heard of Archie Buckley's observations, nor of the mysterious bell sounds in the Himalayas and other places, and they were much fascinated to hear all that from me.

(First published in *Bigfoot Co-op*, October 2001, pp. 3–4.)

EVIDENCE FROM THE CARPATHIANS

The Carpathians is a mountain chain in Central Europe, embracing parts of Poland, Slovakia, Hungary, Romania, and Ukraine. It's a watershed for the Baltic and the Black Seas, well wooded, and in some areas still rich in wildlife. Hominological evidence from the region (namely, two cases of homins male and female, captured in the 18th century) is cited in my book *In the Footsteps of the Russian Snowman*, pp. 162–166. Evidence from the 19th century is absent in my files, but there is some from the 20th, provided by a pen-friend named Vyacheslav Zinov. In 1981, he and his friend hiked in the mountains of the Transcarpathian Region of Ukraine (the Region's central city is Uzhgorod) and quite by chance touched on the subject of "snowman" in a chat with an old local man, named Vasil Dobron, aged 70.

When Dobron was 20 (so it must have been in the 1930s), he pastured sheep in the mountains and had heard from the old men that "devils" and "goblins" were sometimes running in the forest, that they were big (two metres tall), covered with black hair, but otherwise man-like. They sometimes stole sheep, but were afraid of dogs.

It was toward the end of summer, the weather was dry, so Dobron took a vessel and went down to fetch water from the river. He was armed with a hunting gun. When he reached the steep slope from which a path led down to the river he saw below "a man in a fur coat and leather trousers sitting on the bank and drinking water." Vasil Dobron:

I made the gun ready and ran down the path. At first he did not see me, but when there were about 50 metres between us he stood up. As I was approaching he turned toward me and looked at me. I stopped. There were 25-30 metres between us. I aimed the gun at him and asked: "Who are you? Aren't you a bandit? A socialist run away from prison?" [At the time, that part of Ukraine belonged to Czechoslovakia, i.e., it was not under Soviet power—D.B.]

Vyacheslav Zinov sent me his sketch depicting the theme of a tapestry he saw in a museum. The creature in the upper corner is locally known as "woodman". (Opposite page)

The stranger was silent. Then he began mumbling and howling.

Only then did I realize he was not a human being. It was his black hair covering his body that I'd taken for a fur coat. He was about 190 centimetres tall, arms as thick as a girl's legs, the face also covered with hair, except the eyes and the nose. I then cried: "Get away, devil!" and fired at him out of fear. He tore along the river bank faster than a horse, went up a rock like a goat and vanished in the forest. Ever since I've always prayed in the morning and in the evening, and thought that if I had not worn a cross I wouldn't have prevailed over that devil.

A second case was after the war, perhaps in 1955. I went bear hunting with a carbine. Went up high in the mountains and suddenly heard a bear roaring. I approached cautiously through the brush, listening all the time. The roar came from one place. I figured the bear killed an elk or something and was gorging. Well, I thought, I'll get him. I went further and saw a she-bear trying in vain to climb up a thin tree, clawing the bark and roaring angrily. And up in the tree was another creature, probably a young bear. Coming closer, carbine at ready, I saw it was not a bear but a human or a devil in the tree. He was also making sounds, sort of hissing and grumbling. Now it looked just like the devil I'd seen at the river, only smaller, one metre and a half tall, a young devil that is. Also all in black hair. He stood up full height on a branch ready to jump to a bigger tree while the she-bear was almost ready to break the thin tree. The young devil than jumped but failed to reach the other tree and fell to the ground, somersaulted and tore off on two legs so that even lumps of earth flew up from under his feet, and the she-bear darted after him. I crossed myself and ran in the opposite direction. Such is an eyewitness's story from the Carpathians of the 20th century, with its familiar motif of "devilry," gun shooting, and homin/ursus antagonism.

(First printed in *Bigfoot Co-op*, October 2001, pp. 5–6.)

HOMINS BETWEEN MOSCOW AND ST. PETERSBURG

In 1996, when *In the Footsteps of the Russian Snowman*, was published, I happened to read a booklet which made me fear my book missed the most important story of all. The booklet had been supplied by a colleague who bought it in a provincial town. It was written by an Oleg Ivanov, titled *Avdoshki*, published at the author's expense, in 1996, in Malaya Vishera. The latter is a town on the railroad Moscow-St. Petersburg, not far from the city of Novgorod.

The booklet bewildered me a great deal. Its impact was like that of Albert Ostman's story. I mean the claimed encounters were about as close as those of Ostman, or rather those of Jane Goodall with chimpanzees or Dian Fossey with gorillas. Could I believe that? With new, liberal times in Russia all sorts of sensations had flooded the media, the kind we used to see in your tabloids. And yet some bells in the booklet seemed to be ringing true. I had never heard of Oleg Ivanov. A decade and a half earlier Moscow hominologists were hoodwinked by another Ivanov, living in a village some 200 km from Moscow. He also claimed close encounters with snowmen in the woods around his village. It took us months to conclude the man was not mentally balanced. Was Ivanov number two a repeat of number one? I hastened to invite him to our seminar in Moscow.

Now more about the booklet itself. "Avdoshki" is the plural of "avdoshka," a local endearing or jocular name for the Russian "leshy" (wood goblin). The introduction is written by the author's cousin, Vera Senoyedova, who mentions two sightings by her father, and relates a local legend about a beautiful village girl kidnapped by a "man of the forest." When the girl's fiancé found her at last in the woods, she refused to go home, saying: "I live with the woodman. He has bewitched me." The young man killed both the girl and the wildman and brought their corpses to the village. The priest of the village said to the girl's father:

"Your daughter had sold herself to the devil. Take their bodies back to the forest. They can't be buried at the cemetery." So, according to legend, the girl and the wildman are buried side by side in the forest. The booklet's first chapter is titled The First Encounter. It happened in 1960, when Oleg Ivanov was 12 years old. He and his friend Tolik went fishing and came across huge manlike footprints, which they followed and came in view of four hairy creatures in the forest, two big and two small. The boys took fright and, while fleeing, ran into a bog and started sinking. They cried desperately for help, and suddenly it did come .... No, not from the wildmen, but from an unfamiliar man. He cut a pole, threw it to the boys, and pulled them out onto firm ground. Having saved them, the stranger showed the boys the way home. Oleg ran home barefoot because his rubber high boots remained in the quagmire. This earned him a good thrashing from his father.

A subsequent chapter is devoted to the stranger who saved the author's life. He is called Alexander Komlev, aged 40 at the time, and nicknamed "Professor" by the boys. This man is not only the main character of the booklet but, if Ivanov is to be believed, the unchallenged hero of world hominology. "Professor" is claimed to have spent 20 years observing the "forest people" in the manner Jane Goodall observed wild chimps. He saw not only how they lived but also how and where they died. He followed them for hundreds of miles on migration routes. He was a successful "match-maker" among the avdoshkas, helping them to meet and "marry," in order to counteract the adverse effect of their falling numbers.

Sounds like science fiction, doesn't it? If not, why hadn't we heard of Alexander Komlev before? Ivanov gives a weighty reason. "Professor" had worked at a scientific research institute, and in 1953, during Stalinist repressions, was exiled to the Arkhangelsk Region, in the north, where he slaved cutting timber. He escaped from the prison camp, and roaming through the forest encountered "forest people". His fascination with them was so great that he switched direction of research for the rest of his life. For this purpose, but also under the pressure of circumstances, he adopted their way of life, which greatly facilitated his contact with them. In a secretive way the fugitive joined civilization, having probably changed his name. So Alexander Komlev is not his real name. The real name is not known. Understandably, "Professor" was not talkative about his past, and information on it was gleaned by Ivanov from sundry bits of conversation when he and "Professor" became friends. During winters "Professor" worked at various jobs, mostly on construction sites, and devoted all his summers to life with the avdoshkas. He and Oleg met from time to time in the forest, being in pursuit of their common interest. And sometimes Oleg received letters from Komlev, when the latter travelled far and wide, following his hairy wards.

Quote: "In the summer of 1976, I went off on a business trip to the city of Perm. When I came back Pavel Nikiforov told me that "Professor" had died. The hospital buried him as a person without relatives.... Later on, the cemetery was enlarged, new graves appeared in that place, and the grave of "Professor" no longer exists. I was told that before he departed he came and sat on a bench by my house, wishing to hand to me his old black bag with his notes. Having learned that I was absent he went to the forest. Pavel Nikiforov wanted to take the bag and pass it to me, but Komlev refused."

What a plot for a novel, eh? Looks like perfect fiction, but a "Professor" is also mentioned by Vera Senoyedova in an Introduction, and Ivanov refers in the booklet to other real people who claim to have met Alexander Komlev. So you can imagine how eagerly I looked forward to Ivanov coming to Moscow and talking at our seminar. I asked him to bring along his friend and co-witness Tolik, but he wrote back that Tolik was no longer alive, having been poisoned to death by sub-standard vodka (a common cause of death over here; thank goodness Oleg is not a drunkard). I asked him to bring and show us a letter by "Professor," but he replied that "Professor" had asked him to destroy his letters, and Oleg did. Damn it!

Upon coming to Moscow, Ivanov turned out to be a big, strong man, with snow-white hair. He says it turned white when he was 15 and met a male avdoshka face to face for the first time. The shock was such that it made him ill for a long time and his hair became white as a result. Some people at the seminar took Ivanov's story to be a piece of artistic prose based on a copious reading of the "snowman" literature. I was inclined to take it for a mixture of truth and fiction, seeing the latter clearly in some places and doubting in others. Ivanov did admit when we met that he had added some fiction to a true story, saying he was advised to do so to increase sales of the booklet. He seems to be quite indifferent to the damage this does to the value of his story for hominology. And I never got a clear answer from him why he had never

Oleg Ivanov signing copies of his book in a public library. He claims his white hair is the result of a face to face encounter with a wildman.

tried to contact us, hominologists, in Moscow. (Why Komlev did not advertise his discoveries is clear enough.) All in all, Ivanov's visit to Moscow did not dispel some of my colleagues' skepticism and the uncertainty of others. So this summer I asked a member of the seminar, Marina Smolyaninova, to go to Malaya Vishera to try to find other witnesses, besides Oleg Ivanov. I also asked her to search for some documentation of Alexander Komlev's existence (a record in the hospital for example.)

Marina was fairly successful on the first point, having interviewed not only a number of presumed local eyewitnesses but also a very important outsider. He is Dmitri Panov, 62, a retired engineer, residing in St. Petersburg, who had bought a house in a village not far from Malaya Vishera. He claims a good avdoshka sighting while gathering mushrooms in a swampy spot in the forest in July, 1998. He also saw what he took to be the creature's tracks.

Marina's report at the last seminar has favourably swayed the members' opinion. All agree now the Malaya Vishera area calls for serious fieldwork. The question is where to get the staff and the money, with us poor veterans growing poorer and older, and young blood not forthcoming under the country's harsh economic conditions. I called for further efforts to substantiate with documents Komlev's existence (Marina was not successful on this score the first time) and to neatly separate truth from fiction in the booklet. If only a half of what Ivanov says is true (and he insists almost all is true, with very little exception), it's fantastic. Alexander Komlev's still unrecognized feat should become an inspiration for all dedicated workers in hominology. (First published in *Bigfoot Co-op*, December 1999,pp.3-7)

GOBLINS AND BROWNIES IN THE FLESH
HOW I PEEPED INTO THE "GOBLIN UNIVERSE"

As a young man I devoted much thought to the plight of my countrymen and people in general. Along with others I thought that so-called human nature had a lot to do with the destiny of mankind. Human nature is the result of man's origin and evolution; hence I became keenly interested in anthropology and problems of anthropogenesis. In 1964 I read an article by Professor Boris Porshnev, claiming the present-day existence of Neanderthals. The claim greatly surprised and intrigued me. So I met the professor, read his voluminous book on "relict hominoids" (1963), and found his arguments weighty and persuasive. What remained to be checked, I thought, was the veracity of purported eyewitnesses to whom Porshnev referred, or rather the very existence of such witnesses. Their alleged presence in the Caucasus was most incredible. It sounded no less fantastic than, say, relict hominids in California! Yet Porshnev's colleague, French-born Marie-Jeanne Koffmann (usually called simply Zhanna in Russia), was investigating the matter and collecting eyewitness accounts right in the central north Caucasus Soviet republic of Kabardino-Balkaria. So in the summer of 1964 I joined Koffmann's expedition in Kabarda, where the object of her search was called "almasty."

Furry Fellows in the Mirror of Fantasy

The expedition became an eye-opening event in my life. It turned out that people claiming sightings and repeated close encounters with the almasty did really exist, and not only among the natives of the Caucasus, but also among newcomers and strangers to local customs and traditions. With great amazement I became suddenly conscious of a tremendous "knowledge gap" in science: marvellous and priceless information was in the possession of lay people and absent among scientists. And it was a time of "legend come to life" for me, because many things which I had taken for mythology turned out to be stark reality.

To my surprise, the local people saw nothing unusual or surprising in the existence of almasty; on the contrary, they were puzzled by our ignorance and surprise. Their explanations of the phenomenon ranged from purely natural to purely supernatural. One local man said, "There are wild goats, wild sheep, wild pigs; why not wild people?" On the other hand, an old Kabardian Moslem gave us this explanation: "All around us are invisible ghosts and spirits. When an evil spirit grows old it becomes visible and turns into a shaitan [devil]. That's how almasty comes about." "A shaitan-pensioner," wisecracked one of our group. "That's right," said the old man without a hint of a smile.

Expedition leader M. J. Koffmann (left) and your author sporting Caucasian shepherds' cloaks, beside Koffmann's mini-car, the ever-ready prize for almasty. Village of Pervomaiskoye, July 1964.

I was surprised even more upon hearing that the notion of "devil" was applied to the almasty by ethnic Russian witnesses, unfamiliar with the local folklore and mythology. A Russian man told me that when he was making hay and went to a nearby lake for water, he came across a tent of reeds from which hairy legs stuck out. Then a hairy wild man appeared from the tent and walked away. The witness had never heard the word "almasty" and used the Russian word "chort" (devil) to indicate what he saw.

Another ethnic Russian, livestock specialist Nadezhda Serikova, related a dramatic episode of her encounter with almasty in the winter of 1956. Having arrived in the Caucasus from central Russia, she rented lodgings in the Kabardian village of Zalukokoazhe and one night was frightened nearly to death by an almasty who quietly entered her room. When she noticed him the creature was squatting beside her bed and seemed ready to jump at her. The young woman became paralyzed with horror but managed to utter, "Whence you here?" At which the intruder dashed out of the room, leaving behind a choking stench. The rest of the night Nadezhda could neither sleep nor move. In the morning, her Kabardian woman neighbour, surprised that Nadezhda did not go to work, came in and asked, "What's the matter?" "I saw the devil at night," answered the Russian woman. After hearing the explanation, the Kabardian woman said, "Don't you worry. It's not really a devil. It was an almasty. He won't hurt you. He is fed by a family in the neighbourhood and stays in their lumber-room in the daytime." Nadezhda did not know what "almasty" meant and asked the Kabardian to explain. The latter tried to recall the exact Russian word for that kind of almasty and soon remembered: "domovoy," which literally means "domestic one," but is usually translated into English by dictionaries as "brownie."

The witness gave me the most detailed description of the creature, leaving no doubt in my mind that what she had seen was neither a hoaxer nor an ape that had run away from a circus. Nadezhda was not religious (which was not unusual in the atheistic Soviet Union), so I asked her why on earth she took an almasty for a devil. She answered, "I had never seen such a creature, but when I was a little girl my grandmother taught me to pray and used to say that devils will punish people who do not pray. So, seeing that creature, I immediately remembered grandmother and her words about devils."

That was my introduction to the reality of the "devils" and "brownies." The story of an almasty living in a lumber-room was confirmed to me by other villagers besides Nadezhda Serikova, but my attempts to resolve the problem by asking the owner of the lumber-room himself came to nothing. He denied any knowledge of almasty. Neighbours can spread rumour and gossip a lot, but coming to grips with actual contactees is a different matter. Following ancient traditions and taboos they flatly deny any contacts with homins and even their very existence. If you see a group of Kabardians on a village street and start asking them questions about almasty, they first look at you in surprise and then women start leaving the group, as if you said something indecent. There was also a rumour of an almasty fed by a family in another village, that of Pervomaiskoye. It was confided to Koffmann by her Kabardian friends, but the family in question was not Kabardian, but of a different nationality, namely Karachai. Relatives of Koffmann's friend Muhaddin (Misha for short) lived in Pervomaiskoye and informed him that their next-door Karachai neighbours were feeding a male almasty that stayed in the daytime in the loft of their house. The creature had been sighted as recently as a month before. The Karachai family consisted of four sisters whom Misha referred to simply as "the girls," although they were not young at all. They had fine names: Beecha, Jaga, Batyk and Mariam. The latter was a Communist Party member and Deputy of the local Soviet, a very prestigious distinction at the time.

When Zhanna Koffmann got wind of that she said to Muhaddin: "Misha, help me get that almasty. Tell 'the girls' the State will give them a lot of money for it. And I will give you my car if you pull off the deal." She had a Zaparozhets mini-car and it was then an attractive offer. So Muhaddin discussed the matter with his relatives, who were first appalled by the idea; but when he said to them, "Look, it's not a Kabardian but a Karachai almasty that I propose to sell," the relatives consented. Then Misha went to Koffmann and said, "All right, Zhanna, I will help you get a Karachai almasty. Let's go to Pervomaiskoye." In high spirits and full of

Zhanna, ever tinkering with the car engine, after rough rides on unpaved mountain roads, Kabarda hills in background. Expedition base at village of Sarmakovo, Kabarda, June 1964.

hope, Muhaddin, Koffmann, I, and two other members of our team speeded up to Pervomaiskoye. It seemed that for the first time ethnic frictions and rivalries prevailing in the Caucasus would serve a useful purpose. We stopped over at the house of Muhaddin's relatives and he went to negotiate behind closed doors with "the girls." He was met by the Soviet Deputy and Communist Party member Mariam and said to her, "My relatives and your next-door neighbours have told me that you've been having a hard time keeping that almasty of yours. Zhanna [her name was known to everyone in Kabarda] has come to Pervomaiskoye with me. She says you will get big money, enough for the four of you in old age, if you turn over your almasty to the State."

Mariam hesitated and went to ask her three sisters, who answered with a unanimous and unconditional "nyet." Despite these setbacks, on my next, 1965, expedition to the Caucasus, I was still hopeful of a chance to present an almasty to science by dint of an obliging contactee. It was with this hope that I made the acquaintance of a tall and robust Kabardian named Anen Psonukhov, aged 52, a resident of Zalukokoazhe. Several villagers confided to me that Anen "cohabits with an almasty woman." To prove that it was not an empty rumour, they made the following points:

1)   Anen is a bachelor;
2)   He lives alone and never allows anybody to enter his home, the windows of which are always shuttered and curtained. Once, when some men tried to enter his home, Anen, a pitchfork in hand, chased them away;
3)   His late mother was known to be in contact with almastys;

A female almasty was seen in and around his orchard, most recently that very summer. On hearing that, I recalled the words of a young Kabardian named Pate, from the village of Sarmakovo, who gave me an account of his two quite realistic and credible sightings, and then added that a friend of his was cohabiting with an almasty.

"How come?" – "Yes, she visits him three times a year. He has four children by her."

"Where are they?" – "They stay with her in the wild."

"How is he dating her?" – "By means of little sticks." (?)

"So she doesn't speak?" – "She can say one word in Kabardian."

"Which?" – "Give!"

Quite a useful word for an almasty, I thought, although I doubted very much that part of Pata's story. In my diary it was marked "fantastic" and I thought it unworthy of investigation.

The Anen case gave me a second chance. Provided with his home address, I went down to see for myself. Unlike other houses, facing the village street, his old home was hidden in the middle of a large and densely overgrown orchard at the very end of the settlement, next to the cemetery and a pasture. For the next three days I would stubbornly come to that place to "lecture" the alleged contactee. And for three days, against all the strict rules of Caucasian hospitality, Anen would fail, not only to invite me inside his home, but even inside his garden. Every time I had to call him out and talk to him in the street. I must say that in all my subsequent travels I have never experienced such an inhospitable stance by a local man.

The gist of my talk was the importance of almasty for science and the great reward to anyone who would help with the discovery. The gist of his retort was that almasty was nonexistent, it was nothing but an invention by those who spread rumours and slander about him. Our conversation went as follows: "Why don't you let people in and prove them wrong?"

"Because I live alone, my rooms are untidy. I don't want others to see that." (Yet the clothes on Anen were clean and tidy.). "All right, you haven't seen an almasty, but people say they have seen one and in your very orchard. So let me stay there at night and maybe I'll happen to see it, too." "No, that would be bad."

"Why? Please explain!"

Koffmann (standing behind the cart) with Kabardians of Sarmakovo village, members of Ali Kardanov family who rented rooms for expedition base, Kabarda, May 1974. Old quadruped, standing in front, belonged to Koffmann and happened to be called Fox.

Silence from Anen. By the way, other local people never refused to allow me to stay day and night in their gardens and orchards after a reported sighting there. After three days of hard "bargaining," it became clear to me that if Anen was really in contact with a female almasty, he would not avow it for any riches in the world, and not only because of the traditional taboo but because he was said to be cohabiting with her.

If victory proved as elusive as the almasty itself, then at least I managed to collect some interesting local beliefs regarding almasty-human contacts. A young woman confided to me what she heard from the old men: "Almasty man is less likely to become attracted to people. He is tetchy and if offended would leave the homestead. Almasty woman, on the contrary, is tender and attached to her human master, and if she becomes his wife, she does not stand another woman in the house. If her master dies, she weeps bitterly."

I was told that if an almasty regularly visits a homestead, the dogs get accustomed to it and don't bark. One man told me: "Almasty would never show up to a hero or a coward, only to

Expedition members, in search of almasty bones, heading to a huge crack in rock face. Second in line, Bayanov; third Koffmann, July 1964.

one in between. Why? Because the hero will shoot it and the coward will get sick." Almasty is believed to be capable of "mind reading" at any distance: "As soon as you leave Moscow for the Caucasus, he already knows it." I met an 80-year-old man, Ibrahim Bombasir, a Persian, who was born in Mosul (north Iraq). He was taken prisoner by the Russians in World War I, got married in Kabarda and remained there for good. His Russian was very poor, so he told me through an interpreter that his family in Mosul kept a female almasty as a domestic servant. He was then a boy of ten. He said a needle was stuck into her breast and she could not get it out. While the needle remained there she would not leave people. She asked everybody to get it out. I inquired how she was asking that and was told: "In Arabic." He also added something that impressed him as a young boy but sounded incomprehensible to me, probably because of inadequate translation: "When she sleeps blood [is seen]." Later I was told by Kabardians that the almasty sleeping place on the floor is stained with blood. Ah, the menses, I guessed.

According to legend, Kabardians have a different ploy to keep the female almasty servant from leaving her job. It is necessary to tear out a hair from her head and hide it. She will remain with people until the hair is found. The rest of the tale is usually this: While the people

Author holds a widely available item of almasty food.

were away the almasty remained with their child and made it show her where the hair was hidden. Having gotten it, she threw the child into the boiling water (or milk) and made away.

Another crime by almasty was revealed to me as a fact. A man told me that his grandfather had gone to bathe in a river and never returned. Almasty killed him. "How? Why do you think it was almasty?" - "People said almasty tickled him to death." I was skeptical, but later, studying published folklore, became reconciled to the idea of tickling-to-death homins. (See *In the Footsteps of the Russian Snowman*, pp.173-74.)

I was told that, having spotted people, almasty would stand still, sometimes for a long time, and would never immediately run on a surprise encounter but would first step quietly backward. And that viewed from behind an almasty seems to be without arms, because they are hanging in front. Nearly all locals, including children, when asked to describe almasty, would first of all say, "Their eyes are different from ours," and put two fingers of both hands in a vertical, not horizontal, position to their eyes. The exact anatomical meaning of this gesture remains a riddle to this day. There were almasty sightings by the locals in their gardens and orchards at the very time of my presence in Kabarda, and what impressed the eyewitnesses was the unbelievable speed of running by almasty, especially young ones, when they chose to run.

I should not create the impression that collecting relevant information was always simple and easy. Looking for eyewitnesses, you are referred to someone else, and that person would deny that the sighting occurred recently, as you were first told; it happened long ago and most details were forgotten. Once I was directed to a witness who said to me: "Yes, I saved an almasty from the dogs on a pasture."

"Please describe it." - "I can't."

"Why?" - "I didn't look at it."

"Why?" - "Was not interested."

There is not enough space in this paper to describe all I learned on my first two expeditions to the Caucasus; for example, the story by an ethnic Russian who claimed to have seen in 1928 or 1929, when he was young, a hairy, stocky, and swarthy three-year-old boy, born by a woman allegedly kidnapped by a "bear." According to the man, the boy was taken from his mother by the authorities and sent to an institution in Moscow. True or not, it would be worthwhile to examine the records of corresponding institutions not only in Russia but across the world, with an eye to their possible hairy inmates.

As a result of those two expeditions I came to the following four conclusions:

1)   Almasty is a reality;
2)   Almasty has not matured for civilization;
3)   Civilization has not matured for almasty;

Porshnev was correct in his theory that the so-called "popular demons," such as "devils," "goblins," "brownies," etc., etc., were a reflection of what he termed "relict hominoids" in the flesh. "Your snowman is nothing but a wood goblin" [i.e., a mere superstition] charged his critics. "Yes, a wood goblin," answered the professor, "only the other way around. The wood goblin is a snowman, i.e., a paleoanthropological relic."

Back in Moscow (and here I reiterate what I told Craig Heinselman in our 2001 interview), I plunged into reading literature on folklore, demonology, and the history of religion. I was fascinated by what opened to my eyes, my mind having already been opened by Porshnev's theory and what I had learned in the expedition. It became clear to me that folklore and demonology, or what anthropologist John Napier called the Goblin Universe, is the richest source of hominology, very realistic but totally misunderstood and misinterpreted by academic specialists on folklore and mythology. Soon I came up with a work whose title could be translated into English as *In Defense of Devilry*. The work was never published in Soviet years and no folklorist ever agreed to cooperate with me, despite my friendly approaches.

When the country's political situation began to change, I enlarged my original work, changed the title to *Wood Goblin Dubbed Monkey: A Comparative Study in Demonology*, and after addressing in vain many publishers, at last succeeded in finding one who published it in 1991. I sorted out in it volumes of published folklore of the many peoples in the Soviet Union, focusing on the most realistic descriptions of the appearance, behaviour, and habits of their "demons." Folklore not only supports what we learn from eyewitnesses, but provides details and particulars that I never heard from them, because it contains observations and memories amassed and compressed over hundreds of years.

In a recent message to me, Keith Foster, a keen Bigfooter from Colorado, refers to Theodore Roosevelt's book, *Wilderness Hunter* (1893), to the effect that "Roosevelt's native companion did not want to go into a certain area for fear of the 'devils' there. Roosevelt called them 'forest hobgoblins.'" I am glad to see such similarities in the "demonology" of Russia and America. This is yet another feather in the hat of hominology.

PART II.

WOOD GOBLIN DUBBED MONKEY:

A COMPARATIVE STUDY IN DEMONOLOGY

The following is a summary of my book in Russian on folklore and demonology as seen and analyzed from the viewpoint of hominology. Also discussed are some relevant points that came up after the book's publication in 1991. First some words about the title. Folklore informants often compare wood goblins and other folk demons with apes and monkeys. In the Chuvash language, of the ethnic people in the Volga area, one and the same word, "arsuri," means both wood goblin and monkey, even though monkeys are native neither to the local woods nor to the whole of Russia. A Chuvash folklorist, the author of a scholarly work on the arsuri, finds this circumstance very strange and inexplicable, but for the hominologist the matter is no riddle at all. I think the word arsuri for the wood goblin is the ancient and original term, and, subsequently, when the Chuvash became aware of foreign arboreal animals resembling their goblins, they applied to those animals the name of their goblins. Another name for their wood demon is "upate" which translates as "half-man."

It is quite probable that the Greek word "pithekos" (ape, monkey) was also originally applied to the homin, because etymologically it is connected with the Latin "foedus" (abominable), the Lithuanian "baisus" (horrible) and the Russian "bes" (devil). H. W. Janson, in his book *Apes and Ape Lore in the Middle Ages and the Renaissance*, writes that, "the ape was to be viewed as the kin of demons and monsters, rather than as an 'ordinary' animal…" (p. 75). According to primatologist Eman Friedman, it was the presumed demonological connection of apes and monkeys that so delayed the development of primatology, which acquired a scientific basis only in the 19th century.

Here is another example from my book. An old hunter in the backwoods of Siberia told a scholar, "I don't know if monkeys exist or may be made up. But I have seen the leshy [Russian wood goblin] more than once with my own eyes." Why did he mention monkeys in this case and doubt their existence? Because he had seen them only in pictures and they reminded him of the creature seen more than once in the flesh. The scholar, Professor K. Platonov, in his book, *Psychology of Religion* (1967), cites the old hunter's words as an example of "outright superstition."

Academic folklorists and demonologists refer to the "heroes" of their books, i.e., "devils," "goblins," "brownies," etc., by such names as "fabulous beings," "creatures of fantasy," "irreal characters," "mental constructions," etc. Accordingly, they focus attention on the fabulous and imaginary. In this respect, the hominologist's objective is the opposite of theirs. To get at goblin biology and ethology he has to amass and sort out as much folklore material as possible (from as many lands and regions as possible), taking into account first and foremost not what folklorists say, but what their folk informants related. That is why it has to be a "Comparative Study."

And the hominologist is not deterred or deceived by folk terminology, for he is well aware that folklore calmly applies "irreal names" to real beings. A telling example of this charming practice is offered by John McKinnon in his book *In Search of the Red Ape* (1974). In Borneo, in 1969, during an outing in the jungle, the author suddenly "stopped dead," amazed at what he saw. It was a footprint so like a man's yet so definitely not a man's that his skin crept and he felt a strong desire to head home. Back at camp McKinnon asked his Malay boatman what animal could make such tracks. "Without a moment's hesitation he replied 'Batutut,' but when I [McKinnon] asked him to describe the beast he said it was not an animal but a type of ghost." It follows that ghosts, spirits, and other "irreal characters" do not necessarily levitate, leaving no foot tracks on the ground.

So how does the hominologist tell reality from fantasy in folklore and demonology? In the same way an educated person tells real things from imaginary ones in fairy-tales and legends. The hominologist is helped in this task by his knowledge of homins who combine both human and simian traits, being however neither apes nor *Homo sapiens* humans. That is yet another reason for a comparative study.

It should also be mentioned that the names "snowman," "relict hominoid," or any eyewitness accounts collected by hominologists are not to be found in my book. It includes nothing but the published material by professional folklorists, ethnographers, and lexicographers. I did this on purpose in order to beat the opposition with their own weapon – by showing that folklore and demonology alone, seen through the eyes of hominology, graphically reveal the reality of homins. When such material is put side by side with the eyewitness accounts, footprints, and photographic evidence collected by hominologists, the positive conclusion becomes irresistible.

The Biblical Connection

Among historical examples cited in the book, references to the Bible may be of special significance for readers in the West because of the Holy Book's ubiquity in Europe and America. The beings of interest to us are mentioned, for example, in Isaiah 13:21 and 34:14, i.e., in a prophecy against Babylon. The prophet says that Babylon shall be destroyed, turned into a waste land, and "wild animals of the desert" shall come to live there.

Along with such denizens of the desert as ostriches, jackals, and hyenas, the Bible in Russian mentions "the leshy" (wood goblin)! How come wood goblins in the desert? The question intrigued me and begged an answer. In search of it I discovered that the earliest edition of the Bible in Russia (in old Slavic) has "bes" (devil) instead of "leshy" in those verses in Isaiah. I then looked up the Authorized Version of Isaiah in English and discovered "satyrs" in the corresponding places. So I opened *Encyclopedia Britannica*, 1961, vol. 20, p. 11, and read, in part, the following:

Satyrs, in Greek mythology, spirits half-man, half-beast. [...] In Italy often identified with the fauni. In the Authorized Version of Isaiah xiii. 21, xxxiv. 14 the word "satyr" is used to render the Hebrew "se'irim" (hairy ones). A kind of demon or supernatural being known to Hebrew folklore as inhabiting waste places is meant; [...]. They correspond to the "shaggy demon of the mountain pass" (azabb al- 'akaba) of old Arab superstition. So what did the "hairy ones" alias the "shaggy demon of the mountain pass" alias wood goblins alias satyrs alias devils have to do with the ruins of Babylon? Various translations of the Bible answer as follows: they "will leap about," they "will dance," they "shall call to each other," they "shall cry out to one another." Well, Isaiah would have made a good hominologist, I thought. After all, it was not he who called the hairy ones by such names as goblins, satyrs and devils. He used the term derived from the creatures' biological characteristic.

I then happened to look up the New International Version of the Holy Bible, and what did I see? "Wild goats" instead of "satyrs!" "And there wild goats will leap about...", "and wild goats will bleat to each other." What a leap from reality!

Folklore on the Origins of Demons

Hebrew folklore has it that God created the se'irim on the Sabbath eve, and therefore did not have time to make them fully human. But Russian peasants had a different opinion on the matter. When the peasant's son inquired, "Daddy, what is meant by the devil, the leshy, the domovoy? What is the difference between them?" The adult peasant answered, "There is really no difference. They say that when God created man, Satan was eager to create, too, but no matter how hard he tried he could only make devils, not men. When God saw that Satan had already produced several devils, He ordered Archangel Gabriel to dump Satan and his goods from heaven. Gabriel did so. The devil that fell on a wood became the leshy (wood goblin), another, that fell on a field, became the polevoy (field Jewish demon, a "hairy one" in the original Hebrew text of the Bible, and "devil," "satyr," "wild goat" and "he-goat" in various translated Bibles. (Illustration borrowed from the *Universal Jewish Encyclopedia*, article "Demons.") goblin), and a third, that fell on a house, became the domovoy (domestic demon, brownie). That's how they came about and got different names. But actually all devils are alike."

In Bielorussia folklorists recorded the following legend: Adam and Eve had a dozen pairs of children. When God came to look at them, they showed Him six pairs, and hid the other six pairs under an oak. So, like we come from those six pairs shown to God, they (the demons) come from the other six pairs. Their number is the same as ours, only they are invisible because they are hidden from God. A Moslem tale, "On the Origin of Almasty, Jinn and Div," relates that Adam and Eve had an argument. He said that children originate from him. She said they originate from her. To resolve the problem, they agreed to abstain from sex for a certain time, keeping their semen separately. From Adam's semen came living men, and Eve's fluids produced creatures that turned into Almastys, Jinns and Divs.

The "shaitan-pensioner" version, related by a Kabardian Moslem and cited in Part I of this work, relates to this topic as well, but it is not included in my book, which refers only to published material. Less civilized people, living in the lap of nature, had a different and more realistic view on the subject. Thus the Mansi, living in the taiga of Siberia, say that in making people, gods used two materials: clay and larch timber. As soon as people made of larch were produced, they dashed into the forest. Those are "menkvs" (wood goblins). Slow moving beings, made of clay, became ordinary people. Their lifespan is short; arms made of clay, legs made of clay, what's the use of them? If man falls into water, he drowns; if the weather is hot, water comes out of him. If men were made of larch, they would be hardier and wouldn't drown in the water. There are many other folklore versions of the theme, including the belief that demons arise from dead people who were not buried or were buried the wrong way. What is interesting and important for the hominologist in such tales and legends is people's wish to explain both great likeness and great difference between man and demon, and not the essence of the explanations, arising from fantasy and superstition.

The Proverbial Connection
Folklorists define the proverb in this way: An apt and colorful expression summarizing people's observations and reflections regarding various sides of real life. Citing this definition in my book, I note that the proverb has two meanings: one direct and literal, referring to "various sides of real life," and the other indirect and figurative, applied to various episodes and developments of social life. Thus, when people say "It never rains but it pours," or "A bird in the hand is worth two in the bush," or "One shouldn't look a gift horse in the mouth," they use literal, real life meanings in a figurative sense.

So I ask what is the real meaning of the numerous proverbs and sayings of all peoples of the world referring to the devil and other demons. The Russians say, "The devil is not so ugly [or fearsome] as he is painted." The English say, "The devil is not so black as he is painted" and "to paint the devil blacker than he is." The Russians say, "The devil is swarthy from birth, not from the sun." They also say "Brown devil, grry devil, still a devil." Does this not mean that the creators of these proverbs did know the look of the devil?

The Russian equivalent of the English, "Still waters run deep," is "Devils dwell in a quiet slough (pool)." For the hominologist the real meaning of the proverb is quite clear. The famous 19th century lexicographer Vladimir Dahl offers other proverbs and sayings reflecting the devil's aquatic preferences. "To be led to the devil, like the devil to the marsh, "Given a marsh, given the devils," "When devils dive nothing but bubbles arise," "A job [a work assignment] is not a devil, won't disappear into the water," "Worms in the earth, devils in the water, crooks in the court, where can a man go?"

Some more sayings from Vladimir Dahl's *Dictionary of the Russian Language*: "You are as big as the devil [or leshy] but still small in the mind," "You are clever and strong but can't beat the leshy," "Leshy is mute but vociferous," "To roar like a leshy", "Infected with the devil's fleas and lice," "The devil brushed himself and lost his brush." An Arab proverb goes "Azrata min ghoul" (stinking like a ghoul); also quite a familiar sign. A synonym for "demon" in Russian is "unclean spirit." Demons collectively are referred to as "nechistaya sila" (unclean power).

When the Kabardians say "to catch the almasty by head hair," they mean to pull a thing off. The advice and wish "Go to the devil!" and "The devil take you [him, her]" seem to be international. When a needed person appears at last after a long wait the Russians say, "Where has the devil been carrying you?" Enlightened by the Albert Ostman case, the hominologist knows that the latter saying is a reflection of real life as well.

Morphology and Manners

Folklore on demons confirmed all I knew about the homin anatomy and behavior and added things I did not know. The demonic beings are hairy manlike bipeds, often bigger and always stronger than man. There are male and female demons, as well as their offspring. A shock of hair is sometimes mentioned on the heads of males, but bald-headed demons are on record as well. Females boast of long-hanging or flying head hair, sometimes disheveled, sometimes brushed.

The Komi people in the north of Russia say their wood goblins have hair-covered ears. One folklore item in Siberia mentions hair on female breasts. And an item on the Chuvash female wood goblin tells of a hair covered body "except the genitalia," which is a simian characteristic! The hair colour ranges from black to white, with lots of browns and reds, and is likened to the fur of animals native to the particular geographic area (reindeer, bear, camel, goat, buffalo).

The attribute of hairiness is present in the local names of demons, from the Hebrew "se'irim," to the medieval European "pilosus," to the Russian "volosatik" and "volosatka" (literally "hairy one" for male and female).

The colour of the skin is swarthy, with a reddish, or yellowish, or greyish tinge. The pointed, cone-shaped head is a usual feature, even reflected in the names of Russian devils and goblins: "shishko," "shishiga," from "shishka" (cone). The eyes appear big at night when they shine "like stars." Facial features are not, to put it mildly, attractive, since folklore uses the word "muzzle" in reference to a demon's face. Lack of a neck is mentioned in one item from Siberia.

Folklore dwells a lot on the enormous size of a female demon's breasts, calling them "huge" and even "frightening." Mentioned is the size of "about one arshin," an old Russian measure which equals 71 centimetres, or 28 inches. It's noteworthy that hugely hypertrophied breasts, so-called "mamma pendula," hanging down to the middle of the thigh, are sometimes registered in human females, probably as an atavistic trait. In many cases, from different geographic areas of Europe and Asia, the enormous demoniac mammae are said to be carried thrown over the shoulders. Accordingly, there is an observation in folklore that female creatures carry infants on the back and suckle them with breasts thrown over the shoulders. As for *Homo sapiens*, women with breasts thrown over the shoulders are reported among the aborigines of Australia and Africa.

"Devil's Footprints" is the archaeologists' name for a set of petroglyphs (rock carvings) in Karelia (in the west of Russia, bordering on Finland). The scene is a marvellous relic of the heathen past, when the homin was worshipped as the lord of nature and offered bountiful sacrifices. He is shown in the lower right corner of the picture, with a number of true homin features, including the exaggerated big foot. The enormous phallus is not a reflection of anatomy, but rather a symbol of fertility and maybe of satyriasis. The ancient artist carved not only the figure of his god but also a set of his footprints coming across a mass of sacrificed animals, all of which represent the true local fauna. I call this picture of petroglyphs "Bigfoot of Karelia." The illustration is borrowed from the book in Russian *Risunki na skalakh* (*Pictures on the Rocks*) by Yuri Savvateyev, published in Petrozavodsk, capital of Karelia, in 1967.

Demons in Russia are fond of tree-climbing, swinging on the branches, and diving from trees on the river bank into the water. They are excellent swimmers and divers, as well as jumpers and runners. They also love dancing and merrymaking, especially all kinds of pranks, so that Russian peasants called them "jokesters" and "pranksters." A favourite prank of rusalkas was to catch wild geese on the river and entangle the feathers of their wings so that the birds could not fly. Or they would let the fish out of the fishermen's net and fill the latter with slime and water-plants, or divert themselves by putting out a fishermen's or hunters' campfire with the water dripping from their hair covering.

Human-Demon Interactions
In heathen times, the demons were not devils and goblins but "gods" and "lords of nature." People worshipped them not out of superstition but for quite sensible and pragmatic reasons. Going to hunt or to fish they entered the territories of those wild hairy giants, and seeking a *modus vivendi* with them, people had to sacrifice a part of their trophies and catches to the homins. That is the origin of religious sacrifices, whose echoes are still reverberating in folklore.

Bigfoot of Karelia at his best and his footprint that well resembles that of his North American counterpart.

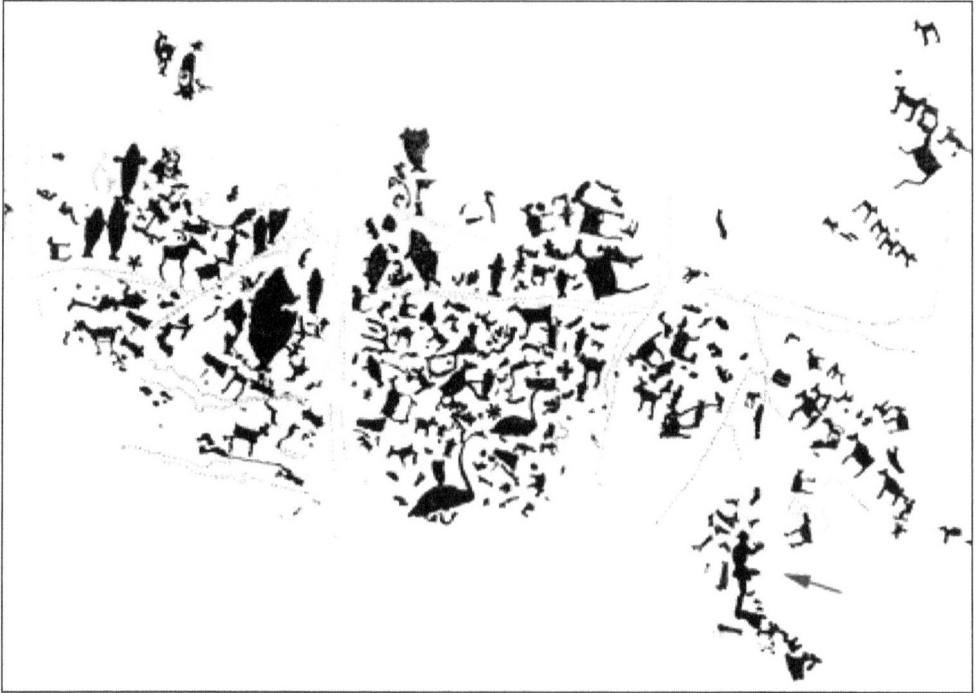

"*Devil's Footprints*" is the archaeologists' name for a set of petroglyphs (rock carvings) in Karelia (in the west of Russia, bordering on Finland). The scene is a marvelous relic of the heathen past, when the homin was worshipped as the lord of nature and offered bountiful sacrifices. He is shown in the lower right corner of the picture, with a number of true homin features, including the exaggerated big foot. The enormous phallus is not a reflection of anatomy, but rather a symbol of fertility and maybe of satyriasis. The ancient artist carved not only the figure of his god but also a set of his footprints coming across a mass of sacrificed animals, all of which represent the true local fauna. I call this picture of petroglyphs "Bigfoot of Karelia." The illustration is borrowed from the book in Russian *Risunki na skalakh* (Pictures on the Rocks) by Yuri Savvateyev, published in Petrozavodsk, capital of Karelia, in 1967.

One folklore item from the European part of Russia, cited in my book, says that in olden days hunters "had to prepare gifts for the 'lord of the forest' for allowing them to hunt on his property." In later times the relationship "progressed" and an item from Siberia says that hunters there engaged in barter trade with wood goblins: the latter supply squirrels and get generous gifts of vodka in exchange. It is most remarkable that squirrel bodies are delivered at night and if the hunters fail to skin them before morning, "the squirrels revive and run away."

Folklore strongly recommends hunters not to build their cabins on the forest path of the wood goblin. And custom forbids whistling in the forest and in the home so as not to alert and invite the goblin. Folk demons also actively interact with fishermen. That homins partake (i.e., steal) of fishermen's catches is well on record, but that they can also help people catch fish was news to me. According to Georgian folklore, all fish in the river are controlled by a water goblin. If a fisherman leaves food and a jug of wine on the bank and speaks nicely of the demon, he will send a lot of fish into the net.

A Mordva fisherman (in the Volga area) discovered a crying goblin child in the fishing net and let it go. Ever since he always had good catches. Ethnic Russian fishermen would throw a bast-shoe into the water and yell: "Hey, devil, drive fish into our net!" But the demons' greatest contractors were herdsmen. It is reported that in Russia they made secret "contracts" with wood goblins who helped pasture the herd, find lost cows, and protect them from wolves and bears. The service was paid for with food and animals from the herd. Such deals were popular with the peasants, but kept strictly secret because they were viewed as very sinful by the Orthodox Church. It is worth mentioning that in ancient Rome fauni were said to protect herds from wolves, and a celebration was held in their honour on the 15th of February, called Lupercalia. Another kind of interaction and category of homin whom I call "visiting demons" are those who approach human habitation for one reason or a combination of them. The most common is food, another clothes, a third the warmth of the hearth. An item from Tajikistan says that when the children asked their mother to give them more pancakes for supper, the mother answered, "If I give you more, what shall we leave for the adjina? She will come at night, and finding nothing may become angry." There are stories in Tajikistan that when the cry of an infant is suddenly heard from a barn, it means that a demon has given birth. People give food to her, "she eats, takes the baby, and goes away."

In Georgia, the ancient clan of Naraani was said to have befriended a dev. They "fed him well," leaving food warm in the ashes of the hearth. When the family went to sleep, he would come and have his fill. If food is not offered, the demons would steal it, all kinds of it, especially vegetables and fruits from gardens and orchards. As a rule, demons are seen naked, but there are many exceptions, and clothing is the next item of interest for them to come into contact with humans. It is advised, when encountering a goblin in the wood, to offer it bread or a piece of clothing, even a torn-off sleeve if nothing else is available. On record are Ukrainian and Bielorussian songs telling how rusalkas beg human girls to give them shirts, no matter how old or tattered. No wonder, demons usually sport threadbare garments, often worn the wrong side out. As a result, when Russians saw a man in a shirt worn inside out, they used to say: "Look, he is (dressed) like a leshy!" The leshy were said to approach campfires built by lumberjacks or hunters in order to warm themselves in cold weather, and it is said that they

Bald demon depicted on a Greek vase.

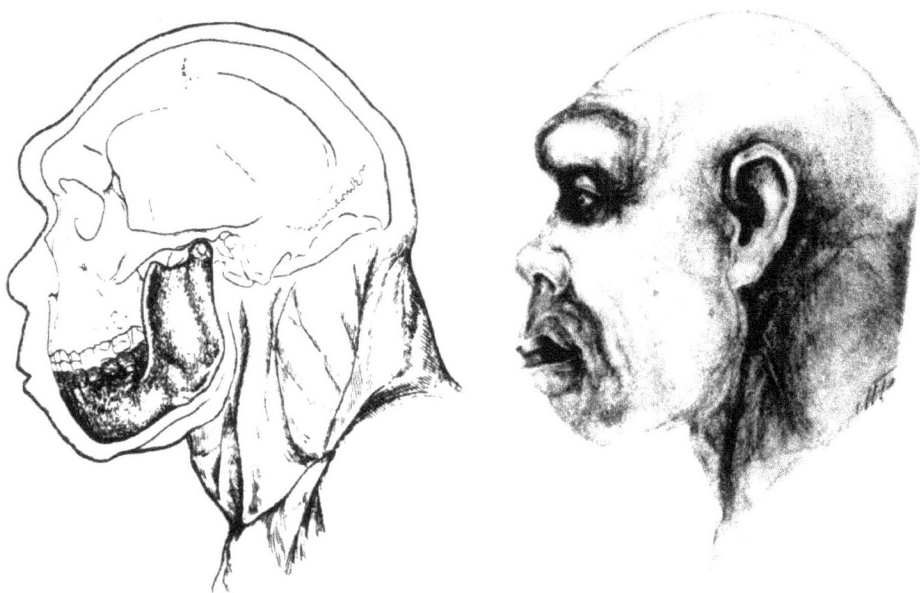

Reconstruction of the head of a paleoanthropus based on the fossil cranium, bearing resemblance to heads of demons.

"turned away their muzzles," apparently because of the bright light. They also took care that flying sparks did not touch their hair.

Seeking warmth they also entered peasant bath huts and barns for crops stocked there. It is reported that a leshy, festooned with icicles, entered a barn and put out a fire with melting ice. In contrast, in the summer they would come up to a campfire not for warmth but to put it out. Folklore is insistent that demons love human children. Hiding from adults, they often come in view of children and even play with them when adults are not around. They are also said to calm down crying babies and, inevitably, as a result of such fondness occasionally take human kids with them. In Bielorussia, a wood goblin was "charged" with stealing a cradle with a baby and hiding it in a birch tree. In the Novgorod province, a boy of 13 was kidnapped by a wood goblin. Four years later the boy returned naked and unable to speak. As mentioned earlier, a Mordva fisherman released a young water demon caught in the net. And there is a Georgian story about an old man who came at night in the wood across a crying boy about 9 years old. He took the boy home and when he and his wife looked at the foundling in the light of the fire burning in the middle of the hut, they realized it was a "chinka" (wood goblin), because he was hairy all over and had red eyes. The old woman began to scold the old man for bringing in a goblin. They tied him up to a bench and showed him to many people in the morning. All agreed that it was a chinka. When untied, the young goblin escaped.

Their Mortality

There was a time, which lasted far longer than the whole of written history, when humans were in the minority and homins in the majority. Then, thanks to agriculture and animal husbandry, human numbers substantially increased and the ratio began to reverse. It was then that kings and high priests, first in Persia, later in Israel and other lands, forbade the worship of "unclean half-man half-beasts," condemned them as "pagan gods," and introduced monotheistic religion instead of polytheistic. The hairy homin was turned into a "devil" and declared an enemy. The echo of those events is heard most clearly in the Persian epic Shah Namah, based on popular legends and traditions. It describes fierce battles waged by the kings of the country against an enemy called alternatively "divs" and "devils." Though the latter displayed miracles of physical force, they battled with their bare hands against human warriors wielding swords and spears. Inevitably, pagan gods suffered heavy casualties, proving beyond doubt their mortality.

Geographer and traveller Pausanias (2nd century A. D.), in his *Description of Greece*, says that the silenus race must be mortal, since their graves are known. He also says that when satyrs grow old, they are called silenoi. There are many examples of demon killings in folklore. According to one item from Siberia, a reduction in wood goblin numbers there was due to the appearance of hunting guns. Some tales relate that hunters, having killed a demon, cut off parts of its body, sometimes the head, as souvenirs and valuable trophies. Obviously, encounters with human beings wielding firearms boded no good for "mythical beings" and that is a reason for their legendary seclusion.

There are also plenty of beliefs that demon killers suffer inevitable retribution for the deed. Chuvash folklore intimates that in a village where "upate" (half-man) were killed, population no longer increased. Tatars had similar beliefs, and when they saw a little poor village, they used to say, "Shurale kargagan" (condemned by shurale, the latter word meaning wood goblin). An example from Azerbaijan mentions a hunter who fired pointblank at a "biaban-ghouli," who fell to the ground, then stood up and ran away, leaving behind a bloody trail. After that, the hunter sold his gun and never hunted again. Asked why, he answered, "After that all my children died." A parallel First Nations tale was published in 1929 in Canada by J. W. Burns and reprinted by John Green in *The Sasquatch File*, 1973, p. 11.

Cases of demons imprisoned by humans are also numerous in folklore. A creature, especially young, could get entangled, as already mentioned, in a fishing net. To catch migratory birds, the Russians used to hang a huge net on the trees of a forest vista. It happened sometimes that instead of wild ducks and geese, the hunters found a devil in the net. The technical term for that kind of net is "pereves." So there appeared a proverb, "popalsya kak bes v pereves," (caught like a devil in a net). From Tatar folklore we learn that the inhabitants of a village, tired from the tricks by a shurale (wood goblin) that troubled their herd of horses every night, spread tar on the back of the best horse and by this ploy caught a she-demon who had tried to ride that horse.

But the surest and most ancient method of catching demons was by intoxicating them with wine, of course. In ancient Greece it was used by King Midas, who caught a silenus; in Italy by King Numa Pompilius, who caught a faun. Being so rare and impressive, these events were recorded by legend. The only modification in the method in Russia is that wine is replaced by vodka. A tale from Abkhazia had it that a wood goblin that meddled with hunters' traps was caught only after imbibing a bucketful of vodka.

The Sexual Connection

Folklore and demonology present this as one of the most prominent factors in human-demon relations. To begin with the ancient world, according to legend the Babylonian King Gilgamesh habituated and befriended the half-man half-beast Enkidu with the help of the priestess of the goddess of love, Ishtar. Enkidu is said to have been shaggy with "hair that sprouted like grain," he ate with the gazelles and drank with the wild beasts at their waterholes. He protected wild animals from hunters, so a hunter went to King Gilgamesh with a request for help. The king recommended that the hunter take a priestess of Ishtar with him to the waterhole and instruct her to take off her clothes, thus enticing Enkidu away from his animal friends. The ruse succeeded and the wildman enjoyed the woman's favours for a week, being gradually persuaded to eat bread and drink wine with the shepherds. He became their friend Assyro–Babylonian demon Humbaba, lord of cedar forests in the mountains, who did not allow people to cut them. According to legend, King Gilgamesh, helped by his befriended wildman Enkidu, fiercely battled with Humbaba and killed him, and helped them by driving lions away from the flocks. Subsequently Enkidu found himself in the palace of Gilgamesh and became the king's best friend and aid in hunting. He also helped Gilgamesh in fighting the monstrous demon Humbaba, actually a wildman in the forested mountains of Lebanon.

Lustfulness was a distinguishing trait of satyrs in ancient Greece. Historian Diodorus Siculus wrote that, "this animal [!] shamelessly seeks cross-breeding." The situation is reflected and recorded in the medical terms "satyriasis" and "nymphomania."

But for readers in the West, most significant and impressive is one more reference to the *Holy Bible*. Among the commandments by the Lord that Moses gave to Israel was this: "And they shall no more sacrifice their victims to devils, with whom they have committed fornication. It shall be an ordinance for ever to them and their posterity." (Leviticus 17:7, *The Holy Bible*, Douay Version, reproduced from the first edition of *The Old Testament*, printed at Douay in 1609.) Another translation in *The Holy Bible*, London, 1850: "And they shall no more offer their sacrifices unto devils, after whom they have gone a whoring. This shall be a statute for ever unto them throughout their generations."

A third version, published in *The New English Bible*, Oxford, 1970: "They shall no longer sacrifice their slaughtered beasts to the demons whom they wantonly follow."

Let us note that, according to the Hebrew text, Moses did not use the words "devils" or "demons" in this commandment by the Lord. Again the term "se'irim" (hairy ones) was used, which presented a sticking point for the translators. "Hairy ones," and moreover sacrifices to and fornication with them, called for an explanation; "wild goats" would not fit in this case. So "devils" and "demons" were found to be preferable terms, for who does not know that devils and demons are seducers and perverters of mankind?

The Assyro–Babylonian demon Humbaba, lord of cedar forests in the mountains, who did not allow people to cut them.

Christianity also condemned "pagan gods" for lustfulness. Saint Augustine wrote that fauns and satyrs, "called at present incubuses," have intercourse with women. "This has been testified to by so many people and so positively that it would be insolent to deny this." In the Middle Ages in Europe, many victims of the Inquisition were tortured and condemned to burn for sex with demons.

In Asia, the 12th century Persian scholar Nizami al-Arudi wrote that "the Nasnas, a creature inhabiting the plains of Turkestan, of erect carriage and vertical stature, […] is very curious about man. […] And if it sees a lonely man it abducts him and is said to be able to conceive by him. This, after mankind, is the highest of animals…" Modern scholars say the Nasnas is an imaginary creature, a kind of faun. Sexual relations with demons is a topic present in all works on folklore that I read and referred to in my book. In Tajik folklore, the female demon "pari" seeks the love of a hunter and pays him with wild goats that she sends him in gratitude. In Chuvash folklore, the female arsuri (goblin dubbed monkey) would run in the wood in front of a man, laughing impudently, showing him her genitalia and beckoning to him. The name "arsuri" is applied by the Chuvash to a shameless woman.

In Circassian folklore it is said that the shaitan and his female partner jinne can be caught. However it is not advisable to catch a shaitan because he will offer strong resistance. Jinne is a different matter. If caught, she can be used as a woman. Sometimes she herself is seeking sex with humans, coming to herdsmen for the purpose. In Bielorussian folklore there is a beautiful poetic incantation intended for young male peasants in case they are accosted by an enamoured rusalka. It is pointed out that the man should not look at her, but at the ground, and say the following (in my rather inadequate translation): Water dweller, wood denizen, wild, unruly and whimsical girl! Go away, get away, don't show up at my homestead! […] I kissed the golden cross and abide by the Christian faith, so can't mix with you. Go to the pine forest, to the forest lord. He has prepared a bed of moss and grass and is waiting for you. You are to sleep with him, not with a Christian like me. Amen.

The most characteristic trait of rusalkas, known from folklore and poetry to all Russians, is their habit of accosting a young man bathing in a lake or river, and, with much delight and merriment, 'tickling him to death' (i.e., until he drowns). And that is exactly what the 'madwoman' in the case of Turgenev was prepared to do: 'touched his neck, his back and his legs with little cacklings of delight.' Had Turgenev not been 'a splendid swimmer,' Russian and world literature would have suffered a heavy loss from the hands of a rusalka. The business of tickling, as part of lovemaking, is ascribed not only to Russian rusalkas, but also to their counterparts in the folklore of Tatars, Bashkirs, Kazakhs, etc. (Let's recall a case in Kabarda that I related in Part I of this work.) And what is most interesting and important, it is also typical of anthropoid apes, as observed by the famous English primatologist Jane Goodall. (…) Returning to rusalkas, the danger of drowning from their caresses was once so real for Russian countrymen that people invented a very simple but potent means of defense: just a pin or needle held at ready while bathing. Folklore has it that it is enough to give rusalka a pin-prick or show her a needle to make her flee. (Ibid., pp. 173, 174).

Crossbreeding

The basic difference of demons from all real creatures, including apes and monkeys, is their desire of sexual relations with man. Clearly, this circumstance is responsible for their unprecedented and unique role in the history of mankind. A Russian specialist on oriental folklore and the *Koran* wrote in 1893 about the demons called "jinn": "The peculiarity of their nature is that they can have sexual intercourse with people." A natural question then is: What comes as a result of such intercourse? Folklore is quite talkative on this score. An item from Siberia: "Sometimes a she-devil cohabits with hunters in the forest and becomes pregnant from them, but she tears the infant apart at its very birth." The Circassian jinne can also kill her crossbreed baby, in case her human husband reveals her presence to his neighbours. A success story in crossbreeding is reported by Kazakh folklore, telling of a horse herdsman who encountered a female almasty in the steppe and thought, "Be it a shaitan or a human, it doesn't matter." He lived with her and "they had three children born to them."

Bashkir folklore explains the origin of the name of the Shaitan-Kudey clan by the fact that once a brave Bashkir caught and married a female shaitan and their posterity formed the said clan. Nogai folklore notes the rapid growth and unusual strength of the offspring of their legendary hunter Kutlukai and his almasty wife. Their son became a national hero and all Nogai nobility descend from him. If we give credence in this respect to folklore, then hominology is faced with the question: What is the genetic status of "demons," i.e., homins, in relation to *Homo sapiens*?

"Good" species are not supposed to produce fertile crossbreeds. Still, division into species and subspecies of closely related organisms is often a matter of speculation and agreement. Primatologists are aware of fertile hybrids of different monkey species. Another case in point is the example of wolves and coyotes, considered to be different species. Yet they carry the same number of chromosomes and there exist no genetic barriers to their interbreeding. If not for behavioural differences, which keep them separate, one species would have long ago absorbed the other. The homin-human situation appears to be similar; the barrier to crossbreeding is neurological and behavioral, not genetic. For these reasons it can be overcome in principle and in practice, but the process has been "invisible" and very protracted.

One more example in favour of this view is a quote from *Essays on Russian Mythology* (1916) by D. K. Zelenin: "People believe that if a rusalka is made to wear the cross, she will become a human being. Such cases are reported from the Vladimir Province, where two boys married baptized rusalkas."

As regards North America, Dr. Ed Fusch reports crossbreeds between Indians and the "Stick Indians" (Sasquatch, "Night People") in S'cwen'yti and the Stick Indians of the Colvilles (1992). (Posted by Bobbie Short on her Bigfoot Encounters site and supplied to me by the late Don Davis.)

The Domovoy

Regarding contact with humans, demons can be divided into those:

1)   who avoid any contacts (Russian folklore calls them "free" and "free roaming" beings);
2)   who meet with people occasionally (I call them "visiting demons"). Reasons for contact, as already mentioned, can be food handouts or payment for certain services or "barter trade"; warmth of the hearth, sexual contacts;
3)   who are staying permanently on a homestead.

The latter subdivision includes:

a)   she-demons "married" to humans and,
b)   former "visiting demons," grown old and unable to provide for themselves on their own.

For obvious reasons, category "3a" is shrouded in great secrecy and there is little information on it. Category "3b" is less cryptic and provides some interesting material. The general Russian term for a demon dwelling in a homestead is "domovoy" (literally, "domestic one"). There are male and female "domestic ones," but most information is about the male.

An 18th century book, *Descriptions of Old Slavic Heathen Fables*, has this to say about the domovoys: "These imaginary half-gods were called 'geniuses' by the ancients, the Slavs called them 'protectors of places and homes,' while modern superstitious simpletons take them for 'domestic devils.'"

Domovoy is described as an old, sometimes very old, man, hairy all over, and with a pointed, cone-shaped head. He lives in the stable or the cattle-shed, and as noted by folklorists, "deals more with the livestock than with people"; "caring for the cattle is his most frequently mentioned function in folklore."

The great 19th century lexicographer Vladimir Dahl, in his work, *On the Beliefs, Superstitions and Prejudices of the Russian People*, wrote that: Generally speaking, domovoy is not a malicious character, but rather a mischievous one. If he likes a person or a person's home, he becomes an obedient servant; but if he dislikes someone, he can evict that person or even cause his death. His service can be like this: cleaning, sweeping and tidying up in the house at night; above all he likes horses, cleaning and brushing them, and plaiting their manes and tails; sometimes he mounts a steed and rides from one end of the village to the other. Sometimes domovoy plays pranks on women, especially if they are silly and loudmouthed, [...]. Results of his pranks can be seen in the morning, for example, all dishes can be found in the slops bucket, stools and benches broken or piled up in a corner of the room.

It is remarkable that domovoy does not like mirrors; some think that mirrors can repel him from the room where he likes to play pranks [...]. In some regions nobody would pronounce the word 'domovoy' out of fear; that is why he has so many other names, including the honorary appellation 'grandfather.'

Russian domovoy. A drawing by artist Ivan Bilibin who studied and illustrated Russian folklore. The drawing was made in 1934 long before the birth of hominology. The domovoy is shown inside a peasant home. Note his coned head and long finger nails

At night domovoy can stroke a sleeping person's face with his hand, which feels furry, and with long cold fingernails. In the winter one can see his tracks in the snow near the stable, but the maker of them is only seen on rare occasions. "Domovoy hates the curious," says Dahl. He describes a special religious procedure which, according to peasant beliefs, helps in seeing a domovoy. The latter is then observed in the light of a candle crouched and hiding in a corner of a cattle-shed or a stable. "Then you can talk to him." In his Dictionary, Vladimir Dahl says that, "Domovoy can be seen on Good Sunday's night in the cattle-shed; he is shaggy, but nothing else can be remembered because he knocks out memory."

Still, not everybody's memory is completely knocked out, for other folklorists add certain details to those supplied by Dahl. Such, for example, as "domovoy is about the size of a bear and covered with long soft fur of a dark brown color. But it is impossible to see his figure in detail because he quickly disappears." Another folklorist writes that,

"He is like a man of medium height, stooping, wide-shouldered, stocky, covered with long hair (in colour can be dark or white or skewbald)." An item from Siberia says that domovoy can be seen "in the image of a man resembling an ape depicted in pictures, but only much more ugly than a monstrous ape."

To avoid coming face-to-face with such a monster, Russian peasants had the custom of repeated coughing when going out into the yard at night. As for domovoy's vocal ability, Dahl writes that the "grandfather" can tease horses by neighing like a horse. Another folklorist says domovoy can "frighten people at night by yelling or crying." Sounds made by domovoy were believed to be prophetic: if he laughs, it's a good omen, and if he makes "hoo, hoo, hoo!," it's a bad omen. It was mentioned earlier that domestic demons were also called "protectors of places and homes." An item from Siberia, supporting this belief, goes like this: Domovoy does not like it when someone enters his territory without permission. For example, if a stranger comes to a house to spend the night, he should address domovoy with the words, 'Grandfather, let me spend the night here.' Otherwise domovoy can do bad things to the stranger at night; can press him or even throw out of the house. He especially dislikes tipsy strangers. Should a drunken man spend the night in somebody else's home without asking domovoy for permission, the latter would not fail to throw the man out. Such cases are known, and the victims were frozen to death in the yard, or got the feet and hands frozen if this happened in the winter.

But most of all the domovoy cares for cattle and one of his many appellations is, "cattle feeder." "If domovoy loves a horse or a cow, or sheep, he steals hay for them from the homestead owner if the latter does not feed his animals well. If the owner has no hay at all and the animals remain hungry, domovoy goes to another homestead and steals hay there for his animals." There are even stories about "domovoy fights over hay which they steal from each other. In some cases domovoys would appeal to humans for help. […] In the Kaluga Province peasants said that when domovoys are fighting, it is necessary to cry: 'Hey, our own, beat that stranger!'"

Domovoy's love of cattle was not entirely altruistic, of course. "A housewife, going into the yard or cattle-shed, would catch him milking a cow, but on seeing her he would immediately disappear." A salient feature of domovoys noted by folklore is their cryptic character: "Domovoy hates the curious." By leading a nocturnal and secluded way of life they managed to escape observation not only by scholars and educated people, but even by most peasants amongst whom they were living, remaining always mysterious and legendary creatures. There are many references in folklore to the leshy (wood goblin) as big as Bigfoot, but no mention of similar big domovoys. Apparently giant homins were too frightening and gluttonous for the role of a domestic demon. So there must have been selection of candidates of appropriate size for the domovoy niche.

Vladimir Dahl cites a proverb which is rhymed in Russian and translates: (domovoy) "has abandoned the devil but has not joined people either." The word "devil" implies here a giant homin free roaming in the wild. And I see at least two reasons for domovoy's failure to "join people." Firstly, his advanced age, when it is too late to learn human ways; secondly, people's overly emotional behaviour in the presence of the domestic demon. On the whole, folklore studies confirmed and clarified for me some things I learned on expeditions to the Caucasus, as described in Part I. Both folklore and field investigations have convinced me that the domovoy is still a reality.

The Brownie
According to the Russian-English dictionary, the English for "domovoy" is "brownie." Having learned that, I began to look for literature on the subject, and was delighted to discover in the best public library catalog a pointer to, *The Brownies: Their Book*, by Palmer Cox, published in New York in 1887. Yet great was my disappointment when I opened the book; it turned out to contain only verses which had nothing to do with brownies in the flesh. Later I read the following about this book in *Encyclopedia Britannica*: In 1883 the Brownies created by Palmer Cox, author and illustrator for *St. Nicholas Magazine*, were introduced to American children. Suggested by Scottish legends but modified to fit the contemporaneous scene, Cox's creatures of fantasy delighted children for 30 years. His series of drawings, "The Brownies," in *St. Nicholas Magazine* depicted the astonishing adventures of a race of benevolent little people. The only bit of prose in Cox's book was this introduction: Brownies, like fairies and goblins, are imaginary little spirits, who are supposed to delight in harmless pranks and helpful deeds. They work and sport while weary households sleep, and never allow themselves to be seen by mortal eyes.

Having found no special work on the theme, I had nothing but dictionaries and encyclopedias to go by. Their entries on "brownie" have been written and "modified" by folklore scholars, but even so present certain points of interest for the hominologist. The following is what I read and copied after publication of my book on folklore in 1991: *The Concise Oxford Dictionary of Current English,* first edition 1911: brownie: Benevolent shaggy goblin haunting house & doing household work secretly. *The Oxford English Dictionary*, second edition, vol. 2, Oxford, 1989: brownie. Also browny, and with capital initial. (denominative of BROWN, with somewhat of diminutive force). A 'wee brown man' often appears in Scottish ballads and fairy tales. A benevolent spirit or goblin, of shaggy appearance, supposed to haunt old houses, esp. farmhouses, in Scotland, and sometimes to perform useful household work while the family were asleep.

Webster's New International Dictionary, 1947: brownie: (From its supposed tawny or swarthy color). A good-natured goblin supposed to perform helpful services by night, such as threshing, churning, and sweeping. *The Everyman's Encyclopaedia*, London, New York, 1913, Vol. 3: Brownie, in the folklore of Scotland a goblin of the most obliging kind. He was never seen, but was only known by the good deeds which he did. He usually attached himself to some farmhouse in the country, and he was only noted by the voluntary labour which he performed during the night. He would churn, or thrash the corn, or clean all the dairy utensils, or perform some equally good-natured labour. His work was always done at night. The country people had great faith in the good works of the B. and believed in him implicitly. His reward was usually a dish of cream. The B. bears a strong resemblance to Robin Goodfellow in the Eng. and the Kobold of Ger. literature, whilst some comparison can be made between him and the household gods of the Roms. And of the domovoy. The Bs. were often the cause of the mysterious disappearance of things, and in this respect can be compared with the Jans, or Jennis, of the Arabs, and also to the pixies of South-western England. Practically every known folklore has its special fairy which can be compared to the brownie.

The New Encyclopedia Britannica, Vol. 2, Chicago, 1993: Brownie, in English and Scottish folklore, a small industrious fairy or hobgoblin believed to inhabit houses and barns. Rarely seen, he was often heard at night, cleaning and doing housework; he also sometimes mischievously disarranged rooms. He would ride for the midwife, and in Cornwall he caused swarming bees to settle quickly. Cream or bread and milk might be left for him, but other gifts offended him. If one made him a suit of clothes, he would put it on and then vanish, never to return. The boggart of Yorkshire and the bogle of Scotland are hostile, mischievous brownies indistinguishable for poltergeists. See also puck.

The Encyclopedia Americana, International Edition, Vol. 4, New York, 1973: Brownie, a household spirit or goblin of English and Scottish folklore. Usually pictured as a tiny old man wearing a brown hood and coat, the brownie would attach himself to families and help with the chores. At night, while the family slept, the brownie would sweep rooms, clean pots and pans, and occasionally help with farm animals. Stories were told of a brownie riding horseback to fetch the midwife at child birth or helping his master to win at checkers. Mischievous as well as helpful, brownies were thought to take revenge, when criticized, by breaking dishes, spilling or souring the milk, or turning the animals loose. A helpful brownie would have a bowl of milk or cream and a special cake left for him, but any other kind of reward or wages would only anger him. If given a new suit of clothes, the brownie would put them on, chanting, "Gie brownie coat, gie brownie sork / Ye'll get nae mair o'brownie's work," and disappear, never to return. Similarities can be seen between the brownie and the boggart, or bogle, also in the folklore of Scotland, and such household spirits as the Kobold in Germany and the nisse in the Scandinavian countries.

Their Gifts and Abilities

The history of man's relations with homins is full of ambivalence. The wild hairy bipeds were believed at one time or another, or at the same time, to be gods, semi-gods, devils, half-men and wildmen. Accordingly, views on their gifts and abilities have been varied and contradictory. One exception though is the unanimity of opinion regarding their physical endowment. All popular demons of both sexes are far better athletes than humans. Many folk tales relate of athletic competitions between man and demon, and every time man would resort to ruse and trickery to "win" the round. On record is Pliny the Elder's phrase in *Natural History*: "the Satyrs have nothing of ordinary humanity about them except human shape." The hominologist, at his present stage of knowledge, tends to both agree and disagree with the ancient scholar. The beings in question are undoubtedly very different from ordinary humanity, and at the same time they are like human beings not only in shape but in many other respects as well. The ancients believed satyrs to be gods and semi-gods, which did not prevent Hesiod from saying that these "brothers of mountain nymphs [were] an idle and worthless race." Idle…if this means that satyrs and their ilk do not earn a living by labour, it is correct. For all we know today, they lead an animal way of life. We also know today that some animals make and use tools that help them obtain nourishment. How about demons in this respect?

There is mention of clubs in the hands of wood goblins, but no mention of stone tools, just use of stones as projectiles. There are though references to tools taken from man. Rusalkas, for example, were seen with a pestle in the hand; they were often described combing their hair with combs, apparently taken from peasant bath huts which they visited; one item said the comb was made of a fish backbone.

A peasant once observed a rusalka standing in the water and looking into it as if into a mirror, smartening herself up. This shows, I wrote, how immensely close the rusalka intellect is to human. Folklore avers that rusalkas make wreaths of flowers, sedge, and tree branches, and put them on their heads. Let us also note that satyrs, nymphs, fauns, etc., are often depicted adorned with wreaths. Pan, the great god of flocks and shepherds, when tired of striking panic into man, would start playing on a flute. There are also pictures of satyrs on Greek vases doing the same. Pan is even credited with inventing the shepherd's flute, the syrinx. Satyrs, nymphs, oriental paris, and Russian rusalkas love dancing and merrymaking, which is credible enough, but I always doubted that demons not only dance but also play music and invented a musical instrument. So I wondered why the Greeks credited them with such gifts. Recently I happened to read Dr. Henner Fahrenbach's report on sasquatches imitating "even short phrases on a flute." This prompted me to think that when a Greek shepherd played on a flute, Pan and company, well hidden in the wood, simply imitated the sounds, and hence the origin of the legend.

Demons can wear clothes, given by humans or stolen from them.

The clothes are usually old, tattered, and worn inside-out. There is mention of wood goblins tearing off bast from trees and trying to make bast shoes (maybe in imitation of similar work by peasants). One item tells of a rusalka that made a cradle for her baby out of a birch-tree bark. In this connection let us recall Albert Ostman's words about sasquatches: "...they had some kind of blankets woven of narrow strips of cedar bark, packed with dry moss. They looked very practical and warm – with no need of washing."

I mentioned already various activities of demons helping humans - in hunting, fishing, pasturing, as well as in household work. Such activities are viewed very positively in folklore, with only a few exceptions. For example, regarding the Georgian dev mentioned earlier, it is said that when people were making hay on a hill, during the night the dev carried all the haystacks to the hilltop, while hay was needed in the valley below. "The people thought to themselves: 'Why wouldn't he carry the stacks down instead of uphill?' The next night the dev brought all the hay down."

The work of household she-demons is highly praised, but it is noted that they can't bake bread because they burn their hands. In regard of fire, it is clear that demons are not afraid of it: they approach campfires and hearths to warm themselves and they are able to put out fire, but are never said to be able to make it. Demons can laugh; in sorrow their women and children would weep. They can sing, whistle, and imitate cries of various animals and voices of people (males, females, and babies). As for the crucial question of speech, the answer in folklore is generally negative. Several examples to this effect are cited in my book, including the method, recommended by the Jewish Talmud, of telling a demon in the dark. If you happen to run into someone in the dark and can't tell who it is in front of you, the Talmud recommends saying "Shalom!" (Hello). If the greeting is not returned, chances are you are facing a demon. The same device is mentioned in Georgian folklore, using Georgian "Gamarjoba!" instead of "Shalom."

Folklore mentions demons resorting to gestures and fingers when communicating with humans. Vladimir Dahl writes that demons "sing without words," that their mumbling heard from a distance can be taken for speech, and peasants would interpret it in a jocular way (as if meaning "Walked, found, lost" or "Worse off every year"), but when coming face-to-face with a demon it would become clear that he is speechless. Discussing communication abilities of demons-alias-homins, we have to take into consideration the long-held views in favour of their so-called extrasensory perception. At the 1978 Sasquatch conference in Vancouver, Dr. James R. Butler contributed a paper entitled "The Theoretical Importance of Higher Sensory Perceptions in the Sasquatch Phenomenon." He wrote:

"The term 'telepathy' (feeling from a distance) was coined by Frederick W. Myers as early as 1882 to denote 'the communication of impressions of any kind from one mind to another, independent of the recognized channels of sense.' [...] Our present civilization has perhaps overemphasized the value of the cerebral cortex because of our reliance on language and our insistence upon rationality. Also, the absence of selective environmental pressures has not genetically favored the continued development of HSP. [...] There is increasing documentation supporting the existence of unknown sensory channels in both human beings and other animals. If we accept this documentation, we would have to theoretically accept the probability of its occurrence in a Sasquatch. [...] It is hopeful that the Sasquatch investigation will soon shift from the pages of mythology into the physical and behavioral sciences. When increased emphasis is placed upon direct behavioral observations of Sasquatches, collecting data from field observations may not be as easy as it sounds unless we are prepared to apply new methodologies aligned with the problems imposed by HSPs." (*In The Sasquatch and Other Unknown Hominoids*, ed. by V. Markotic and G. Krantz, Calgary, 1984, pp. 207, 213, 215.)

It is also of relevance here what Arnold J. Toynbee, a well-known British historian, had to say on the subject of language and telepathy: Man shares with some other species of living creature the powers of communicating with his fellows telepathically. In human society, however, this faculty has been pushed into the margin of intercourse by language. This more effective medium of communication is possessed by all human beings in all societies and is one of the distinctive marks of being human. In spite of our command of language, telepathy is still an indispensable means of communication for human beings too. [...] However, language is a more copious means of communication than telepathy is. Like telepathy, language can communicate feelings and impulses, but it can also communicate thoughts, which telepathy can convey, if at all, only when they have a strong emotional charge - and emotion is the enemy of intellectual clarity and objectivity. (*Change and Habit* by Arnold J. Toynbee, Oxford University Press, London, 1966, p. 16.)

A depiction of a Jewish demon

We have learned recently from Boris Porshnev's archive that he accepted the possibility of telepathic abilities in relict hominids. There are certain hints and signs in folklore and demonology, including the material of this work, suggesting the presence of homins' hypnotic and telepathic powers. Similar signs are also present in accounts of witnesses collected by investigators. Such evidence, along with sporadically reported indications of homins' speech faculty, is the subject of both on-going and future studies.

* * *

Folklore is the richest source of information for the hominologist and, at the same time, an obstacle that has to be overcome on the way to the truth. Wood Goblin Dubbed Monkey serves this double aim. The book ends up with the question: "Will goblins help the world of science to open its eyes on what was clear to Boris Porshnev over twenty years ago?"

STILL ON THE TRACK OF UNKNOWN ANIMALS

T
he Centre for Fortean Zoology, or CFZ, is a non profit-making organisation founded in 1992 with the aim of being a clearing house for information, and coordinating research into mystery animals around the world.

We also study out of place animals, rare and aberrant animal behaviour, and Zooform Phenomena; little-understood "things" that appear to be animals, but which are in fact nothing of the sort, and not even alive (at least in the way we understand the term).

Not only are we the biggest organisation of our type in the world, but - or so we like to think - we are the best. We are certainly the only truly global cryptozoological research organisation, and we carry out our investigations using a strictly scientific set of guidelines. We are expanding all the time and looking to recruit new members to help us in our research into mysterious animals and strange creatures across the globe.

Why should you join us? Because, if you are genuinely interested in trying to solve the last great mysteries of Mother Nature, there is nobody better than us with whom to do it.

Members get a four-issue subscription to our journal *Animals & Men*. Each issue contains nearly 100 pages packed with news, articles, letters, research papers, field reports, and even a gossip column! The magazine is Royal Octavo in format with a full colour cover. You also have access to one of the world's largest collections of resource material dealing with cryptozoology and allied disciplines, and people from the CFZ membership regularly take part in fieldwork and expeditions around the world.

The CFZ is managed by a three-man board of trustees, with a non-profit making trust registered with HM Government Stamp Office. The board of trustees is supported by a Permanent Directorate of full and part-time staff, and advised by a Consultancy Board of specialists - many of whom are world-renowned experts in their particular field. We have regional representatives across the UK, the USA, and many other parts of the world, and are affiliated with

You'll find that the people at the CFZ are friendly and approachable. We have a thriving forum on the website which is the hub of an ever-growing electronic community. You will soon find your feet. Many members of the CFZ Permanent Directorate started off as ordinary members, and now work full-time chasing monsters around the world.

Write to us, e-mail us, or telephone us. The list of future projects on the website is not exhaustive. If you have a good idea for an investigation, please tell us. We may well be able to help.

We are always looking for volunteers to join us. If you see a project that interests you, do not hesitate to get in touch with us. Under certain circumstances we can help provide funding for your trip. If you look on the future projects section of the website, you can see some of the projects that we have pencilled in for the next few years.

In 2003 and 2004 we sent three-man expeditions to Sumatra looking for Orang-Pendek - a semi-legendary bipedal ape. The same three went to Mongolia in 2005. All three members started off merely subscribers to the CFZ magazine. Next time it could be you!

We have no magic sources of income. All our funds come from donations, membership fees, and sales of our publications and merchandise. We are always looking for corporate sponsorship, and other sources of revenue. If you have any ideas for fund-raising please let us know. However, unlike other cryptozoological organisations in the past, we do not live in an intellectual ivory tower. We are not afraid to get our hands dirty, and furthermore we are not one of those organisations where the membership have to raise money so that a privileged few can go on expensive foreign trips. Our research teams, both in the UK and abroad, consist of a mixture of experienced and inexperienced personnel. We are truly a community, and work on the premise that the benefits of CFZ membership are open to all.

Reports of our investigations are published on our website as soon as they are available. Preliminary reports are posted within days of the project finishing.

Each year we publish a 200 page yearbook

We have a thriving YouTube channel, CFZtv, which has well over two hundred self-made documentaries, lecture appearances, and episodes of our monthly webTV show. We have a daily online magazine, which has over a million hits each year.

Each year since 2000 we have held our annual convention - the Weird Weekend. It is three days of lectures, workshops, and excursions. But most importantly it is a chance for members of the CFZ to meet each other, and to talk with the members of the permanent directorate in a relaxed and informal setting and preferably with a pint of beer in one hand. Since 2006 - the Weird Weekend has been bigger and better and held on the third weekend in August in the idyllic rural location of Woolsery in North Devon.

Since relocating to North Devon in 2005 we have become ever more closely involved with other community organisations, and we hope that this trend will continue. We have also worked closely with Police Forces across the UK as consultants for animal mutilation cases, and we intend to forge closer links with the coastguard and other community services. We want to work closely with those who regularly travel into the Bristol Channel, so that if the recent trend of exotic animal visitors to our coastal waters continues, we can be out there as soon as possible.

Apart from having been the only Fortean Zoological organisation in the world to have consistently published material on all aspects of the subject for over a decade, we have achieved the following concrete results:

• Disproved the myth relating to the headless so-called sea-serpent carcass of Durgan beach in Cornwall 1975
• Disproved the story

of the 1988 puma skull of Lustleigh Cleave

- Carried out the only in-depth research ever into the mythos of the Cornish Owlman.
- Made the first records of a tropical species of lamprey
- Made the first records of a luminous cave gnat larva in Thailand
- Discovered a possible new species of British mammal - the beech marten
- In 1994-6 carried out the first archival fortean zoological survey of Hong Kong
- In the year 2000, CFZ theories were confirmed when a new species of lizard was added to the British List
- Identified the monster of Martin Mere in Lancashire as a giant wels catfish
- Expanded the known range of Armitage's skink in the Gambia by 80%
- Obtained photographic evidence of the remains of Europe's largest known pike
- Carried out the first ever in-depth study of the ninki-nanka
- Carried out the first attempt to breed Puerto Rican cave snails in captivity
- Were the first European explorers to visit the `lost valley` in Sumatra
- Published the first ever evidence for a new tribe of pygmies in Guyana
- Published the first evidence for a new species of caiman in Guyana

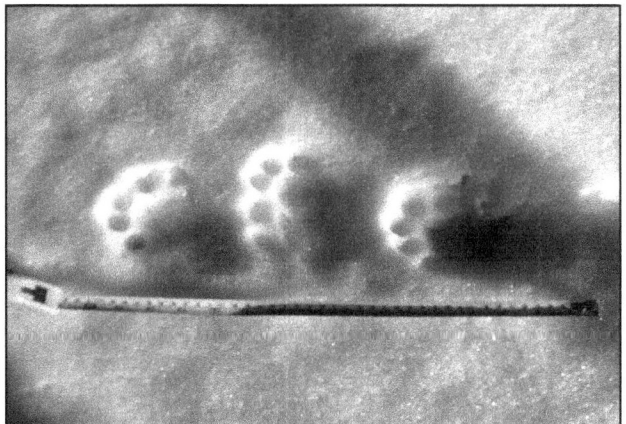

on a monster-haunted lake in Ireland for the first time

• Had a sighting of orang pendek in Sumatra in 2009
• Found leopard hair, subsequently identified by DNA analysis, from rural North Devon in 2010
• Brought back hairs which appear to be from an unknown primate in Sumatra
• Published some of the best evidence ever for the almasty in southern Russia

CFZ Expeditions and Investigations include:

• 1998 Puerto Rico, Florida, Mexico (Chupacabras)
• 1999 Nevada (Bigfoot)
• 2000 Thailand (Naga)
• 2002 Martin Mere (Giant catfish)
• 2002 Cleveland (Wallaby mutilation)
• 2003 Bolam Lake (BHM Reports)

- 2003 Sumatra (Orang Pendek)
- 2003 Texas (Bigfoot; giant snapping turtles)
- 2004 Sumatra (Orang Pendek; cigau, a sabre-toothed cat)
- 2004 Illinois (Black panthers; cicada swarm)
- 2004 Texas (Mystery blue dog)
- Loch Morar (Monster)
- 2004 Puerto Rico (Chupacabras; carnivorous cave snails)
- 2005 Belize (Affiliate expedition for hairy dwarfs)
- 2005 Loch Ness (Monster)
- 2005 Mongolia (Allghoi Khorkhoi aka Mongolian death worm)

- 2006 Gambia (Gambo - Gambian sea monster , Ninki Nanka and Armitage's skink
- 2006 Llangorse Lake (Giant pike, giant eels)
- 2006 Windermere (Giant eels)
- 2007 Coniston Water (Giant eels)
- 2007 Guyana (Giant anaconda, didi, water tiger)
- 2008 Russia (Almasty)
- 2009 Sumatra (Orang pendek)
- 2009 Republic of Ireland (Lake Monster)
- 2010 Texas (Blue Dogs)
- 2010 India (Mande Burung)
- 2011 Sumatra (Orang-pendek)

For details of current membership fees, current expeditions and investigations, and voluntary posts within the CFZ that need your help, please do not hesitate to contact us.

The Centre for Fortean Zoology,
Myrtle Cottage,
Woolfardisworthy,
Bideford, North Devon
EX39 5QR

Telephone 01237 431413
Fax+44 (0)7006-074-925
eMail info@cfz.org.uk

Websites:

www.cfz.org.uk
www.weirdweekend.org

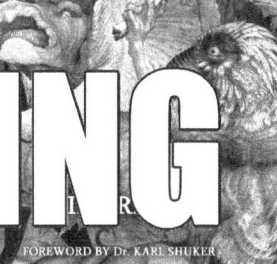

ANIMALS & MEN ISSUES 16-20
THE JOURNAL OF THE CENTRE FOR FORTEAN ZOOLOGY
NEW HORIZONS
Edited by Jon Downes

BIG CATS LOOSE IN BRITAIN

PREDATOR DEATHMATCH
NICK MOLLOY
WITH ILLUSTRATIONS BY ANTHONY WALLIS

Edited by
Jonathan Downes and Richard Freeman

FOREWORD BY Dr. KARL SHUKER

A DAINTREE DIARY
Tales from Travels Daintree
tropical North
CARL PORTMAN

THE COLLECTED POEMS
Dr Karl P.N. Shuker

STRANGELYSTRANGE
ly normal
an anthology of writings by
ANDY ROBERTS

THE WORLD'S WEIRDEST PUBLISHING COMPANY

HOW TO START A PUBLISHING EMPIRE

Unlike most mainstream publishers, we have a non-commercial remit, and our mission statement claims that "we publish books because they deserve to be published, not because we think that we can make money out of them". Our motto is the Latin Tag *Pro bona causa facimus* (we do it for good reason), a slogan taken from a children's book *The Case of the Silver Egg* by the late Desmond Skirrow.

WIKIPEDIA: "The first book published was in 1988. *Take this Brother may it Serve you Well* was a guide to Beatles bootlegs by Jonathan Downes. It sold quite well, but was hampered by very poor production values, being photocopied, and held together by a plastic clip binder. In 1988 A5 clip binders were hard to get hold of, so the publishers took A4 binders and cut them in half with a hacksaw. It now reaches surprisingly high prices second hand.

The production quality improved slightly over the years, and after 1999 all the books produced were ringbound with laminated colour covers. In 2004, however, they signed an agreement with Lightning Source, and all books are now produced perfect bound, with full colour covers."

Until 2010 all our books, the majority of which are/were on the subject of mystery animals and allied disciplines, were published by `CFZ Press`, the publishing arm of the Centre for Fortean Zoology (CFZ), and we urged our readers and followers to draw a discreet veil over the books that we published that were completely off topic to the CFZ.

However, in 2010 we decided that enough was enough and launched a second imprint, `Fortean Words` which aims to cover a wide range of non animal-related esoteric subjects. Other imprints will be launched as and when we feel like it, however the basic ethos of the company remains the same: Our job is to publish books and magazines that we feel are worth publishing, whether or not they are going to sell. Money is, after all - as my dear old Mama once told me - a rather vulgar subject, and she would be rolling in her grave if she thought that her eldest son was somehow in `trade`.

Luckily, so far our tastes have turned out not to be that rarified after all, and we have sold far more books than anyone ever thought that we would, so there is a moral in there somewhere…

Jon Downes,
Woolsery, North Devon
July 2010

CFZ PRESS

Other Books in Print

Wildman! by Redfern, Nick
Globsters by Newton, Michael
Cats of Magic, Mythology and Mystery Shuker, by Karl P. N
Those Amazing Newfoundland Dogs by Bondeson, Jan
The Mystery Animals of Pennsylvania by Gable, Andrew
Sea Serpent Carcasses - Scotland from the Stronsa Monster to Loch Ness by Glen Vaudrey
The CFZ Yearbook 2012 edited by Jonathan and Corinna Downes
ORANG PENDEK: Sumatra's Forgotten Ape by Richard Freeman
THE MYSTERY ANIMALS OF THE BRITISH ISLES: London by Neil Arnold
CFZ EXPEDITION REPORT: India 2010 by Richard Freeman *et al*
The Cryptid Creatures of Florida by Scott Marlow
Dead of Night by Lee Walker
The Mystery Animals of the British Isles: The Northern Isles by Glen Vaudrey
THE MYSTERY ANIMALS OF THE BRTISH ISLES: Gloucestershire and Worcestershire by
Paul Williams
When Bigfoot Attacks by Michael Newton
Weird Waters – The Mystery Animals of Scandinavia: Lake and Sea Monsters by Lars Thomas
The Inhumanoids by Barton Nunnelly
Monstrum! A Wizard's Tale by Tony "Doc" Shiels
CFZ Yearbook 2011 edited by Jonathan Downes
Karl Shuker's Alien Zoo by Shuker, Dr Karl P.N
Tetrapod Zoology Book One by Naish, Dr Darren
The Mystery Animals of Ireland by Gary Cunningham and Ronan Coghlan
Monsters of Texas by Gerhard, Ken
The Great Yokai Encyclopaedia by Freeman, Richard
NEW HORIZONS: Animals & Men *issues 16-20 Collected Editions Vol. 4*
by Downes, Jonathan
A Daintree Diary -
Tales from Travels to the Daintree Rainforest in tropical north Queensland, Australia
by Portman, Carl
Strangely Strange but Oddly Normal by Roberts, Andy

by Downes, Jonathan
The Smaller Mystery Carnivores of the Westcountry by Downes, Jonathan
CFZ EXPEDITION REPORT: Gambia 2006 by Richard Freeman *et al*, Shuker, Karl (fwd)
The Owlman and Others by Jonathan Downes
The Blackdown Mystery by Downes, Jonathan
Big Cats in Britain Yearbook 2006 by Fraser, Mark (Ed)
Fragrant Harbours - Distant Rivers by Downes, John T
Only Fools and Goatsuckers by Downes, Jonathan
Monster of the Mere by Jonathan Downes
Dragons:More than a Myth by Freeman, Richard Alan
Granfer's Bible Stories by Downes, John Tweddell
Monster Hunter by Downes, Jonathan

CFZ Classics is a new venture for us. There are many seminal works that are either unavailable today, or not available with the production values which we would like to see. So, following the old adage that if you want to get something done do it yourself, this is exactly what we have done.

Desiderius Erasmus Roterodamus (b. October 18th 1466, d. July 2nd 1536) said: "When I have a little money, I buy books; and if I have any left, I buy food and clothes," and we are much the same. Only, we are in the lucky position of being able to share our books with the wider world. CFZ Classics is a conduit through which we cannot just re-issue titles which we feel still have much to offer the cryptozoological and Fortean research communities of the 21st Century, but we are adding footnotes, supplementary essays, and other material where we deem it appropriate.

Headhunters of The Amazon by Fritz W Up de Graff (1902)

Fortean Words

The Centre for Fortean Zoology has for several years led the field in Fortean publishing. CFZ Press is the only publishing company specialising in books on monsters and mystery animals. CFZ Press has published more books on this subject than any other company in history and has attracted such well known authors as Andy Roberts, Nick Redfern, Michael Newton, Dr Karl Shuker, Neil Arnold, Dr Darren Naish, Jon Downes, Ken Gerhard and Richard Freeman.

Now CFZ Press are launching a new imprint. Fortean Words is a new line of books dealing with Fortean subjects other than cryptozoology, which is - after all - the subject the CFZ are best known for. Fortean Words is being launched with a spectacular multi-volume series called *Haunted Skies* which covers British UFO sightings between 1940 and 2010. Former policeman John Hanson and his long-suffering partner Dawn Holloway have compiled a peerless library of sighting reports, many that have not been made public before.

Other books include a look at the Berwyn Mountains UFO case by renowned Fortean Andy Roberts and a series of forthcoming books by transatlantic researcher Nick Redfern. CFZ Press are dedicated to maintaining the fine quality of their works with Fortean Words. New authors tackling new subjects will always be encouraged, and we hope that our books will continue to be as ground-breaking and popular as ever.

Haunted Skies Volume One 1940-1959 by John Hanson and Dawn Holloway
Haunted Skies Volume Two 1960-1965 by John Hanson and Dawn Holloway
Haunted Skies Volume Three 1965-1967 by John Hanson and Dawn Holloway
Haunted Skies Volume Four 1968-1971 by John Hanson and Dawn Holloway
Haunted Skies Volume Five 1972-1974 by John Hanson and Dawn Holloway
Haunted Skies Volume Six 1975-1977 by John Hanson and Dawn Holloway
Grave Concerns by Kai Roberts

Police and the Paranormal by Andy Owens
Dead of Night by Lee Walker
Space Girl Dead on Spaghetti Junction - an anthology by Nick Redfern
I Fort the Lore - an anthology by Paul Screeton
UFO Down - the Berwyn Mountains UFO Crash by Andy Roberts
The Grail by Ronan Coghlan
UFO Warminster - Cradle of Contract by Kevin Goodman
Quest for the Hexham Heads by Paul Screeton

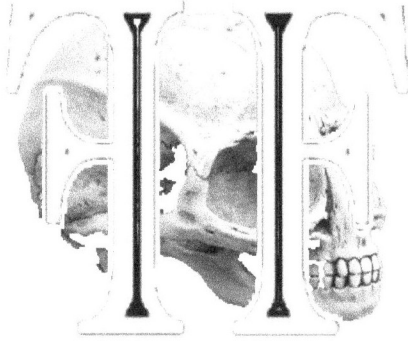

Fortean Fiction

Just before Christmas 2011, we launched our third imprint, this time dedicated to - let's see if you guessed it from the title - fictional books with a Fortean or cryptozoological theme. We have published a few fictional books in the past, but now think that because of our rising reputation as publishers of quality Forteana, that a dedicated fiction imprint was the order of the day.

We launched with four titles:

Green Unpleasant Land by Richard Freeman
Left Behind by Harriet Wadham
Dark Ness by Tabitca Cope
Snap! By Steven Bredice
Death on Dartmoor by Di Francis
Dark Wear by Tabitca Cope
Hyakymonogatari Book 1 by Richard Freeman

www.ingramcontent.com/pod-product-compliance
Lightning Source LLC
Chambersburg PA
CBHW062209270326
41930CB00009B/1692